The Ghost of Jim Crow

THE GHOST OF JIM CROW

How Southern Moderates Used
Brown v. Board of Education
to Stall Civil Rights

Anders Walker

UNIVERSITY PRESS
2009

Oxford University Press, Inc., publishes works that further
Oxford University's objective of excellence
in research, scholarship, and education.

Oxford New York
Auckland   Cape Town   Dar es Salaam   Hong Kong   Karachi
Kuala Lumpur   Madrid   Melbourne   Mexico City   Nairobi
New Delhi   Shanghai   Taipei   Toronto

With offices in
Argentina   Austria   Brazil   Chile   Czech Republic   France   Greece
Guatemala   Hungary   Italy   Japan   Poland   Portugal   Singapore
South Korea   Switzerland   Thailand   Turkey   Ukraine   Vietnam

Published by Oxford University Press, Inc.
198 Madison Avenue, New York, New York 10016
www.oup.com

Library of Congress Cataloging-in-Publication Data

Walker, Anders.
   The ghost of Jim Crow : how southern moderates used Brown v.
Board of Education to stall civil rights / Anders Walker.
   p.   cm.
   Includes bibliographical references and index.
   ISBN 978-0-19-518174-6
1. African Americans—Civil rights—Southern States—History—20th century.
2. Civil rights—Southern States—History—20th century.   3. Brown, Oliver,
1918–1961—Trials, litigation, etc.   4. Topeka (Kan.). Board of Education—Trials,
litigation, etc.   5. Coleman, J. P. (James Plemon), 1914—Political and social views.
6. Hodges, Luther Hartwell, 1898-1974—Political and social views.   7. Collins,
LeRoy—Political and social views.   8. Moderation—Political aspects—Southern
States—History—20th century.   9. Southern States—Race relations—Political
aspects—History—20th century.   10. Southern States—Politics and
government—1951–   I. Title.
   E185.61.W17   2009
   323.1196'073009045—dc22   2008041066

9 8 7 6 5 4 3 2 1

Printed in the United States of America
on acid-free paper

To Jennifer

ACKNOWLEDGMENTS

I doubt that I would have written a book about southern moderates had I not attended a private school in Tallahassee, Florida. Founded in 1968, my alma mater was one of hundreds of private academies to open in the South just as public schools were finally beginning the process of mass desegregation in the region. Perhaps ironically, it never occurred to me in the 1980s that my high school might have been designed to sidestep *Brown* or that resistance to integration had assumed any form other than a violent, defiant one. After stumbling across a book entitled *The Schools That Fear Built*, however, I began to realize not only that my high school had been part of a quiet move to circumvent integration but also that popular portrayals of southern segregationists as violent and hysterical were also incomplete. This led me to become interested in the question of whether there might have been other forms of resistance to integration that emerged in the South in the 1950s and 1960s that did not capture media attention and did not involve outright defiance of the Supreme Court.

In pursuing this question, I met many remarkable people, all of whom deserve credit for this work. One is Robert Sherrill. One of the founding members of the progressive *Texas Observer*, Sherrill lived at the end of a dirt road in Tallahassee when I met him in the summer of 2000. He encouraged me to look beyond local Tallahassee politics to the highest levels of Florida's state government, even to LeRoy Collins, the celebrated moderate governor of Florida from 1955 to 1961. Two men who reinforced this advice were Kent Spriggs, the mayor of Tallahassee in 1984 and 1985, and Phil Parsons, counsel to the speaker of the Florida House of Representatives from 1972 to 1975. During the early days of their legal careers, Parsons and Spriggs had both considered suing the Tallahassee Country Club, a publicly held property, for leasing its eighteen-hole golf course for $1 a year for ninety-nine years to members of a private club, including Collins's family, in 1956. By the time I interviewed Parsons and Spriggs in 2000, the lease was still in effect. It is scheduled to run out in 2055.

Another person who deserves credit for this project is Althamese Barnes, curator of Tallahassee's African American Riley House Museum. Barnes suggested I go through city council minutes from the 1950s, looking for evidence that might explain why Smoky Hollow, a black neighborhood near the capitol, was razed in 1958. In those minutes, I found evidence that LeRoy Collins had taken time out of his busy schedule as governor to write letters to Tallahassee's city council, urging the destruction of Smoky Hollow. At the same time, African American residents of the Hollow claimed that Collins, his father, and his brother all owned property in the neighborhood. Why, I wondered, did he lobby city officials to bulldoze it?

As I began to read through Collins's papers at the Florida State Archives in Tallahassee, I began to suspect that what Collins had become remembered for and what he actually did were two very different things. While projecting a public image of racial moderation, Collins also charged a committee of legal experts to draft legislation designed to help preserve racial segregation in Florida. Over the course of Collins's administration, this committee recommended a significant amount of legislation that appeared to have nothing to do with civil rights. Some of it dealt with state police; some of it had to do with local-state relations; meanwhile, other parts of it were clearly aimed at buying black support for racial segregation through, for example, more black beaches and more scholarships to schools.

Interestingly, other governors joined Collins in this endeavor. One was Luther Hodges, the governor of North Carolina from 1954 to 1961. Another was James P. Coleman, the governor of Mississippi from 1956 to 1960. For information on Coleman, I am indebted to Professor Tahirih Lee at the Florida State University College of Law, who put me in touch with Joshua Morse, former dean of FSU Law School and, from 1963 to 1969, dean of the University of Mississippi School of Law. According to Morse, who tried to promote progressive reform at Ole Miss in the 1960s, some of the most sophisticated segregationists in Mississippi were leaders like Coleman, not extremists like James O. Eastland or Ross Barnett.

While personal interviews proved helpful, the bulk of my source material came from state and university archives. I am particularly indebted to Clinton Bagley, archivist at the Mississippi Department of Archives and History, and also to the North Caroliniana Society for giving me an Archie K. Davis Grant to fund research at the University of North Carolina at Chapel Hill. Further credit goes to the research staffs at the State Archives of Florida, Special Collections at the University of South Florida, Special Collections at the Claude Pepper Library in Tallahassee, the North Carolina

State Archives, the Southern Historical Collection at the University of North Carolina–Chapel Hill, Special Collections at the University of North Carolina–Greensboro, and the Charles W. Capps Jr. Archives at Delta State University in Cleveland, Mississippi.

I gained immeasurable benefits from interactions with scholars as well. At Duke University, I learned from conversations with Larry Goodwyn, Bill Chafe, Raymond Gavins, Malachi Hacohen, Karen Wigen, and Wendy Wall. I also received help from James Coleman and Jerome Culp at Duke Law School. Robert Rodgers Korstad, on the faculty at the History Department and the School of Public Policy at Duke, deserves particular credit for this book. He provided encouragement from the very beginning days of research and has continued to give generously of his time in reading drafts and commenting.

I am also grateful to Glenda Elizabeth Gilmore, Jonathan Holloway, and Robert W. Gordon at Yale University. Gilmore encouraged me to sharpen my analysis, improve my writing, and prepare myself for the inevitable attacks on a project targeting some of the South's "best men." She also read innumerable drafts, made invaluable comments, and encouraged me to place my findings within the larger historiography of the South at the time. Jonathan Holloway and Bob Gordon also provided helpful comments and extensive written commentary at an early stage of the project.

One academic community that deserves particular credit for this book is the legal history colloquium at the New York University School of Law. Thanks to William E. Nelson, R. B. Bernstein, William LaPiana, John Phillip Ried, Harold Forsyth, Dan Hulsebosch, Bernard K. Freamon, Serena Mayeri, and others, I began to see moderate resistance to *Brown* as a distinct type of constitutional politics. This politics sought not simply to resist the Supreme Court, but to provide it with a series of opportunities to bow out of the political thicket, if you will, by modifying its *Brown* holding, thereby influencing its civil rights jurisprudence.

Others who provided helpful comments and advice include Jane Dailey, Tony Badger, David J. Garrow, Adrienne Davis, Steven F. Lawson, David L. Chappell, and Hendrik Hartog, all of whom commented either on drafts or at conferences. I benefited from conversations with Joseph Crespino, whose concept of strategic accommodation in the political context informed my own notion of strategic constitutionalism in the legal context. I also owe thanks to Dorothy Schultz, Robert Panzarella, and Dolores Jones-Brown at the John Jay College of Criminal Justice, all of whom helped me sharpen my analysis of the role that the state and particularly the police played in the story of southern resistance to civil rights. Fred Bloom, Eric Miller, and Joel Goldstein at the Saint Louis University School of Law provided helpful comments and constitutional analysis. Susan Ferber at Oxford University

Press played a particularly critical role in guiding the book through several substantive revisions and providing invaluable comments along the way. Finally, I would like to thank Jennifer Walker for putting up with what turned out to be several years of clutter and false promises regarding the actual completion date of this book.

CONTENTS

The Ghost of Jim Crow

INTRODUCTION: SOUTHERNERS
OF THE TRUE SOUTH

On September 23, 1957, Florida Governor LeRoy Collins stood up before an audience at the lavish Cloister Hotel on Sea Island, Georgia, and warned the South not to wrap itself in a "confederate blanket."[1] The warning would not have been particularly remarkable except that Collins spoke at the height of massive resistance to integration, a crisis dramatized by Arkansas Governor Orval Faubus's refusal to desegregate Little Rock's Central High School earlier that month. As Faubus rebuffed both the president and the Supreme Court, Collins received a request from Luther Hodges, the governor of North Carolina, entreating him to deliver an antiextremist, moderating speech at the upcoming Southern Governors' Conference on Sea Island.[2]

Unfortunately, just as Hodges introduced Collins to a packed room at the Cloister, proclaiming him to be a "southerner of the true South," news of racial violence exploded at Little Rock's Central High.[3] On the very morning that Collins spoke, nine black students entered the school, prompting white mobs to attack African Americans in the street.[4] Outraged, President Eisenhower ordered the 101st Airborne into the city, forever shaping northern perceptions of the South as a land of violent extremists, intent on the brutal repression of blacks.[5]

While the story of racial extremism in the 1950s South is well documented, less familiar is the manner in which southern governors like LeRoy Collins and Luther Hodges sought to counterbalance extremism and manage the desegregation crisis.[6] Yet, both governors rejected massive resistance and worked hard to assemble a response to *Brown v. Board of Education* that was peaceful, legal, and attuned to northern sensibilities. In fact, both governors excelled at the amount of legislation they were able to push through their state legislatures, effectively using popular unease over racial integration as a fulcrum for reform. Rather than view *Brown* as a death sentence for the southern way of life, they took it as an opportunity to improve that life, join the economic success of the nation, and jettison Jim Crow for a more expansive, more omnipotent state.

That *Brown* contributed to a modernization and expansion of state power in the South is not well known. Proponents of massive resistance denounced the federal government's civil rights imperatives as intrusive meddling, making it appear as if centralization in all forms was unpalatable. Yet, many of the statist reforms endorsed by Hodges and Collins in the 1950s spread across the South in the 1960s. Remarkably, few of these reforms dealt with schools. While both Collins and Hodges endorsed elaborate schemes to assign students to schools based on factors other than race, they also promoted the expansion and centralization of state police, the modernization of state judiciaries, and the reconfiguration of welfare regulations and family law.

Rather than simply disorganized acts of racial revenge, modifications in welfare law, adoption law, marriage law, police jurisdiction, and judicial administration formed interlocking pieces of a complex puzzle aimed at preventing violence, preserving as much segregation as possible, and complying, formally, with the Supreme Court. Relying on committees of attorneys, Collins and Hodges both became interested not just in preventing racial conflagrations like the riot in Little Rock but also in influencing constitutional doctrine. Hoping that the Court might accept tokenism, particularly if peace could be maintained and uncontroversial efforts to help African Americans were enacted, Collins and Hodges engaged in what might be called a type of strategic constitutionalism aimed at convincing the Supreme Court to qualify its *Brown* holding.

Though headlines wavered, much of the legal work that Collins and Hodges accomplished endured. As this book shows, vestiges of their response to *Brown* can still be seen in the South and much of what they did foreshadowed political and constitutional developments nationally into the 1970s and beyond. Precisely because they understood the importance of avoiding violence and reframing southern racial practices in northern terms, so did their reforms anticipate national trends. Recovering their strategic constitutionalism helps to complement recent explanations of how the defiant South merged seamlessly with the post-civil rights North and West. Rather than just a factor of Nixon's infamous "southern strategy," the South's reconciliation with national norms also reflected the contribution of an indigenous tradition of moderation, racial progressivism, and legal reform.[7]

That two moderate governors from two of the South's most progressive states spearheaded such reform may not be particularly surprising. What is surprising is that their strategies paralleled, and at times even drew inspiration from, Mississippi Governor James Plemon (J. P.) Coleman. Long before Collins and Hodges even entered office, J. P. Coleman traveled to Washington, D.C., to listen to Thurgood Marshall deliver his oral arguments in *Brown* and, anticipating a black victory in the case, returned to Mississippi determined to devise a peaceful, legalist response to the opinion. Coleman, like Collins and Hodges, immediately began to centralize law enforcement, modernize judicial administration, reform family law, and tighten welfare. Like his moderate counterparts, he realized that racial violence would only hurt the South and turned instead to a variety of measures aimed at curtailing the Court's ruling, meanwhile presenting a peaceful, reasonable, even progressive image of the South. Part of this image had to do with helping African Americans improve their lives. Part of it also had to do with advertising black shortcomings, particularly statistics on illegitimacy, crime, and venereal disease, all to communicate to the rest of the country why, precisely, mass integration was imprudent.

Looked at together, Coleman, Collins, and Hodges provide a glimpse of an entire dimension of southern resistance to *Brown* that has gone largely undocumented.[8] By recovering this resistance, we learn at least three things: One, rather than the "hollow hope" that some historians have come to view it as, *Brown* reemerges as an important evolutionary decision that pushed the South to curtail localized policing, rein in vigilante violence, expand welfare technologies, and modernize family law.[9] Two, for the purposes of constitutional theory, Collins, Coleman, and Hodges all show how state leaders embraced a type of strategic constitutionalism that expands our understanding of how Supreme Court decisions influence state law, even law that does not appear, on its face, to have anything to do with the constitutional questions involved. Three, just because Collins, Coleman, and Hodges modernized aspects of the South's legal system does not necessarily mean that they contributed to racial equality. Although their work to end racial violence benefited blacks, many of their efforts to help African Americans discreetly shifted the burden of constitutional change onto black shoulders, held them responsible for their plight, and meanwhile exaggerated the extent to which they suffered from illegitimacy, immorality, and other social ills.

Though focusing on black illegitimacy rates may seem to have little to do with fighting integration in the courts, Collins, Coleman, and Hodges all saw the invocation of a type of socially conservative, moralist politics to be useful in combating *Brown*. Shocked that the Supreme Court had relied on social science evidence to prove that segregation harmed black children, Collins, Coleman, and Hodges themselves all used social science data, particularly illegitimacy rates, to make the counterargument that integration would hurt whites. In so doing, they articulated a defense of the status quo rooted not in repression, but aspiration. Though supportive of legal segregation, they did not perceive Jim Crow to be repressive so much as protective, a bulwark against social ills endemic to black communities. This position, though blind to the limiting impact that segregation had on black life, is worth recovering. It helps explain why southerners who were moderate, reasonable, conscientious and well-intentioned resisted *Brown*. It also helps explain an aspect of the South that studies of massive resistance ignore. Rather than a region inflamed with a desire to subordinate blacks, Collins, Coleman, and Hodges all suggest that southern resistance to *Brown* was also motivated by a desire to protect and preserve a type of racial and cultural pluralism. Indeed, all three governors expressed a discernable respect for black institutions, traditions, and culture, particularly middle class culture, even as they called for the uplift and reform of the lowest echelons of black society. Understanding this pluralist, progressive, yet still segregationist vision is critical to understanding southern moderates, and arguably southern resistance to integration generally. Opposition to *Brown* was not simply based on hate, but also, ironically, on hope—hope that the races could continue to grow, side by side, in a separate, synergistic manner.

By focusing on low black standards as read through illegitimacy rates, for example, each governor tried to influence the manner in which white voters in the North and West perceived black people and counter notions that white southerners possessed an irrational dislike of African Americans due simply to their color. It was not the color of African Americans at all, they claimed, that explained southern resistance to *Brown;* it was the fact that many of the poorest blacks possessed low standards, standards that needed to be raised before integration could occur. Such vague notions of race-related standards, which none of the three went to great lengths to explain, provided a new way of rationalizing resistance to integration, even as they provided each governor with a means of parrying black demands for immediate constitutional change. Aware that constitutional law hinged at least to some extent on "political support," all three governors sought to curry popular support in the North and West by providing a perspective on southern resistance that most white voters might understand.[10]

Looked at together, the perspective of moderates like Collins, Coleman, and Hodges casts new light not only on white resistance to integration but also on the challenges faced by the civil rights movement generally. Though the movement is well known for its manipulation of white racism to achieve federal legislation in the 1960s, it is less well known that white moderates manipulated black stereotypes to preclude movement gains. In fact, few realize that as early as 1955, white moderates like J. P. Coleman and civil rights strategists like Roy Wilkins were actively trying to out-manipulate one another, desperately attempting to cast aspersions onto the opposite race in order to win federal favor. Long before the dramatic showdowns of the 1960s, in other words, white moderates and black activists were deeply engaged in an ideological struggle for the hearts and minds of American voters, and the sympathies of federal officials, outside the South.[11] Given that audiences outside the South did in fact have considerable power to fundamentally alter southern politics, the real struggle over civil rights in the 1950s and 1960s might therefore be said to have taken place not between black activists and white extremists, but between black activists and white moderates.[12] As Martin Luther King Jr. himself observed, the "great stumbling block" to black freedom in the South was not the "White Citizen's Counciler or the Ku Klux Klanner," but the "white moderate."[13]

Returning to the subject of constitutional law, this means that not only did *Brown* trigger a defiant backlash, as constitutional historian Michael J. Klarman has shown, but also it incited a complex process of what constitutional scholar Reva Siegel has called "preservation through transformation."[14] By transforming the legal criteria for segregating students from overt racial classifications to facially neutral, standards-based criteria, not to mention by endorsing legal measures that focused attention on if not actually exaggerated perceived indicia of racial differences, Collins, Coleman, and Hodges all sought to lay the foundations for a new legal idiom through which racial inequality could be maintained in the post-*Brown* era. This idiom, rather than focus on the group-categorical classification of color, relied instead on group-salient criteria like poor academic performance, illegitimacy, and poverty, all of which had a disproportionate impact on blacks. Just as the Civil War pushed the region to develop new legal means of preserving racial stratification—first through Black Codes and later through the elaborate legal system of racial segregation known as Jim Crow—so, too, did *Brown* inspire legal creativity. And just as moderates designed much of Jim Crow's nineteenth-century body, so, too, did moderates design much of its ghost.[15]

To show how this transpired, this book proceeds in four parts. Chapter 1 focuses on J. P. Coleman's response to *Brown* in Mississippi. Specifically, it focuses on Coleman's struggle with Roy Wilkins, director of the NAACP, to project a positive image of the state and to thwart civil rights protest. It also focuses on Coleman's attempts to control white extremism by centralizing law enforcement, modernizing judicial administration, and removing power from local justices of the peace. Finally, it discusses Coleman's efforts to facilitate the continued segregation of schools by shifting classifications from color to moral character. This shift, though dedicated largely to facilitate pupil placement, also became part of Coleman's larger effort to win what he perceived to be a propaganda battle against the NAACP by showcasing social problems endemic to black communities.

Chapter 2 shows how Luther Hodges, inspired by Coleman, developed his own strategies of fighting integration in North Carolina. It begins by discussing Hodges's work with the Pearsall Committee, a committee of legal experts charged with devising legalist strategies for circumventing *Brown*. It then shows how Hodges sought to augment the committee's work by recommending that African Americans accept segregation voluntarily to preserve their traditions and "culture." Alert to the danger that white extremists posed to moderation, Hodges empowered white voters by allowing them to close public schools in their districts, even as he employed the State Bureau of Investigation to intimidate the Ku Klux Klan. Angered by NAACP activism, particularly the exploitation of a juvenile court case involving two African American boys accused of "kissing" two white girls, Hodges worked hard to shift public attention away from white repression and toward black shortcomings, particularly illegitimacy rates.

Chapter 3 focuses on how LeRoy Collins worked with a committee of legal experts to undermine *Brown* in Florida. Specifically, it discusses Collins's use of state troopers and state agencies to monitor both white extremists and black activists. It also describes Collins's attempts to reconfigure segregation in racially neutral ways, including his attempts to shift attention away from black bids for desegregation and toward the need to improve black "standards." Hoping to augment such rhetoric, Collins engaged in a variety of measures designed to place more scrutiny and pressure on the black poor. Though his commitment to segregation seemed ambivalent, a close review of Collins's private letters suggests that he maintained a firm commitment to segregation from the start but did not advertise it, in the hopes that federal courts would be more prone to approving Florida's pupil placement program.

Chapter 4 takes the story into the post-massive resistance era, the 1960s and beyond, when Hodges, Collins, and Coleman all rose to positions in the federal government. Luther Hodges became President John F. Kennedy's secretary of Commerce and LeRoy Collins rose to become head of the Community Relations Service, an agency dedicated to negotiating peaceful conclusions to civil rights demonstrations. Meanwhile, Lyndon Johnson appointed J. P. Coleman to the Fifth Circuit Court of Appeals, where he would find himself presiding over civil rights cases for the next two decades, into the 1980s. Though initially lenient toward black plaintiffs, Coleman hardened his stance as the makeup of the federal judiciary shifted to the right in the 1970s. Specifically, he used pro-law enforcement arguments to limit the contours of civil rights protest, even as he used facially neutral color-blind arguments to deny black claims in educational, economic, and voting contexts.

In telling these stories, I seek to show in this book that the struggle against *Brown* in the American South was not simply a struggle between segregationists and the Supreme Court but also a struggle among segregationists over the best possible strategy for evading and/or influencing the

Court. In this struggle, segregationists who advocated legal defiance against the Court—or what this book terms *extremists*—developed a relatively crude constitutional strategy for preserving segregation, one rooted in outright legal opposition or massive resistance. At the same time, other segregationists rejected outright defiance and, opting for a more sophisticated approach, treated *Brown* as an opportunity to improve their region's image, modernize its governmental apparatus, and attract investment.[16] Segregation, to them, no longer required rigid legal enforcement. It was part of the social fabric of the South, a mode of living that would not disappear with the alteration of a few laws. Further, insofar as black and white culture could be celebrated, segregation might well continue, voluntarily. Minor concessions, such as seats on buses and places at lunch counters, could all be granted without overturning the South's social order. Indeed, even schools could be integrated. As the southern population moved to the suburbs and acquired wealth, district lines could be drawn and private schools formed in a way that would keep integration at a minimum.

1

"MEANS AND METHODS":
J. P. COLEMAN LIMITS *BROWN*
IN MISSISSIPPI

The partially decomposed body floated upside down in the murky water. Its teeth were knocked out, the right side of its face was crushed, and it was tied to a heavy cotton gin fan with barbed wire. Floyd Hodges, only seventeen years old at the time, discovered the body while fishing and went immediately to get the police, not realizing that he had stumbled across what would become one of the most sensational murders in America. The body belonged to an African American teenager from Chicago named Emmett Till, who had been visiting his uncle in Mississippi for the summer. Although the exact reasons for the murder were unclear, police traced it back to an ill-fated interaction between Till and a young white woman named Carolyn Bryant in a general store in the small Delta town of Money. Some claimed that Till whistled at Bryant. Others, including Carolyn herself, claimed that he entered her store and propositioned her. Relying on his wife's account, Bryant's husband enlisted his half-brother J. W. Milam, kidnapped Till from his uncle's house, and killed him.[1]

It was the summer of 1955, and though the killing was a local incident, the savagery of the murder attracted national attention, particularly after Till's mother, Mamie Bradley, ordered the body exhumed from its grave and brought back to Chicago. Once there, Bradley left her son's casket open in a public wake, attracting thousands of viewers. Charles Diggs, a black congressman from Detroit, later explained how a picture of Till's partly decomposed, mangled corpse, reprinted in *Jet* magazine, turned the incident into a national scandal. "I think that was probably one of the greatest media products in the last forty or fifty years," recounted Diggs, "because that picture stimulated a lot of interest and a lot of anger on the part of blacks all over the country."[2]

Though Milam and Bryant were both acquitted of the crime, many white Mississippians were appalled by the murder. "The [Emmett Till] killing must have been the act of a depraved mind, or minds," wrote the *Jackson Daily News*. "The people of Money, where the crime took place, were shocked and appalled. Everyone is in solid agreement that it was a stupid, horrible crime. Intelligent Mississippians can only suppose it came about in the sick mind of men who should be removed from society by due course of law."[3]

One white Mississippian who was particularly distressed by the murder was Attorney General and Governor-elect James Plemon (J. P.) Coleman. Coleman had won Mississippi's Democratic primary only a week before Till's disappearance on a platform of fighting corruption, encouraging economic development, and quietly preserving racially segregated public schools. No demagogue, Coleman had worked with his predecessor, Governor Hugh White, to improve education for blacks, hoping that it might forestall integration. Now he joined White in appointing a special prosecutor specifically for the Till case.[4]

Coleman's interest in seeing Till's murderers brought to justice stemmed from more than simply personal outrage at the brutal crime. It coincided with a promise he had made during his gubernatorial campaign to resolve racial conflicts through formal, peaceful, legal means. If racial issues were not handled lawfully, he feared, then Mississippi's image would suffer, and vital state interests like attracting industry and preserving segregation—two goals that Coleman believed were actually complementary—would be compromised.[5] To him, segregation ensured "peaceable government" precisely because it kept blacks and whites apart, thereby reducing the kind of altercations that resulted in Till's death and ensuring the kind of social stability that outside investors expected.[6] Coleman was already afraid that outside investment was being jeopardized by the *Brown v. Board of Education* decision. To Coleman's mind, *Brown* had exacerbated Mississippi's race relation problems and fueled violence and racial extremism in the state. He clashed with white activists not far from Money who had formed a reactionary political organization called the Citizens' Councils to intimidate African Americans and lobby state leaders like Coleman into adopting extremist anti-integration positions to counter the Supreme Court decision. To the new governor, who refused to join the councils, such maneuvers were ill-considered. "We can't preserve segregation by defying the federal government," Coleman asserted in December 1955. "We must do it by legal means."[7]

Unlike the Citizens' Councils, which rejected the Supreme Court's ruling outright, Coleman took a more lawyerly approach, studying the *Brown* decision for ambiguities, for chances to comply formally with it, meanwhile retaining segregation. In 1952 and 1953, he traveled to Washington, D.C., to observe Thurgood Marshall in oral argument, listen to the justices' questions, and theorize a reasonable, segregationist response. It was at this time that he began to develop pupil placement, a legal plan that removed overt racial classifications from southern state law and replaced them with more neutral classifications that could be used as substitutes for race, such as academic performance and moral background. Anticipating an NAACP victory, Coleman used his position on a governmental body called the Legal Education Advisory Committee to push the South's first placement plan through Mississippi's state legislature in April 1954, a month before *Brown* was handed down. In fact, Mississippi's placement plan, which Coleman helped write, would become a model for similar plans enacted across the South in the 1950s.[8]

Coleman's early conviction that the Supreme Court rulings on race were best handled through legal means distinguished him from better-known political contemporaries in Mississippi, men like U.S. Senator James O. Eastland, who advocated outright rejection of the nation's highest tribunal. Eastland seemed to have little concern for the possibility that defiance and extremism might harm the state's image or hurt its chances for economic growth. Instead, Eastland seemed eager to exaggerate the potential impact of the Supreme Court ruling and claimed, implausibly, that it was part of a Communist plot that would, if not resisted bitterly, destroy the South. He made his views known unabashedly, gambling that white voters in the region would respond to such incendiary, emotional appeals.[9]

Coleman rejected such a shortsighted, politically motivated approach. To him, outright defiance would only jeopardize the region's chances of evading *Brown* and possibly even speed integration in the region.[10] A student of the Civil War, he remained mindful of history, particularly the "dark days of Reconstruction," when the Union army occupied the South and handed power over to northern Republicans, southern sympathizers, and freed slaves. Convinced that such an arrangement had led to political corruption and poor government, Coleman lobbied to replace defiance with a much more strategic form of constitutionalism in the 1950s, one that did not invite a repeat of the past.

This chapter looks at J. P. Coleman's strategic constitutionalism, focusing on the multipronged strategy that he endorsed to deal with *Brown*. It shows how Coleman engaged the NAACP in a propaganda battle over the image of Mississippi in hopes that by projecting a positive image of the state, he might reduce popular support for aggressive enforcement of integration. Coleman simultaneously used centralized state power to control civil rights activists and white extremists, two groups that he thought compromised the state's image and risked even more intrusive federal intervention in southern affairs. He actively tried to buy black support for fighting civil rights, a campaign that Coleman hoped might curb the black attack on segregation in the courts. Finally, he worked to convince the state legislature to enact a variety of evasive laws that formally ended segregation by race, while granting local school boards a variety of subtle opportunities for preserving segregated schools. Examined together, these strategies represented a remarkably creative, extrajudicial approach to resisting *Brown*.[11]

Coleman's response to *Brown* suggests that he sought not simply to resist the ruling but also to orchestrate a reinterpretation of it. Unlike extremists in Mississippi at the time, Coleman tended to see *Brown* as a relatively open-ended decision. One way to interpret it, for example, was as an order for the South to forcibly enroll white and black students in the same schools, which he believed would be a disaster. Another interpretation was that it ordered the South to stop assigning students to schools based on race but still allowed students to choose whether they wanted to attend schools based on race. Under such an arrangement, informal social and economic pressure could be relied on to pressure the races to segregate themselves. A third possible interpretation, one that Coleman found the most compelling, was that *Brown* barred local officials from assigning students to schools based solely on race but did not prevent them from assigning students to schools according to other reasonable criteria that might somehow be linked to race. New state legislation enumerating such criteria, which might refer to socioeconomic background, academic performance, or even health, might, if written carefully enough, survive Supreme Court review, particularly if the South made a reasonable case for why such criteria were necessary. By taking such an approach, Coleman believed that the South could actually engineer a reinterpretation of *Brown* favorable to continued racial separation in public schools. This was particularly true, he thought, if the South took aggressive measures to quell outside "agitators" who came to the region to stir up support for mass, forced integration, as well as white extremists, who inadvertently boosted national support for the NAACP. Both white extremists and civil rights activists, in Coleman's view, worked together in a perverse, symbiotic relationship that did the South a disservice, making it look more brutal, more backward, and ultimately more in need of intrusive federal intervention than it actually was. "Our enemies," he wrote to one constituent in 1958, expect Mississippi to be a "bloody battleground furnishing every excuse for the second military occupation" of the South.[12] To him, aggressive measures needed to be taken to control the battlefield so that agitators could not induce a second Reconstruction. So long as the South remained calm, he told his constituents, the Supreme Court would eventually realize that enforcing *Brown*, at least as the NAACP wanted it to be enforced, was impossible. Instead, he hoped, the Court would realize that it had no option but to endorse placement plans, thereby adopting a relatively restricted interpretation of the Fourteenth Amendment.

Unlike southerners who read *Brown* as a frontal attack on sovereign state law, Coleman read the decision as a call for modifying that law, making it less like an "ox-cart" and more like a "jet plane."[13] Such a move would, he believed, address national concerns that Jim Crow was being used by Soviet propagandists as a weapon in the Cold War and would also satisfy concerns that Jim Crow was turning business away from the South by making the region look backward and unreconstructed. Neither of these concerns convinced Coleman that segregation itself had to end. An active member of the Democratic National Party, Coleman knew full well that de facto segregation existed in the North, particularly in major cities like Chicago and New York, and that white Americans in the North and West were not as liberal on racial issues as many believed. To him, "[p]eople from other parts of the country are just like people from Mississippi," and national opinion was, ultimately, "favorable to our way of thinking."[14] All the South needed to do was become more like the rest of the country: Eliminate overt racial classifications from its state codes, and rearticulate its position on segregation in dispassionate terms that most Americans could understand. It was imperative, for example, that the South abandon the language of white supremacy and turn instead to a type of objective, sociological defense of segregation, much like the argument that the NAACP used to win *Brown.* Coleman believed strongly that Thurgood Marshall's sociological argument, which held that segregation invariably damaged the psychological development of black children, was wrong. In his opinion, segregation allowed black children to learn and grow at their own pace, free from outside interference, whereas throwing them into schools with whites would hurt them by exposing them to white recriminations and put them in a position where they could not compete. This conviction led Coleman to conclude that whites and blacks alike would be better off if the South improved black schools without integrating them. So long as the rest of America could be made to understand this, popular support for aggressive enforcement of *Brown* would evaporate, he hoped, making congressional or executive action against the South unlikely.

By taking a legalist, moderate path of resistance to the Supreme Court, Coleman saw the South as guiding constitutional jurisprudence in favor of a new era of segregation, animated not so much by Jim Crow's legal body as by its ghost. This approach provides a counterpoint to the better-known story of massive resistance in the South in the 1950s, a story dominated by white extremists and defiant organizations like the Mississippi Citizens' Councils. Although the councils became a potent political force, they never convinced Coleman that defiance was a viable means of thwarting the Supreme Court, nor did they prevent him from pushing a variety of decidedly moderate measures through the state legislature. Coleman compromised with extremists in Mississippi on certain issues, but his compromises were strategic, designed to maintain some level of moderate control over the state's legal response to *Brown.* Rather than being a proponent of gradual integration, he saw moderation itself as the best line of defense against gradual integration. A brief look at his background, particularly his extensive legal experience, helps explain how he could be a strong segregationist and a moderate at the same time.[15]

To Jackson via Washington, D.C.

Born on December 9, 1914, James Plemon Coleman grew up on a farm in Ackerman, Mississippi, northeast of Jackson in hill country. Though the descendant of farmers, Coleman decided at an early age that he wanted to become a lawyer, a dream that his grandfather supported by encouraging him to read the *Congressional Record* while young James was still a high school student. Something in the *Record*, which documented speeches, hearings, and legislative activity in Congress, inspired him and led him to borrow law books from the district attorney in Ackerman, Aaron Lane Ford. When Ford ran for a U.S. House seat in 1934, he remembered Coleman— then a student at the University of Mississippi—and asked him to look through the *Congressional Record* for information on his opponent, Thomas Jefferson Busby. Coleman ably documented Busby's absences from particular votes, producing a source of easily accessible campaign data that Ford then used to win the election. Impressed by Coleman's work, Ford invited Coleman to take a job in Washington.[16]

Though not yet a graduate, Coleman left Ole Miss and moved to the nation's capital, where he worked as Ford's secretary by day and attended classes at the George Washington University School of Law by night. For the next four years, he immersed himself in political life, listened to Supreme Court oral arguments, attended congressional debates, and participated in the Little Congress, an organization of young clerks and secretaries that met in the House Caucus room to introduce and debate mock bills. While in the Little Congress, Coleman led a successful challenge to an initiative brought by a young Texan named Lyndon Baines Johnson, a move that won Johnson's respect and sparked a lifelong friendship between the two. When Coleman ran for governor in 1955, Johnson contributed financially to his campaign, and Coleman, in turn, supported Johnson for the presidency in 1956, 1960, and 1964.[17]

Perhaps because of his early contact with nationally minded southerners like Johnson, Coleman never lost sight of the relationship between local politics in the South and national politics, particularly for the Democratic Party. Indeed, Coleman remained convinced that the conservative southern wing of the party had to remain on at least moderately good terms with its more liberal northern wing, lest the South lose important influence in Congress. Two factors arguably contributed to this belief. One was seeing firsthand how the New Deal brought federal largesse to the aid of struggling southern states. A second factor was the election of Mississippi Senator Theodore Bilbo, who beat incumbent Hubert Stephens in 1934. Bilbo, a populist who supported Roosevelt's New Deal, became known for engaging in excessive displays of racial extremism, such as attacking antilynching laws and blasting African Americans for wanting to "mongrelize" the white race.[18] Though Coleman admired certain elements of Bilbo's political style, what he later termed his "common touch," he came to believe that his vitriolic racism did Mississippi a "disservice."[19] Coleman thought that the South should instead project a positive image to the nation, striving to "be on good terms with the people from the North," in order to develop positive national relationships conducive to its own economic and political interests.[20]

While Coleman was in Washington, he observed how President Franklin Delano Roosevelt moved to curb the powers of the Supreme Court in 1937. Angered by a string of Supreme Court rulings striking down New Deal programs, Roosevelt—along with congressional leaders like Senator Sherman Minton of Indiana—threatened a variety of legislative measures to pressure the Court into adopting a less aggressive jurisprudence. These measures included bills requiring a vote of at least seven justices to overrule an act of Congress and increasing the number of justices on the Court, which would give Roosevelt a chance to stack the tribunal with judges favorable to the New Deal.[21]

Although the Supreme Court's subsequent shift in favor of New Deal policies was motivated by more than just Roosevelt's threats, J. P. Coleman saw the shift as a judicial response to extrajudicial political pressure.[22] This reading convinced him, almost twenty years later, that *Brown*, too, could be influenced by political pressure, just not extremism. In fact, it helps explain his belief that the South's best chances lay in communicating its position to the rest of the country in reasonable terms and winning popular and ultimately political support for continued segregation.[23]

Coleman's time in Washington helped prepare him for *Brown* in certain ways; his time back in Mississippi helped prepare him in others. Both of his grandfathers were Confederate soldiers, sparking Coleman's interest in southern and particularly Civil War history. By the time he became governor in 1956, he had accumulated an impressive library of four hundred books on the topic and reminded voters repeatedly of the trials of Reconstruction, when the federal government sent troops to occupy southern states.[24] Conversely, he also reminded voters that the Supreme Court had once been an ally of the South during the decades following the Civil War and could be again. He even published an article on post–Civil War politics that coincided, in many ways, with his campaign to mount a legalist response to the Supreme Court in the 1950s. In it, he showed how

Mississippi leaders in the 1890s had feared that defiance "would bring evils upon the state," not least among them "adverse congressional legislation."[25] At the same time, he made sure to point out that this did not stop state legislators from devising less noticeable, more legalist schemes for denying blacks the right to vote. Building on his understanding of southern history, Coleman tried to make a rational, historically rooted argument for opposing defiance and embracing legalist evasion.[26]

Coleman's view of the South and civil rights was further developed through his own legal career. Shortly after leaving Washington in 1939, he returned home to Ackerman and ran for district attorney, a position that he held until 1946, when he was elected a state circuit judge. After Coleman spent four years on the bench, Governor Fielding Wright appointed the thirty-six-year-old to the Supreme Court of Mississippi. When Mississippi Supreme Court Justice Gus Smith died just two months later, Wright appointed Coleman to serve as attorney general, a position that he would hold until becoming governor in January 1956.[27]

As attorney general, Coleman had perhaps his most defining civil rights experience pre-*Brown*. In 1951, he argued the state's case in favor of executing an alleged black rapist named Willie McGee. First convicted in 1945 for raping a white woman, McGee became an international cause célèbre when a left-leaning, northern-based civil rights organization, the Civil Rights Congress (CRC), discovered that McGee had been having a consensual affair with the alleged victim. The CRC decided not only to take up the case but also to use it as a propaganda tool against the South by sending a full motorcade to Jackson in 1950. Thanks in part to the CRC, McGee gained outside representation from New York attorney and future congresswoman Bella Abzug, who battled J. P. Coleman all the way to the Supreme Court. Coleman's eventual victory over Abzug, securing the execution of Willie McGee, reinforced his conviction that the Court could ultimately be made a southern ally and showed him how outside groups could use southern atrocities to fuel northern propaganda. The McGee case led to demonstrations in Chicago, Detroit, and New York, in addition to letters pleading for McGee's release from political officials as far away as China and the Soviet Union.[28]

Just as Coleman had learned that racial extremism did not help Theodore Bilbo's image nationally, so, too, did the McGee case teach him how perceived racial extremism could draw unwanted publicity and attention to the South in the postwar era. At the same time, his victory affirmed for him that the Supreme Court could be brought to the southern side by adopting a reasonable legalist approach to combating civil rights.

Coleman's battle with the CRC, an organization that had few, if any, ties to blacks in Mississippi, reinforced his view that integration was a radical northern goal, sponsored by left-wing, elitist groups who had little concern for average southern people. To him, such groups only obfuscated the reality that *Brown* was bad for both races and that segregation was a mutually beneficial arrangement. "I am for segregation not because I hate Negroes," he wrote one constituent in 1958, but "because I know from experience, as you do, that it is for the best interest of both races."[29] Segregation, for Coleman, was a "kindness" that made life "easier" for blacks by keeping them protected from white extremists, ultimately representing an "implement of orderly, peaceable government."[30] Not only did it neutralize racial tensions but also segregation allowed blacks to improve their lives free from white interference and control.

Of course, implicit in such a view was an inability to see how segregation actually reinforced racial subordination. Not only did Jim Crow laws separate whites and blacks in public spaces but also they facilitated an often remarkable disparity in resource allocation. For blacks, public accommodations were not only set apart from whites, for example, but were often considerably inferior. Black schools received less money, black neighborhoods received fewer public services, and black chances to rise out of poverty were blocked by obstacles to professional education, licensing, and employment opportunity, not to mention voting. Coleman's inability to see the potentially devastating effects of such barriers to black advancement reflected a deeper prejudice that, while not vitriolic or violent, nevertheless made it impossible for him to understand black demands in Mississippi at the time. Indeed, Coleman was shocked when black leaders who had previously assured white officials that they opposed integration summoned the courage to denounce segregation during a meeting with Governor Hugh White in Jackson in July 1954. Rather than take this as a sign of black frustration with segregation, however, Coleman saw it as evidence that groups like the CRC and NAACP were brainwashing black leaders.[31]

Confident that neither blacks nor whites wanted to send their children to integrated schools, Coleman campaigned for governor of Mississippi in 1955 on a platform of improving schools for both races and encouraging economic development across the state. Committed to the notion that segregation was good for both races, Coleman consciously avoided making ill-considered, negative statements about African Americans and refused to endorse the Citizens' Councils. This was remarkable, given that the councils had, since the summer of 1954, amassed considerable popular support in favor of outright defiance of the Supreme Court. Coleman was the only one of five gubernatorial candidates not to endorse the Councils, a move that he rationalized by emphasizing the importance of serving "all the people" in the state.[32] That he won the election suggests that Mississippi voters, who were overwhelmingly against desegregation, remained open to the idea that there might be more than one way of dealing with the Supreme Court as late as 1955.[33]

Resisting "Nullification"

J. P. Coleman openly signaled his opposition to defiance only two weeks after the *Brown* ruling on June 1, 1954. Responding to concerns about the Supreme Court's desegregation order, Coleman went on Mississippi television and proclaimed confidently that there was "plenty" the state could do to preserve segregated schools without resorting to extremism.[34] He noted that the *Brown* opinion substituted legal authority for "psychological and sociological" opinion and did not mention either how or when the South was to end segregation.[35] This meant, Coleman argued, that the state of Mississippi could legally engage in a variety of measures to preserve segregation by manipulating "normal district boundaries," as well as by assigning students to schools based on "health," "aptitude," and "intelligence."[36]

Convinced that "outside meddlers" had put "a few colored children" up to challenging segregation in the South, Coleman maintained that black students by and large did not want to give up "their own schools," "their own associates," and "their own teachers" simply for the chance to integrate with whites. Not only would such a move be challenged by "well-settled social rules" in Mississippi, he argued, but it would also mark an ill-considered rejection of substantive increases in black teachers' salaries, together with new, greatly improved black facilities in Mississippi. African Americans of "good judgment," contended Coleman, would not exchange "a bird in the hand" for "nothing" in the bush.[37]

Coleman's conviction that blacks lacked commitment to integration contrasted starkly with white extremists' vigorous argument that blacks were eager to integrate because they wanted to engage in interracial sex. Such preposterous claims became the centerpiece of extremist positions like those held by Mississippi Circuit Judge Thomas Pickens Brady in 1954. Brady popularized the view that integration would lead to "amalgamation" in a speech delivered to a group of white citizens in Greenwood, Mississippi, only a few weeks after *Brown* was decided. Lamenting the impact that integration would have on southern society, Brady announced that black activists wanted to "get on the inter-marriage turnpikes" in pursuit of a "social program for amalgamation of the two races" that would "blow out the light" in the "white man's brain."[38] Such claims played on long-standing fears of interracial sex in the South and inspired members of Brady's audience to form the first Citizens' Council in the summer of 1954.[39]

The Citizens' Councils, which eschewed violence but embraced economic coercion and legal defiance, spread quickly through the South and formed the backbone of a larger political movement to reject *Brown* known as massive resistance. Coined by Virginia Senator Harry F. Byrd in 1956, the term *massive resistance* rested on the flawed assumption that the best method of opposing the Supreme Court was outright defiance. This opposition drew dubious constitutional strength from the theory of interposition popularized by Virginia newspaper editor James Jackson Kilpatrick in a series of editorials in November 1955. First devised by James Madison and Thomas Jefferson in the 1790s, interposition held that individual states could substitute, or interpose, their own interpretations of constitutional law for those of the Supreme Court, thereby freeing them of any duty to obey legal rulings like *Brown*. Although such a position had motivated southern leaders like John C. Calhoun during the first half of the nineteenth century and still inspired southerners like Kilpatrick, interposition made little constitutional sense in 1955. At best, it was a formal way of dressing groundless constitutional rebellion in legal language, useful mainly as a rhetorical tool for extremists to gain uninformed votes.[40]

To J. P. Coleman, massive resistance and the extremists who supported it posed just as much a threat to preserving segregation as the outside "meddlers" who were pushing blacks to file ill-considered legal challenges to segregated schools. So long as black activists and white extremists were allowed to operate freely, believed Coleman, they would jeopardize the South's ability to preserve segregation. If they could be kept in check, however, then the federal government could be kept out of southern affairs, allowing the races time to separate themselves. Even if some blacks refused to remain in their own schools, he believed, they could be thwarted quietly by redrawing school district boundaries or even assigning students to schools according to factors that did not refer overtly to their color. Such legalist evasions, coupled with established racial norms, would effectively save segregation in the state.

To drive home the damage that extremists could cause the South, Coleman worked hard to remind white voters in Mississippi that what the South faced in the 1950s was very much like what it had confronted in the 1870s. Once again, he claimed on statewide television in 1954, the South's way of life was being challenged by "individuals of whom not a one ever lived in our state."[41] This challenge had to be met with the same "determination" that Confederate leaders like South Carolina Governor Wade Hampton exhibited during his opposition to Reconstruction. Though Hampton had himself been something of an extremist, Coleman focused instead on his loyal service to the South, arguing that he, too, was deeply committed to southern traditions, arguably even more so than the politically irresponsible proponents of massive resistance.[42]

Determined to avoid defiance, Coleman came into direct conflict with Tom P. Brady and James O. Eastland on December 12, 1955, when they joined Mississippi Congressman John Bell Williams in signing a resolution endorsing nullification of the *Brown* ruling.[43] Nullification, which lacked any legal basis, was, to Coleman, rash: "I am shocked and surprised by this proposal, because history teaches in a long succession of events that such efforts have always failed, and in failing have brought down terrible penalties upon the heads of those who attempted it."[44] To avoid such penalties, the new governor advocated calm. "What I want to do," Coleman told the state's lawmakers, "is to preserve segregation in Mississippi. I am not trying to grab headlines."[45]

Coleman's mention of grabbing headlines was suggestive. Though leaders like Eastland, Williams, and Brady saw interposition as the best possible response to the Supreme Court, it is possible, indeed, likely, that they, too, realized it was constitutionally flimsy. After all, Brady was an experienced judge, and both Eastland and Williams were accomplished attorneys. Their brazen endorsement of nullification may have had less to do with their belief that it would actually stop the Supreme Court than with a more instrumental belief that it could be used to rally white votes. This was certainly true of Eastland and Williams, both of whom relied on white voters to keep them in positions of power, and arguably for Brady as well, who later confessed to being interested in running for governor.[46]

Why might these leaders come to think that extremism would win them votes, even though it had little chance of actually succeeding against the Supreme Court? And how, if they were correct, did J. P. Coleman win the governor's race in 1955? Perhaps the best answer is that popular support for defiance grew in direct relation to grassroots organizing by groups like the Citizens' Councils, who expanded rapidly across the South from 1956 to 1959. Aided by extreme segregationists like James Jackson Kilpatrick, the councils endorsed a program of massive resistance that they then sold to legally unsophisticated voters as a more robust form of constitutionalism than Coleman's placement schemes. Indeed, prior to the rise of the councils, southern voters seemed relatively ambivalent about the best means of dealing with *Brown.* That they overwhelmingly opposed the ruling is relatively certain, yet many voters seemed to have been at least open to the idea that other means of circumventing the Court existed beside defiance. This was certainly true in Mississippi, one of the South's most conservative, racially divided states, as J. P. Coleman's victory attests.

Indeed, Coleman gained a certain amount of success by distinguishing himself from Brady, Eastland, and Williams, sometimes known as the "little three," and instead counseling legalist evasion as the best means of preserving the status quo. Afraid that defiance would compromise Mississippi's ability to keep black children out of white schools, for example, Coleman urged the Legal Education Advisory Committee to "pour cold water on any resolution coming before the new legislature for purposes of nullification of the Supreme Court decision."[47] Though Coleman derided Brady, Eastland, and Williams's means, he did not oppose their ends. "I don't have one iota of fear," he assured white Mississippians, "that we will not have segregation continued in this state."[48]

Remarkably, other politicians in Mississippi agreed. Representative Barron Drewry of Alcorn County, in Mississippi's hill country, praised Coleman's stand against Brady, Eastland, and Williams, all of whom he openly derided. "The people of Mississippi are tired of Eastland's snorting, Williams's bellowing and Brady's braying," explained Drewry. "As a member-elect of the 1956 legislature, I want you to know that I stand solidly behind you in the position you have taken concerning the nullification proposal of the 'little three.'"[49] Unfortunately for Coleman, Drewry's support was not enough to overcome a wave of extremism in the state legislature, fueled by the Citizens' Councils. Only a few days after Coleman blasted the Little Three, former Governor Fielding Wright came out publicly in support of interposition, a move that surprised Coleman and convinced him to compromise. Afraid of alienating legislative support for his moderate program, he signed a symbolic statement of interposition but rejected nullification on the somewhat legalist ground that it, and not interposition, represented outright rejection of the Supreme Court. In response to such waffling, Eastland wrote Kilpatrick that Coleman was simply trying to stay alive politically.[50]

Although Eastland's opinion was probably true, Coleman's willingness to compromise on interposition proved to be little more than a symbolic gesture and did not deter his larger goal of evading *Brown* through non-defiant, legalist means. In fact, the interposition resolution he ultimately signed was arguably a moderate one, calling for "all appropriate measures honorably and constitutionally available" to resist the Supreme Court.[51] Nevertheless, by assuming a more defiant public stance, Coleman managed to appear strong enough on segregation to get a variety of bills enacted that he might not have otherwise, all of which tacitly recognized the legal validity of *Brown*. Does this mean that he alternately feigned both compliance and defiance toward the Supreme Court? In a way, yes. One reading of Coleman's shift to endorse interposition is that he engaged in defiant posturing when it suited him, but he never endorsed defiance as actual legal policy.[52]

Thwarting the NAACP

To J. P. Coleman, the Little Three's move toward nullification only worsened Mississippi's reputation for racial extremism, an image exacerbated by the murder of Emmett Till and a string of other murders targeting civil rights activists that year. The first of these occurred in May, when an African American minister named George W. Lee was shot in his car as he was driving home through the small Delta town of Belzoni. Lee, a member of the NAACP, had been trying to register black voters in Humphreys County and had ignored white requests to refrain. Ike Shelton, the local sheriff, refused to charge anyone for the murder, claiming that he could not tell whether the shotgun pellets in Lee's face were bullets or lead fillings in his teeth. On August 13, an African American named Lamer Smith was killed on the lawn outside Tom P. Brady's courthouse in Brookhaven. Smith had also been active in trying to register black voters. Even though local police witnessed a white man covered in blood leaving the scene of the murder, they took days to arrest anyone. When three men were finally brought before a grand jury, it refused to indict any of them, bolstering the impression that whites in Mississippi tolerated, if not approved of, the killing of black people in the state.[53]

The violence inspired the NAACP to release the pamphlet *M Is for Mississippi and Murder,* which described the killings of Lee, Smith, and Till and called for the federal government to intervene in ending the violence in Mississippi. To fuel the fire, high-ranking officers in the NAACP made public statements decrying Mississippi's violent record. "It would appear from this lynching," announced Roy Wilkins, the NAACP's executive secretary, shortly after the Till killing, "that the state of Mississippi has decided to maintain white supremacy by murdering children. The killers of the boy felt free to lynch him because there is in the entire state no restraining influence of decency, not in the state capital, among the daily newspapers, the clergy nor any segment of the so-called better citizens."[54] Though something of an exaggeration, Roy Wilkins realized that white violence could be used to draw federal intervention into the South. In fact, two weeks after the Little Three signed their nullification resolution, Wilkins wrote to every NAACP branch in the country to suggest that they use the Till murder to lobby Congress into passing legislation authorizing federal intervention in the region. "[P]lease write without further delay to both Senators from your state and to the Congressman from your district," he urged branch leaders, "reminding them of the Till murder and asking that this session of Congress pass civil rights bills to give the Department of Justice authority to act in such cases as the Till killing."[55] Wilkins's tactic—using evidence of southern atrocities to lobby directly for congressional intervention in the South—suggests that at least some strategists in the early civil rights movement were thinking about ways to coerce southern compliance long before the famed direct action campaigns in Birmingham and Selma in 1963 and 1965. Though Wilkins certainly did not advocate direct action protest to provoke such violence, he undoubtedly saw how white extremism could help the black struggle.[56]

So did J. P. Coleman. As early as June 1955, Coleman warned constituents that "Congress might be inclined to implement the desegregation decision with laws" if the South chose to pursue defiance.[57] Such an eventuality would be disastrous, argued Coleman, given Congress's far-reaching powers over federal funding and the jurisdictional reach of federal agents. Conversely, "all the Supreme Court can do," he maintained, "is lay down a rule" from within the interpretation of a case, something that did not lend itself to particularly aggressive enforcement.[58]

Roy Wilkins, perhaps even more than black legal strategists like Thurgood Marshall, knew this. Three weeks after the Little Three signed their interposition resolution and one week before Coleman's inauguration, Roy Wilkins sent the Mississippi governor a telegram requesting that he do more for racial justice in his state. The inspiration behind the message was a magazine article by Alabama journalist William Bradford Huie recounting J. W. Milam and Roy Bryant's shocking confessions to the Emmett Till killing.[59] Given "the admission" of Bryant and Milam, wrote Wilkins to Coleman, "the National Association for the Advancement of Colored People calls upon you to convene the grand jury of Le Flore County for the purpose of a new presentment of the kidnap charges against these self confessed criminals."[60] A new trial on the separate charge of kidnapping, not murder, Wilkins explained, would have far-reaching effects. "If nothing is done to make them pay for at least one of their crimes," lectured Wilkins, "our country will be held up for international ridicule."[61] The reference suggested that he was using international politics, backlit by the Cold War, as a means of pressuring Coleman into helping African Americans.

Did Coleman fear, much less understand, such a move? It is almost certain that he did. After all, he had confronted just such a threat while prosecuting Willie McGee. Now, Wilkins and the NAACP seemed to be applying the tactic of focusing on southern atrocities to try to force the South to change its racial practices. White extremists, Till's brazen killers among them, only facilitated this project, further convincing Coleman of the strategic value of moderation. During his inaugural address on January 17, 1956, he responded to Wilkins and spoke about Huie's article and *M Is for Mississippi and Murder*. "Despite all the propaganda which has been fired against us," explained the new governor, "the country can be assured that the white people of Mississippi are not a race of Negro killers."[62] Realizing that reporters from national newspapers like the *New York Times* and the *Chicago Daily Tribune* were present, Coleman specifically addressed audiences outside the state. "I would like you, our friends outside Mississippi, to know," he continued, "that the great overwhelming majority of the white people of Mississippi are not now guilty and never intend to be guilty of any murder, violence, or any other wrong-doing toward anyone."[63] Coleman then urged his constituents to "keep cool heads and calm judgment in the face of all the provocation which is being hurled upon us." "[W]hile there is no magic remedy for the Supreme Court decision there are multiplied means and methods, all perfectly legal, by which we can and will defeat integration of the races in our state."[64] Offering other options, he called for evasion, not extremism, illustrating his conviction that the best way of preventing integration was through legalist means.

Roy Wilkins took issue with Coleman's suggestion that he and other activists were using white atrocities to force political change.[65] Outraged that Coleman would try to pin racial unrest on "provocation" by civil rights groups, Wilkins wrote to the new governor about the murder of an African American named Clinton Melton on December 3, 1955, in Glendora, Mississippi. According to Wilkins, the NAACP had purposely not intervened in the case, precisely because it hoped that Mississippi authorities might prosecute the killer, Elmore Otis Kimball, who had been identified by three witnesses. Despite the absence of such NAACP "interference," however, an all-white jury still refused to convict. To Wilkins, this meant that Mississippi was "unwilling to administer justice" in cases where African Americans were killed by whites, thereby validating the NAACP's push for "Federal intervention to uphold justice."[66]

Partly in response to Wilkins's letter, Coleman discouraged civil rights activists like the NAACP leader from visiting Mississippi. On April 27, 1956, for example, Coleman wired Adam Clayton Powell, a prominent black congressman from New York City, and Dr. Martin Luther King Jr., an increasingly prominent black minister in Montgomery, Alabama, to request them to stay out of the state.[67] Citing his "duty" as governor, Coleman alerted both men to the fact that conditions in Mississippi were "more tranquil than at any time in recent months" and that their appearance in the state would be "a great disservice to our Negro people."[68] In a prepared statement issued to the public, Coleman went even further, calling both King and Powell "professional agitators" akin to the "carpetbaggers" and "scalawags" who corrupted southern politics after the Civil War.[69] Both had been invited to speak at a meeting in Jackson sponsored by an organization called the Regional Council of Negro Leadership (RCNL).[70] King, in particular, worried Coleman because of his charismatic leadership of a massive bus boycott in Montgomery that had begun in December 1955 and was still in full swing during the spring of 1956. Seeing the avalanche of negative press the boycott generated for Alabama authorities and the greater outpouring of sympathy it generated for the black struggle, Coleman recognized that a similar conflagration in Mississippi might compromise his plans for peaceful evasion of *Brown*. Both King and Powell complied with Coleman's request, asserting that they had never planned to accept the RCNL's invitation.[71] Although this, of course, might have been true, the RCNL still chafed at the governor's move and attacked him for trying to project a façade of tranquility in the state. "The effort being put forth by Governor J. P. Coleman to give the outside world the impression that there is a tranquil state of race relations in Mississippi" must be challenged, lamented the RCNL at its meeting. "As long as the 986,000 Negroes in Mississippi are denied their God given American rights in the field of Education, voting and justice, there will be no tranquil era in Mississippi."[72]

To bolster his peaceful image of Mississippi, Coleman called for measures far beyond polite requests that civil rights activists stay home. Among the subtlest were innovations in the state's law enforcement and criminal justice system. During his inaugural address, for example, he promised that "the full weight of the government will unfailingly be used to the end that Mississippi will be a State of law and not of violence."[73] Acknowledging the negative implications of poor law enforcement like that demonstrated by the sheriffs in Belzoni and Brookhaven, Coleman admonished those in positions of power to conduct government on "a high plane of service, economy, and stability." They must "leave no doubt" that Mississippi was "an outstanding, safe place," where outside investors would feel comfortable "to locate and operate" and where all citizens would receive "fair and equitable treatment under fair and just laws."[74] It was a big promise, one that sought to reassure the nation that Mississippi was committed to peace through centralization of law enforcement. Coleman knew well that one of the weakest links in Mississippi's law enforcement machinery was the local discretion of elected sheriffs who had little interest in presenting a moderate image to the nation or the world, particularly if such an image hindered them in local reelection campaigns.

Centralizing the State's Law Enforcement Power

Convinced that Mississippi needed to rein in violence, Coleman made reforming the state's criminal justice system a central part of his administration. "I shall at the first appropriate opportunity," he announced during his inaugural address, "deliver a special message to the Legislature on the necessity of strengthening and improving all phases of our law enforcement machinery."[75] Up to that point, law enforcement was controlled largely at the local level, which gave the state little power to prevent instances of local defiance. To ameliorate this, Coleman advocated several limitations on local power. One was an unprecedented procedure through which locally appointed authorities and police could be recalled by popular vote. Thirty percent of the voters of any county could, under Coleman's proposed bill, request by petition a recall election of a county official, and 51 percent could recall a police officer. Once such a recall petition was made, a governor-appointed chancery court would be assigned the duty of deciding whether the official or police officer should remain in office. Such a bill defied what one newspaper called Mississippi's traditional "hands off policy when it came to 'interfering' in local affairs."[76]

To further control local affairs, Coleman increased state regulation of local justices of the peace. Such justices, elected by county, handled the vast majority of criminal cases in Mississippi, yet they often possessed little or no legal training. Generally, their salaries were contingent on producing convictions.[77] Justices of the peace had become notorious in Mississippi for charging exorbitant court fees and unreasonable fines for traffic violations and other petty crimes. Part of this stemmed from the fact that they were paid a percentage of the fees they charged, a situation inviting corruption. Coleman made it a goal of his administration to end this corruption and modernize the JP system. "Justices of the peace who want to do right have no need to fear," declared the governor in 1956, "but if JP's resist efforts to improve and modernize their offices, it could result in abolition of the JP court system, and they will have brought it on themselves."[78]

Coleman also strengthened the state highway patrol. State troopers derived their authority from the executive branch of state government, thereby providing Coleman with a law enforcement mechanism capable of overriding local sheriffs and intervening in local affairs. To make Mississippi's highway patrol "second to none," Coleman initiated a substantial reorganization of the patrol, as well as an overall increase in its numbers.[79] He succeeded in obtaining increases in both tag and drivers' license fees throughout the state to fund the expansion.[80] As he reflected many years later, his changes in the highway patrol had direct implications for the relationship between Jackson and other parts of the state, particularly the Citizens' Councils headquarters, the Delta. "For years and years," he explained, "the Mississippi Delta . . . was a fiefdom of its own. They didn't want anybody messing with their business; they ran their own affairs . . . and they just wouldn't permit any—they wouldn't even talk about having—state police."[81] Though state police had long existed in Mississippi, they lacked general jurisdiction and were limited largely to patrolling highways.[82] This meant that local law enforcement officers, particularly sheriffs, possessed almost complete autonomy, a situation that led to a type of "local option" law enforcement, where local police could essentially decide which laws to enforce and which laws to ignore. Because state troopers worked for the governor, they represented a potential threat to this arrangement in that they might be sent to rural counties to enforce state laws. This threat was exacerbated by the fact that many sheriffs made considerable amounts of money by agreeing to turn a blind eye to criminal activity, particularly violations of the state's prohibition against alcohol. Mississippi sheriffs, hoping to preserve their autonomy, lobbied futilely in the state House and Senate against the centralization of law enforcement statewide.[83]

Coleman's success against local sheriffs indicates that his strategy was beginning to draw popular support. Not only were state legislators undermining local police by granting voters the power to remove local satraps from office but also they were augmenting state troopers. This suggests that even as *Brown* incited extremism, it also created a desire to control it. For southern governors with a strategic sensibility like Coleman, popular support for maintaining order created an opportunity to advance bold new initiatives transforming the contours of criminal justice.[84]

Enhancing the reach of Mississippi's state troopers was just one part of Coleman's plan. The most remarkable measure he endorsed was the creation of a state agency called the Mississippi Sovereignty Commission. Established by statute in 1956, the commission was an executive agency given the public charge of using "any lawful, peaceful and constitutional means" to prevent implementation of *Brown*.[85] It possessed police powers, as well as adjudicatory capabilities. For example, members of the Sovereignty Commission could subpoena witnesses and require production of private "books, records, papers or documents."[86] Refusal to produce such evidence could result in imprisonment. Similarly, the commission had the power to use the Hinds County Chancery Court in Jackson "to enforce obedience to any process issued by it" and was further granted broad investigatory powers to look into the records of individuals, corporate entities, and political groups. Finally, the Sovereignty Commission possessed a propaganda wing dedicated to improving Mississippi's image nationally.[87]

Impressive in scope, the Sovereignty Commission replaced the Legal Education Advisory Committee and became an integral part of J. P. Coleman's strategy for maintaining segregation—and tranquility—in Mississippi by controlling both civil rights activists and white extremists. In the spring of 1958, for example, the commission became actively involved in thwarting a Citizens' Council attempt to have Medgar Evers, the head of the NAACP's Mississippi branch, and Executive Secretary Roy Wilkins arrested during an event at a black Masonic lodge in Jackson. The speeches had been planned months in advance to rally black support for civil rights in the state. Prior to the commencement of the speeches, Attorney General Joseph T. Patterson and a Sovereignty Commission investigator, Zack Van Landingham, drove to the lodge "to observe just what appeared to be going on."[88] The Jackson Police Department's Chief of Detectives Meady Pierce approached them, complaining that the Citizens' Council had attempted to sabotage the meeting. "You know what some damn fools have done?" Pierce exclaimed to Patterson and Van Landingham. "They have gone and gotten out warrants for Roy Wilkins and Medgar Evers."[89]

Upon investigation, Patterson and Van Landingham discovered that the Citizens' Council, convinced that "Governor Coleman and State authorities were afraid of Roy Wilkins and Medgar Evers," had obtained a warrant from a sympathetic justice of the peace to arrest the two civil rights leaders.[90] In an effort to derail the council's strategy, Attorney General Patterson contacted Dick King, a high-ranking council official, and warned him that arresting high-profile figures would not aid the cause of white supremacy in the state "because of the national publicity that would follow."[91] Van Landingham then contacted Louis Hollis, director of the Mississippi Citizens' Council, reiterating that the arrests would be bad for Mississippi. While Governor Coleman hurried back to Jackson to deal with the crisis, Hollis followed Van Landingham's advice, contacted other influential council members in the state, and conveyed to them his discussion with the Sovereignty Commission. By the time the speeches were scheduled, the councils had withdrawn their warrant.[92]

Not only did Coleman's Sovereignty Commission control white extremists but also it attempted to control civil rights activists. One method the commission deployed to do this was police surveillance. Almost one year before the Sovereignty Commission saved Medgar Evers from arrest, the commission began tracking his movements around the state. "At the meeting of the State Sovereignty Commission on November 20, 1958," read the minutes of one Sovereignty Commission meeting, "Governor Coleman suggested that spot checks be made of the activities of Medgar Evers, both day and night, to determine whether he is violating any laws."[93] That Coleman ordered the Sovereignty Commission to ensnare Medgar Evers in the violation of petty laws yet shied away from outright arrest at a public speech appears, on the surface, to be paradoxical. Yet, it hints at the deeper logic behind J. P. Coleman's larger civil rights strategy. Afraid of appearing to be a racial extremist, he had no qualms about appearing tough on law enforcement, particularly if such enforcement happened to thwart civil rights activists.

Coleman ordered a particularly bold display of law enforcement power in June 1958, when an African American named Clennon King tried to enroll in summer school at the University of Mississippi. King, a thirty-seven-year-old former professor, would have been the first African American to enroll at the university, predating James Meredith by almost four years. Although he had little trouble entering the campus, King encountered problems when he joined the line to register. Robert Ellis, a university registrar, invited King to his office and promptly asked him to leave campus. King refused, only to find state troopers, operating under Coleman's orders, waiting for him outside. The troopers arrested him, carried him bodily to a waiting car, and then drove him to patrol headquarters, where Public Safety Commissioner Tom Scarborough, at Coleman's request, ordered King examined by psychiatrists.[94] Based on his examination, a state judge ordered King committed to a state mental hospital. Governor Coleman, who orchestrated King's commitment, later told a press conference that the professor would either be confined to a mental hospital or tried for resisting arrest and disturbing the peace.[95]

Coleman's neutralization of Clennon King, which also included an order to seal off Ole Miss's campus so that agitators could not travel to the campus and stir unrest, showcased his penchant for both shrewd and subtle state action.[96] While King clearly had no mental problems, his quick examination and commitment precluded events from escalating to a riot, as they later did at Ole Miss in 1962. Of course, King's story still made it into northern newspapers like the *New York Times*, but it failed to make front-page news. By deftly handling state police and Sovereignty Commission agents, Coleman shut down a public attempt at black protest. He would further refine this strategy to prevent integration as his agents undertook the manipulation of black leaders themselves.

Recruiting Black Informers

On May 15, 1956, J. P. Coleman declared that it was time for the Mississippi State Sovereignty Commission to bring itself into "full effect and fruition" by taking two final steps toward expanding its power.[97] Specifically, the commission decided to allocate state funds to "buy information" from civil rights activists and, concomitantly, to hire black secret agents to serve as the commission's "eyes and ears" in African American communities.[98] The agents used to guide the commission through black political networks otherwise hidden from white view were usually older, middle-class African Americans who held prestigious positions in black colleges and schools and feared, correctly, that integration could lose them their jobs. Once on the Sovereignty Commission's payroll, they performed a variety of tasks, including reporting civil rights activity in their communities and intervening directly to diffuse civil rights protest.

For example, on December 10, 1957, Sovereignty Commission Public Relations Director Hal DeCell reported to Governor Coleman on a meeting in Clarksdale of the Regional Council of Negro Leadership, the same group that had invited Martin Luther King and Adam Clayton Powell to Jackson in 1956. "We had the meeting well covered with some of our Negro friends," asserted DeCell, referring to hired informants, "and will have by the latter part of this week, a complete typewritten report on what went on."[99] That Coleman was getting typewritten reports of RCNL meetings was remarkable. The RCNL, unlike the NAACP, was a relatively isolated, local organization, indicating a high level of state surveillance of black affairs. This also helps to explain how Coleman knew, for example, that King and Powell were scheduled to speak in Jackson and was able to preempt their visit.

The information furnished by the commission helped give Coleman a sense of which parts of the state might need particular attention. In August 1956, for example, Coleman received assurance from a Sovereignty Commission agent named William Liston that whites in Yazoo City were working together with black agents to quell civil rights activity themselves, independent of state help.[100] Liston noted that a black agent named Fred W. Young had called a "meeting of all the Negro teachers" in Yazoo City and warned them that "the fastest way for them to lose the proposed new Negro schools would be for them to engage in N.A.A.C.P. activities."[101] That African Americans were being offered new schools, and that black agents were being used to sell such schools, helps explain Coleman's approach of rewarding black separatism at the same time as it pressured blacks to resist integration.

Although Coleman's willingness to fund black schools was clearly designed to forestall integration, it was also indicative of a larger, perhaps unexpected, effect of *Brown*. As much as *Brown* seemed to pit the races against each other, it also brought moderates of both races closer together, usually by encouraging them to meet and forge compromises.[102] For example, white moderates throughout Mississippi worked hard to form interracial organizations or committees so that black and white leaders could sit down and negotiate deals in lieu of integrating. One such committee in Mississippi drew attention to itself in the summer of 1956, when Liston reported on civil rights in Vicksburg. According to him, an "Inter-racial Committee on Race Relations," composed of "outstanding and rational members of both races," had worked successfully through negotiation and mediation to "control extremists on both sides."[103] One committee member, J. H. White, gained particular praise from Liston for his openness to negotiating with whites, a willingness that might have stemmed from the fact that he was president of all-black Mississippi Vocational College.[104]

To Roy Wilkins, more than a thousand miles away in New York, such black cooperation was contemptible. "Over in Soviet Russia," exclaimed Wilkins during a speech on June 3, 1956, "they had a system of paying children to spy on their parents"; now Mississippi, in his opinion, was doing the same thing.[105] "Spies will tell who smiled at a Negro yesterday," he reported, "or what Negro said he was sick of Jim Crow, or what tired Negro woman said she wished she did not have to stand up while white men sat in the bus."[106] Although black collaboration clearly bothered Wilkins, there was not much he could do to stop it. In fact, some NAACP members in Mississippi even pressured him, threatening to switch sides and work for whites if he did not comply with their demands. One such mercenary was

Gus Courts, a black activist who was shot by a white racist in his own grocery store in Belzoni, Mississippi, in 1955. Unable to find work, Courts accepted money from the NAACP in exchange for delivering speeches and testifying in favor of civil rights legislation in Congress. By April 1957, however, that money had begun to run out, prompting Courts to ask Wilkins for more. Aware of his potential value to segregationists, Courts threatened Wilkins that if the NAACP did not send him $1,500 for a new store, he would switch sides and work for J. P. Coleman. "Must I go back to Mississippi, denounce the N.A.A.C.P. and accept the offers of the South?" Courts wrote Wilkins. "I could have avoided all this by accepting the offers of the Southern Whites but I chose to stand by the N.A.A.C.P. and its program upon its promises."[107] Courts, perhaps because he was the victim of a relatively sensational crime, proved too valuable a spokesperson for the NAACP to lose. Wilkins sent him the money a week later.[108]

Roy Wilkins's willingness to pay Gus Courts cash in exchange for making speeches against white southerners indicated the depth of his commitment to winning a constitutional struggle against the Mississippi Sovereignty Commission and J. P. Coleman on a playing field far removed from the federal courts. Though NAACP lawyers like Thurgood Marshall became better known as crusaders for *Brown*, Wilkins was very much involved in the fight, albeit in a subtler type of propaganda struggle that involved manipulation of hearts and minds. The goal of this struggle was to build popular support, and ultimately congressional and executive resolve, for coercing compliance with *Brown* in the South. The primary opponents of the NAACP in this struggle were southern moderates like Coleman, not white extremists like Eastland and Brady, who helped the NAACP by dis-crediting the South with their absurd declarations of defiance against the Supreme Court and their ridiculous claims that integration would lead to mongrelization and civilizational collapse. Rather than fear them, NAACP agents actually sought to increase the illusion of their influence. On April 29, 1956, for example, A. M. Mackel, a NAACP member from Natchez, Mississippi, wrote a letter to Roy Wilkins suggesting that *they* infiltrate the Citizens' Councils with agents appearing to be white extremists. "A friend of mine," wrote Mackel, "said we should infiltrate the Councils with the same type of propaganda they are putting on us."[109] Mackel suggested that the infiltrators pretend they were outspoken extremists, damaging the councils' image by making "a few 'Hitler' speeches."[110] Though such proposals were not acted on, the extent to which the battle over *Brown* bled into ideological terrain was nevertheless remarkable. Long before young black activists in the Southern Christian Leadership Conference or the Congress of Racial Equality used direct action to win hearts and minds nationally, leaders of the NAACP used other tactics, like the payment of black agents like Mackel and Courts, to achieve a similar end.

To the chagrin of the NAACP, established black leaders often refused to cooperate with NAACP plans, even petitioning to work for Coleman's administration. On November 13, 1958, B. L. Bell, a black school supervisor, wrote to Governor Coleman requesting employment with the Sovereignty Commission.[111] Coleman ordered the commission to investigate Bell to ascertain his reliability and influence. This process included an interview, during which Bell "furnished considerable information and names of individuals in Bolivar County whom he stated were members of the NAACP."[112] After conducting his investigation, a white Sovereignty Commission agent concluded that hiring Bell "has some merit."[113] He recommended paying Bell "$50 a month for a period of 3 months," noting that during this time Bell could monitor civil rights activity in the state and then "furnish any worthwhile information" to the commission.[114]

Political pragmatism, coupled with economic incentives, accounted for much of the Sovereignty Commission's success in attracting black agents. Informants sought money or services in exchange for cooperation. A dramatic example of this occurred when Clyde Kennard, a black former paratrooper, applied for admission to Mississippi Southern, an all-white college in Hattiesburg, in the fall of 1959.[115] The Sovereignty Commission devised a variety of plans to thwart him, none involving dramatic confrontations or violence. One was a full-scale investigation of Kennard's past and anything that could be used to disqualify him, including bad credit, bad moral character, and criminal violations. In pursuit of this end, the commission deployed investigators to search through Kennard's past work record, his past school records, and even vital statistics on his parents' marriage.[116]

The commission also recruited a taskforce of black ministers and educators to discourage Kennard from submitting his application. As one commission investigator wrote, "[I]t was suggested to these individuals that since they were leaders of their race in the community and since they were in favor of maintaining segregated schools, that it might serve a useful purpose if they would constitute themselves as a committee to call on Clyde Kennard and persuade him that it was for the best interest of all concerned that he withdraw and desist from filing an application for admission to Mississippi Southern College."[117] In exchange for their betrayal of Kennard, the black ministers and educators gave the Sovereignty Commission an implicit list of demands, not least of which was construction of an all-black junior college in Hattiesburg. "It is interesting to note," continued the Sovereignty Commission report, "that all three of the Negro educators when interviewed on separate occasions, brought into the conversation their need for a Negro Junior College in [Hattiesburg]. The inference was inescapable that they were attempting to bargain in a subtle manner."[118]

One of the more skillful bargainers was J. H. White, the same individual who had been recommended to the commission for helping subvert civil rights in Vicksburg. To avert a crisis at Mississippi Southern, White suggested that the Sovereignty Commission order the college's president, Dr. McCain, to find some way of bringing Kennard to Jackson where, by apparent accident, he could run into Governor Coleman. An impromptu meeting with Coleman, argued White, would appease Kennard (who, according to White, only wanted attention), especially if the governor promised to deliver the college.[119] Though Kennard would end up being arrested and jailed by local authorities for reckless driving and theft, J. H. White's not-so-subtle insistence on a black college in Hattiesburg provides a glimpse into the type of realpolitik that permeated race relations in Mississippi in the 1950s.[120] Rather than unsuspecting Uncle Toms, the black employees of the Sovereignty Commission banked on the hope that by aligning themselves with the state they could preserve their jobs, as well as gain benefits for themselves and the black community. The NAACP, to many of them, was an alien, even dangerous, force. Not only did it risk inviting a white crackdown but also it represented a challenge to their power. Instead of embracing the civil rights organization, some black leaders opted to go around it, engaging in accommodation with white authorities. Precisely because he was willing to engage in accommodation, Coleman used black informers to help him preempt direct action protest and subvert civil rights activism in the state.

Of course, violence remained a constant threat to black activism in Mississippi. Yet, as activists-for-hire like Gus Courts illustrate, white violence had a certain perverse currency in the civil rights world. While it clearly threatened black lives, it also helped the black cause, providing the NAACP with clear evidence that segregation was far from the system of "peaceable" government that J. P. Coleman tried to project. This led Coleman to rail against the manner in which the NAACP paraded victims of white violence like Courts around the country to win sympathy for the black cause. In March 1957, Coleman even traveled to Washington to testify against Wilkins and his tactics before a U.S. Senate subcommittee considering a civil rights bill.

Committed to equating Mississippi with murder, Roy Wilkins told the Senate subcommittee how Gus Courts had been "shot and seriously wounded" by a white man in his own store in Belzoni, Mississippi, simply for trying to vote.[121] Such acts of racial violence, lamented Wilkins, were not being solved by local authorities and demanded federal action.[122] Coleman, who had been trying to improve Mississippi's criminal justice system to avoid such eventualities, testified that accounts of racial violence in Mississippi, including Courts's shooting, were exaggerated.[123] Complaining that Mississippi had become a "whipping boy," Coleman testified that white Mississippians "do not deserve a blanket indictment just because there were 4 Negroes killed by the whites in that State in 1955, while the Negroes were busily engaged killing 159 of their own number."[124] Coleman's emphasis on black criminality represented a new way of deflecting attention from racially motivated killings, not to mention the shortcomings of local law enforcement. Of course, Coleman did not mention that he was, at that very moment, engaged in trying to improve such law enforcement. Perhaps he felt that such a concession would lend credence to Wilkins's point. Instead, he attacked the manner in which the NAACP used white-on-black killings as chess pieces in "national politics,"[125] while neglecting to mention black-on-black murders, presumably because they were not as politically relevant.[126] Trying to paint Wilkins as a propagandist, Coleman struggled to reassure the subcommittee that federal legislation would not "aid the Negro" at all and instead would become a "continuous source of agitation, uproar, tumult, and domestic discord."[127] Here we catch a glimpse of the manner in which Coleman perceived civil rights gains to jeopardize larger state interests, most notably the preservation of peace and tranquility. Here also we see evidence of how Coleman and Wilkins fought publicly over whether federal intervention should be increased in the state, long before the direct action campaigns of 1963 and 1965.

Despite his best efforts, Coleman's testimony did not prevent the enactment of the 1957 Civil Rights Act. Desperate to get some kind of civil rights legislation passed, Senator Lyndon Johnson, with an eye on the presidency, made a series of compromises to push the bill through. Though weakened by concessions, the act reaffirmed Coleman's conviction that civil rights groups could strategically use white violence to win more robust federal enforcement of *Brown.*

Influencing the National Media

Coleman's trip to Washington in March 1957 was not his only attempt to influence congressional opinion of the South. Beginning in 1956, he encouraged the State Sovereignty Commission to devise creative ways to improve Mississippi's image in the North and West, in hopes that by increasing popular support nationally, he could reduce political support for the NAACP. In October 1956, Coleman invited a group of newspaper editors and publishers from New England to tour Mississippi in hopes of changing their opinions about the state. After meeting the newsmen personally at the Jackson airport, Coleman arranged for bus trips and steamboat rides to almost a dozen Mississippi cities. Many of the newsmen, representing publications like the *Darien Review* and the *Petersborough Transcript*, left impressed. According to one editor's ensuing story, pleasant "receptions" at antebellum plantation homes made the trip both enjoyable and memorable.[128]

Though the New England editors' tour did not stop the 1957 Civil Rights Act, it did raise the ire of NAACP Secretary Roy Wilkins. As soon as he heard of the plan, he wrote a letter to each journalist scheduled to take the trip. After commending them for going after "a first-hand view of what goes on in Mississippi," he warned "that the sponsors of conducted tours" tended to show guests only "those aspects of the community which they wish tourists to see."[129] Wilkins implored the editors to ask whites about the conditions that African Americans faced in the state, questions regarding voting, political opportunity, and jobs. "We would suggest, also," continued Wilkins, "that if your sponsors will permit you to do so, you try to talk freely with some Negro citizens of Mississippi, although it is likely that if a white Mississippi sponsor is present, the replies to questions may be more diplomatic than informative."[130] Along with the letter, Wilkins enclosed a copy of *M Is for Mississippi and Murder.*[131]

Though a tour of Mississippi by editors from small New England newspapers might seem inconsequential, the fact that Roy Wilkins took it upon himself to write to each of the editors suggests that it was not. In fact, Wilkins's interest in the tour, coupled with Coleman's decision to host it, indicates just how intensely the two struggled over conflicting images of the South. These images, in turn, contributed to their constitutional struggle over *Brown* precisely because they helped each leader promote positions that they hoped voters would respond to, either by demanding or, in Coleman's case, rejecting federal enforcement of the ruling. Both were relatively aware that such legislation required marshaling popular support, which they struggled to garner long before the momentous Civil Rights Acts of 1964 and 1965. Coleman and Wilkins both suggest that the constitutional struggle over *Brown* in the 1950s was not simply a matter of white defiance against NAACP gains in the federal courts but also an ideological struggle over the hearts and minds of American voters.

Hoping to win this struggle, the Sovereignty Commission continued its propaganda campaign. In 1958, it mailed more than 200,000 letters outside the state to advertise Mississippi as an attractive frontier for business investment.[132] It also printed pamphlets with titles like "All Mississippi Asks Is Fairness and a Chance to Present Its Side of the Case" and distributed them nationally to local newspapers and chambers of commerce.[133] Hal DeCell, the Sovereignty Commission's public relations director, traveled to meetings of the National Editorial Association, hoping to establish further contacts with editors in the North and West.[134] Recognizing the emerging significance of television to national politics, the commission tried to recast Mississippi in the eyes of national network audiences. It offered technical advisers, for example, to producers interested in doing documentaries on the state and actually provided one for a piece on Emmett Till.[135]

How are such measures to be assessed? One way to analyze Coleman's efforts to present a positive image of Mississippi in the 1950s, including his propaganda clashes with Roy Wilkins, is to compare him with Orval Faubus, the otherwise moderate governor of Arkansas at the same time. Faubus initially showed relatively little interest in managing affairs at the local level and even allowed a school board to admit black students to a white school in Hoxie. Although this made Faubus appear much more moderate than J. P. Coleman, he quickly transformed his image when a local school board in Little Rock decided to admit nine black students to all-white Central High School. As extremists in the state began to publicize the school board's decision, Faubus took a bold, ill-considered move and ordered the National Guard to surround Central High and turn the black students away. Almost overnight, Faubus became known as an extremist willing to use military force to defy the U.S. Supreme Court and drew unwanted negative attention to the state. This attention increased when Faubus called off the National Guard and left the black students at the mercy of an unruly mob. As violence erupted in the streets of Little Rock, prompting President Dwight D. Eisenhower to send the 101st Airborne into the city to restore calm, national opinion shifted dramatically against extremists in the South, prompting even the Supreme Court to step in and denounce massive resistance in a 1958 opinion holding that states could not simply "annul" Supreme Court rulings.[136]

In J. P. Coleman's view, the entire event should never have happened and could easily have been avoided. Faubus, in his opinion, had deliberately traded short-term political support among extremists in Arkansas for long-term gains against the Supreme Court and the NAACP. The NAACP, he believed, gained legitimacy thanks to Faubus's defiant antics, which emboldened the Court to make an unprecedented stand against overt segregation in the South. If Faubus had pursued a strategy like Coleman's, designed to control potential unrest at the local level, then events would never have reached the chaotic point that they ultimately did.[137]

Only two months after the Supreme Court decided against massive resistance in *Cooper v. Aaron*, it turned around and approved a placement plan modeled after the one that Coleman had helped design in Mississippi.[138] Affirming the holding of a district court in Alabama, the Supreme Court upheld a placement statute that allowed local officials to assign students to schools based on a variety of factors, including their "home environment" and "moral conduct."[139] Though the Court made it clear that the statute could later be found unconstitutional in its application, it was, it decided, not unconstitutional on its face. This holding, in *Shuttlesworth v. Birmingham*, marked a substantial victory for Coleman's approach to *Brown*, no less so because it came on the heels of *Aaron*, which prohibited nullification schemes that operated "openly and directly," as well as those that nullified "indirectly" by way of "evasive schemes."[140] Did this mean that the Court did not consider what Coleman was doing to be evasive? It is hard to say. The Court mentioned nothing expressly in its opinion but did rely on the lower court's decision, which expressly noted that "no intellectually honest" person could deny that placement schemes had emerged in direct response to *Brown*.[141] According to Supreme Court historian Michael J. Klarman, a minority of justices did want to strike down the statute but were overruled by a majority who recognized the statute's intent, realized it would be hard to strike down in the future, but still voted to uphold it.[142] That the specter of defiance in the South at the time probably convinced the Court to accept such moderate subterfuges is no doubt true, but so, too, is the fact that Coleman's view of constitutional process was probably correct. Just as he promised, there were measures that states could take to prevent integration that were nondefiant and likely to win Supreme Court approval. To understand just how subtle some of these measures were, it is helpful to look more closely at Coleman's endorsement of pupil placement in Mississippi.

Targeting Black Moral Background

In September 1957, while Orval Faubus brought the attention of the world to Little Rock by provoking the federal occupation of Central High School, J. P Coleman worked on a much calmer, more sophisticated method of circumventing mass integration. The strategy hinged on a legalist measure called pupil placement, a mechanism for assigning students to schools based not on their color but on vague criteria like "morals, community welfare, and health."[143] Coleman had begun work on such a plan in 1953 and would continue to work on its implementation while an active member of Mississippi's Legal Education Advisory Commission (LEAC). The LEAC, which had been formed by Coleman's predecessor Hugh White, was vested with the authority to "recommend courses of action for consideration by the Legislature" so that Mississippi could "maintain separate education and separate schools for the white and colored race."[144] It was established, somewhat remarkably, on April 5, 1954, more than a month before the Supreme Court handed down its decision in *Brown*.[145]

Worried that the Supreme Court might rule in favor of the NAACP, Coleman joined other state officials in devising legalist means of evading the ruling long before the rise of massive resistance. In so doing, the LEAC worked hard to come up with strategies for evading the opinion that would not run afoul of Supreme Court review, even drawing inspiration from the NAACP's *Brown* briefs. Coleman learned of the content of such briefs after traveling to Washington to sit in on both phases of oral argument in the

Brown case. After listening to the NAACP make what he believed were unconvincing arguments that segregating children in school harmed blacks, Coleman returned to Mississippi convinced that the South could preserve segregation by making the precise opposite case, namely, that integration, for a variety of reasons, harmed whites. Central to making such an argument, however, was to challenge the type of psychological and sociological evidence that the NAACP had used to build its case in *Brown* with equally compelling sociological evidence against it. This, in Coleman's opinion, would not be particularly hard to do. After all, the NAACP had relied on a variety of creative, methodologically shaky "tests" to prove that segregation harmed black children. Perhaps the most notorious of such tests, conducted by sociologist Kenneth B. Clark, presented black children with colored dolls and then asked them which doll they found more desirable. Though more black children in the North chose the white doll, suggesting that southern black children were actually better adjusted than their northern, nonsegregated counterparts, the Supreme Court bought Clark's evidence, citing it in footnote 11 of its opinion.

Footnote 11, to J. P. Coleman, meant at least two things. First, the Court had relied more on "psychological and sociological authorities" than on law to reach the conclusion it wanted. Second, similar "sociological and psychological" evidence might be marshaled by the South to get the Court to modify or limit its *Brown* ruling. Pupil placement, which rationalized the assignment of students to schools based on sociological factors, not race, provided the legalist mechanism through which to accomplish this. Critical to this, argued Coleman to his constituents, was the fact that Mississippi's pupil placement plan made "no reference to race" and instead sought to "put children in schools according to their 'best interest.'"[146] The people in charge of deciding that interest were, of course, white school board officials who gained the authority to assign black students to black schools not according to their skin color but "strictly on a basis of welfare, public health, safety and morals."[147]

Although placement plans would eventually come under Supreme Court scrutiny in 1968, they were more sophisticated, and ultimately more realistic, than massive resistance as a means of evading the Court. Forms of pupil placement had, for example, long existed in the United States.[148] Even though they seemed to promote gradualism by authorizing small numbers of blacks in white schools, Coleman remained adamant that social pressure alone would keep most black students from ever applying to white institutions. Placement plans would then be used to take care of the rest. Of course, admitting negligible, token numbers of black students to white schools could also have the strategic effect of reinforcing segregation by convincing federal courts that the South was complying with federal law even though, in essence, it was not.[149]

Pupil placement laws had another advantage. They enabled moderates to reconcile continued segregation with legitimate, reasonable, even moral goals. If students were assigned to schools simply because of their race, for example, observers in the North and West might argue that such a practice was superficial and fundamentally unfair. However, if students happened to be assigned to particular schools because they suffered from deficiencies that had nothing to do with race, then that evoked a more reasonable standard. What parents, after all, would want their children to be exposed to negative influences, regardless of the racial implications?

Evidence of just how far Mississippi took the link between pupil placement and extraneous factors like health and moral background emerged in January 1956. That month, Coleman recommended augmenting Mississippi's placement statute with a measure that sought to reinforce negative sociological evidence of black shortcomings. This measure, which seemed completely unrelated to either segregation or race, abolished common law marriage.[150] Common law marriage, according to Mississippi law, was any relationship in which a man and a woman made an informal agreement to "become husband and wife" and then proceeded to enter into a state of "cohabitation" without obtaining a formal marriage license.[151] Whether a couple was in a common law marriage could be proven by introducing evidence that the couple lived together and "held themselves out" as married by, for example, telling friends and family that they were husband and wife.[152]

What, if anything, did this have to do with race? Evidence suggests that Mississippi legislators, along with J. P. Coleman, believed that abolishing common law marriage would bolster the state's attempt to keep black children out of white schools based on questions of moral background. "[I]t is expected to bolster the state's use of a 1954 pupil assignment law based on morals, health, and welfare of the community," reported Vanderbilt University Law School's civil rights watch group, the *Southern School News.* "Of the 56,724 babies born in Mississippi in 1953, 7,337 were born out of wedlock, and of that number 7,070 were Negroes."[153] Under Mississippi's pupil placement plan, factors such as illegitimacy could be used to assign students to schools based on moral character. "LEAC members," reported the Baton Rouge *Morning Advocate,* "said the bill would aid segregation by permitting the state to segregate on a basis of 'unfavorable moral background' instead of on a basis of race."[154] "Under the law," the *Advocate* continued, "illegitimate Negro children would be considered as having 'unfavorable moral background' and could be kept out of white schools."[155]

How did determining "unfavorable moral background" relate to abolishing common law marriage? One possibility is that white leaders like Coleman hoped that abolishing common law marriage would end black marriages, artificially boost black illegitimacy rates, and give local school boards more options to keep black students out of white schools.[156] Under such a theory, however, African Americans needed to have a higher rate of common law marriage than whites, something that was difficult to establish, given the absence of reporting by those who did not gain formal marriage licenses. In fact, statistical evidence of black births during the years immediately following enactment of the law suggests that the common law marriage bill actually had little, if any, impact on black illegitimacy rates in the state.[157]

Perhaps a more likely possibility is that by abolishing common law marriage, state officials ultimately sought to make it easier to reject black applications to white schools solely on the basis of illegitimacy. In 1955, for example, there were 7,557 reported illegitimate black births in the state and only 286 recorded illegitimate white births.[158] Although such numbers could easily have been skewed by higher rates of adoption among whites, they still reflected a type of statistical measurement that could be used by the state to neutrally perpetuate segregation. By invalidating common law marriage, in other words, the state removed a likely defense that an admittedly large number of illegitimate black children might try to make to get into white schools, namely, that their parents were in fact married and only lacked a formal marriage license.[159] Local school boards could simply require black students to produce a copy of their parents' marriage license, something that upward of 20 percent of black children would be unable to do.[160]

The invalidation of common law marriage reveals the extent to which J. P. Coleman was willing to go, both theoretically and practically, toward reconfiguring segregation in the state.[161] It also reveals how legal concepts drawn from seemingly unrelated fields of law, like family law, could become embroiled in the larger controversy over basic constitutional rights.[162] Although no other state followed Mississippi in outlawing common law marriage, many hoped that alternate criteria like moral background could be used to keep black students out of white schools and survive federal court review.[163] Although the odds of this happening looked slim after the Fifth Circuit Court of Appeals struck down a placement law in Louisiana in 1956, the Supreme Court of the United States eventually upheld an Alabama placement statute modeled after Mississippi's law in 1958.[164] The Supreme Court made sure to reserve the right to strike down such placement laws in the future, but it refused to do so for the next decade, suggesting that black rights were contingent on a variety of subconstitutional criteria, like whether African Americans were married.[165]

Civil rights leaders tried to respond to the moral indictments that pupil placement plans hinged on. Martin Luther King Jr., for example, suggested in 1958 that black activists mount a two-pronged approach to gain their constitutional rights: by protesting legal discrimination directly and by countering white attacks on black moral behavior or culture by raising black "standards." "By improving our standards here and now," King asserted in 1958, "we will go a long way toward breaking down the arguments of the segregationist."[166] "[W]e must work on two fronts," he continued. "On the one hand, we must continue to resist the system of segregation which is the basic cause of our lagging standards; on the other hand we must work constructively to improve the standards themselves. There must be a rhythmic alteration between attacking the causes and healing the effects."[167] King's allusion to a rhythmic alteration meant that blacks needed to wage a particularly difficult struggle, one that sought to challenge both the law and white impressions of black behavior. To him, whatever gaps existed between whites and blacks were a direct result not of racial inferiority but of decades of segregation. That whites refused to acknowledge this meant that African Americans had to do more than just win legal battles; they had to actually shift the perception of race itself in the South.

Rewriting the State Constitution

Manipulating popular perception, independent of making arguments in court, represented a type of constitutionalism that would become increasingly central to the black struggle in the 1960s. So long as J. P. Coleman was able to present reasonable defenses of obstructionist tactics, meanwhile convincing Mississippi's state legislature to expand facially neutral opportunities for keeping black students out of white schools, he created the possibility for legal victory in the region. This was because the Supreme Court, ultimately, did not have to go beyond a superficial review of statutory language in determining compliance with *Brown*. If southern states could convince the Court that *Brown* simply demanded an end to overt racial classifications in state law, for example, then they could remove any mention of such classifications from their state codes, while still engaging in discrimination. The likelihood of this was made even greater if the region could make a reasonable appeal to the nation that it was upholding moral standards and not discriminating unfairly on the basis of race.

Mississippi's invalidation of common law marriage, of course, tried to do just that. Even though civil rights activists arguably recognized the manner in which such a measure augmented pupil placement, it was by itself completely neutral. Many states both inside and outside the South had long done away with the arrangement, making Mississippi look, if anything, like it was catching up to national trends. Subtlety, in this case, and not sensation appealed to legislators as a reasonable way of resisting civil rights.

While J. P. Coleman touted pupil placement as a means of avoiding *Brown*, he also scrambled to remove overt racial classifications from other areas of public law. Perhaps the most flagrant was Section 207 of the state constitution, which held "separate schools shall be maintained for children of the white and colored race."[168] On August 2, 1957, Coleman wrote to Speaker Walter Sillers of the Mississippi House of Representatives to warn him that if Section 207 were not removed, it would jeopardize the state's placement plan. Noting that he had been careful "not to give any tangible expression" to the problem that Section 207 posed, Coleman explained to Sillers that Mississippi could not "sustain the validity of our Pupil Assignment Law as long as Section 207 is in our Constitution."[169] Federal courts, according to Coleman, would focus on the provision and use it to invalidate any school bill that regulated the admission of students to schools, regardless of whether it mentioned race. If this happened, Coleman lamented, then all his work evading *Brown* would "come down like a house of cards."[170] Specifically, Coleman noted a recent Fourth Circuit Court of Appeals ruling asserting the validity of North Carolina's pupil placement plan and emphasized that Mississippi could survive federal review as well if it removed all overt references to race from its state law.[171] "The only thing to do is to get Section 207 out of Constitution," Coleman explained to Sillers, "and then revamp all our school laws to eliminate reference to race."[172] The first step in this process was not a constitutional amendment but a convention that would, in Coleman's opinion, make it easier to disguise the fact that the state was eliminating Section 207. If it did not try to hide this, Coleman feared the state might "afford every argument in the world to the NAACP and our other adversaries to say that the people of Mississippi had voted it out at the secrecy of the ballot box."[173] To avoid this, Coleman recommended "a general revision" that would not focus on "this particular problem."[174]

Coleman had other reasons to propose a general revision of the state's constitution. Among other things, he hoped a new constitution would enable the state to reapportion its legislature, which up to that point was heavily weighted in favor of the Delta, not the more populous districts to the south. The Delta's power skewed state politics, Coleman believed, by making the Mississippi legislature more racially extremist and less moderate than it might otherwise have been, both direct products of the region's plantation past. Due in part to its impact on reapportionment, Coleman's bid for a constitutional convention ultimately failed. Interestingly, it also failed because of Section 207. Citizens' Council leaders claimed, for example, that by removing Section 207, Coleman was actually trying to abolish segregation in the state. Such a literal reading of the plan, of course, failed to recognize Coleman's strategic insight into constitutional process. Yet, less sophisticated voters across the state had little understanding of strategic constitutionalism and began to suspect that Coleman was trying to open the doors of white schools to blacks. This led, inevitably, to a growing perception that Coleman was soft on segregation—an ironic position, given the lengths that he went to preserve it.[175]

Failing to change the state's constitution was not the only setback that Coleman encountered while governor. In April 1959, during his final year in office, Mack Charles Parker, a black man arrested for raping a pregnant, twenty-three-year-old white woman, was kidnapped from the Poplarville, Mississippi, jail by a band of hooded whites. Several days later, his corpse was found floating in the Pearl River. Four years had passed since the lynching of Emmett Till, and although there had been a lull in racial violence, Parker's murder stirred old fears, particularly in J. P. Coleman.[176] To Coleman, Parker's murder created yet another opportunity for civil rights groups like the NAACP to generate propaganda favoring more aggressive federal legislation in the South. Already, the Senate Judiciary Committee was conducting hearings on a second proposed civil rights bill, which Coleman was desperate to stop. Parker's murder, Coleman feared, would add momentum to the bill, particularly because it involved the flagrant kidnapping of a prisoner from a county jail. This brazen act of defiance, Coleman worried, would support long-standing NAACP claims that racial violence was tacitly sanctioned by southern state officials, a claim that, if true, bolstered the case for federal intervention in the region.

Coleman also was concerned that Parker's killing could destabilize a precarious equilibrium between moderate strategies of resistance to *Brown* and the Supreme Court. Since the murder of Emmett Till, for example, there had not been one case of integration in the state. In fact, in 1958 the Supreme Court had even invalidated massive resistance and tentatively endorsed pupil placement, two developments that boded well for Coleman's moderate approach.[177] Of course, if the Court began to suspect that national support for aggressive enforcement of civil rights in Mississippi was growing, then it might feel pressure to revisit placement plans and perhaps even invalidate them. Coleman, naturally, did not want this to happen. In many ways, he stood on the verge of victory over both the NAACP and the Citizens' Councils, a position that drove him to take a particularly adamant stance against the vigilante killing of Mack Charles Parker. In a controversial move that sought to preempt the NAACP's demands for federal intervention in the South, Coleman requested that the federal government intervene in the case, even inviting the FBI to investigate the Parker kidnapping and murder. In a letter to southern governors, he asked them to join him in a conference to "come up with the best possible solution" for preventing similar acts of racial violence in the future.[178] Such a meeting, he hoped, would send a clear message to the country that southern officials did not endorse racial violence and, he hoped, deflect any negative publicity created by the crime.

Interestingly, southern governors disagreed over whether such a stance was necessary. Some, like Virginia Governor Lindsay Almond, supported Coleman's proposal. "I share your view," wrote Almond, "that the time is now for the Governors of the southern states to sit down in conference and discuss this matter, resolving our views to the end that law and order shall and must prevail throughout the Southland."[179] Other governors, however, declined. "Without second, sober thought," noted South Carolina Governor Ernest F. Hollings, "my immediate reaction is 'no.'"[180] According to Hollings, the furor over the Parker killing was "not near so bad as your letter indicates," and a top-level meeting of southern governors would only "give credence" to allegations by civil rights groups like the NAACP that "something really is wrong with the South."[181]

Hollings's response was arguably naive. By refusing to meet, he and other governors were probably only giving the NAACP more opportunities to make the South look recalcitrant. Of course, not all southern governors understood as well as Coleman did just how determined black activists were to use white violence to their own advantage. In fact, the divergence of opinion between Hollings and Almond was indicative of a larger rift forming between southern leaders at the time. To most, like Almond, the days of massive resistance were over, and a new era of resistance was beginning, one in which the South needed to pursue legalist evasion while taking aggressive action to control racial violence and project a positive national image. To others, however, defiance was still desirable, if for no other reason than that it won votes. Hollings, for example, had won a battle against University of South Carolina President Donald Russell in 1958 by blasting him for being soft on segregation.[182] Now, he made a point to reject Coleman's meeting, fearing that it could be taken as a concession to the NAACP.

Disappointed, Coleman traveled to Washington to testify against the second civil rights bill in three years and found himself bombarded by questions about Mack Charles Parker. "How [did] they get the key?" asked Colorado Senator John A. Carroll, referring to the manner in which the mob gained access to the prisoner. "Was there a conspiracy on the part of the bailiff or the jailers?"[183] H. Slayman Jr., the subcommittee's chief counsel, asked Coleman why a grand jury hearing to indict the suspects would not be held until November, a delay that Coleman attributed to scheduling. Further questions revolved around black voting rights, black rights to a jury trial, and even whether the Mississippi State Sovereignty Commission was involved. Coleman tried desperately to bring the focus of the committee back to the proposed civil rights bill, but with little success. He ended up making a somewhat futile reference to the degree of support that he had received among African Americans in Mississippi for the public schools he had built—a non sequitur that had little to do with the subcommittee's main topic of interest.[184]

Despite this frustrating incident, J. P. Coleman's four years in office proved remarkably successful. He managed to push key pieces of legislation through the Mississippi House and Senate that increased the centralized power of the state's law enforcement capabilities while providing local officials with opportunities to keep black children out of white schools. Coleman also enjoyed considerable success in neutralizing potentially combustible racial protests. He subverted the applications of Clyde Kennard and Clennon King, who might have triggered riots. He also worked hard to keep activists like Martin Luther King Jr. out of the state, to buy information, and to some extent even to gain support from black leaders.

Perhaps Coleman's biggest failure lay in his inability to retain the confidence of white voters. Despite the many accomplishments of his administration, white voters replaced him with an outspoken segregationist and Citizens' Councils member named Ross Barnett in 1960. Coleman may have suffered from his own cleverness. Though he was astute in predicting much of what would happen in the 1960s and adept at forming legalist strategies, many white voters in the state concluded that he was weak on segregation. While clearly superior to massive resistance in constitutional terms, Coleman's strategies were by no means clear to voters, perhaps because they were not defiant enough. His emphasis on legalist evasion, coupled with his formalist compliance with the Supreme Court, understandably appeared more conciliatory than strategic.

The next chapter looks at how Luther Hodges, the governor of North Carolina, took Coleman's inspiration and built on it, forging his own even more successful moderate response to evading the Supreme Court's *Brown* ruling by effectively handling white voters in his state.

2

"LEGAL MEANS": LUTHER HODGES
LIMITS *BROWN* IN NORTH CAROLINA

Raleigh is almost eight hundred miles by car from Jackson, a distance matched, some might say, by differences in political climate. Even in the 1950s, many southerners would probably agree that Raleigh was not quite as conservative as Jackson, was more progressive, and was more interested in technological innovation and economic growth. Yet, while Mississippi Governor J. P. Coleman struggled to evade the Supreme Court's ruling in *Brown v. Board of Education*, North Carolina Governor Luther Hodges took notes.

Hodges had been personally intrigued by Mississippi's approach to circumventing integration since he became governor, in November 1954. A month after he took office, the North Carolina governor wrote directly to J. P. Coleman's boss at the time, Mississippi Governor Hugh White. "I was very sorry that I could not get down to the Governors' Conference at Boca Raton and have an opportunity to renew my acquaintance with you and get some advice from an old timer," wrote Hodges to White, but "[a]t your convenience would you let me know how you are coming along with your segregation problem. I know you have made some progress on the so-called 'Mississippi, or Assignment Plan.'"[1]

In response, White sent Hodges a courtesy copy of Mississippi's plan for assigning students to schools based not on their color but on other racially "neutral" criteria.[2] Hodges used the statute as a model to develop a bill that he personally introduced to the General Assembly in January 1955, selling it as a way to avoid "the mixing of the races," yet still "meet the requirements" of *Brown*.[3] When North Carolina's legislature adopted a modified version of the plan later that spring, Hodges had one of his advisors invite Ney Gore, the director of the Mississippi State Sovereignty Commission, to Raleigh to help work out the details of how placement would actually work.[4]

Not convinced that pupil placement alone would preserve segregation, Hodges enacted other strategies, which to a remarkable degree corresponded to measures that J. P. Coleman took in Mississippi. For example, he used a centralized state agency, the North Carolina State Bureau of Investigation, to monitor black activists and control white extremists, not unlike Mississippi's Sovereignty Commission. Just as Coleman feared that acts of racial extremism might compromise the South's image, so, too, did Hodges worry that the national press might focus on isolated racial incidents to produce a skewed image of North Carolina. Interested in appealing to the nation, Hodges worked hard to reframe segregation as a legal arrangement that helped African Americans by protecting them from white interference and preserving racial peace. At the same time, Hodges advanced the idea that integration was an alien, northern concept that would only lead to violence and unrest, much like Coleman did in his state.

Yet, Hodges differed from Coleman in at least two ways. He placed greater emphasis on appealing to average voters, ensuring that white and black voters alike felt they had some say in the desegregation controversy. For example, he advocated legal mechanisms called "safety valves" that allowed white voters to close school systems if they did not trust the manner in which he proposed to handle them. He also endorsed a popular referendum on a desegregation plan that he and a group of handpicked legal advisors put together to evade the Supreme Court. Continuing this emphasis on localism, Hodges even tried to encourage African Americans to choose black schools willingly by endorsing a plan that he called "voluntary segregation." To promote such an idea, Hodges offered a set of incentives and costs. He argued that if blacks voluntarily remained in their own schools, they would receive superior facilities and also be able to better preserve their own culture and traditions than if they enrolled their children in school with whites. Conversely, if blacks did not voluntarily go to segregated schools, Hodges warned, then they would be responsible for school closures, robbing their children of educational opportunities in the process.

When African American leaders made it clear that they would not segregate themselves voluntarily, Hodges shifted attention away from black civil rights claims and toward black shortcomings, particularly illegitimacy rates, eventually arguing for punitive, antiwelfare measures that had a disproportionate impact on blacks. Here again, Hodges and Coleman converged. Hodges's turn to illegitimacy rates, like Coleman's, reflected an attempt to shift the terms of the debate over *Brown* away from white repression and toward black shortcomings, thereby introducing a new fiscally and morally conservative idiom for rationalizing resistance to integration. Yet, partly due to North Carolina's long history of progressivism, this move became bitterly contested both by those who wanted harsher measures leveled against blacks and by others who wanted none. Some state leaders, for example, demanded that unwed mothers be sterilized. Others, like Hodges, recommended that they be subjected to increased state monitoring and control. Meanwhile, advocates of adoption argued that draconian measures, particularly if they were race-neutral, should be stopped, partly because they might end up negatively affecting whites.

Looked at as a whole, North Carolina's response to *Brown* represented a type of strategic constitutionalism that tried both to project a positive image of the state to the rest of the country and to convince the Supreme Court to reinterpret *Brown* in its favor. Rather than an isolated corollary to this strategy, North Carolina's battles over welfare regulations sought to augment it. By shifting attention to black illegitimacy rates, state leaders like Hodges hoped to present a reasonable case to the nation by explaining precisely why whites did not want to send their children to integrated schools. Hodges also hoped to place more obstacles in the road to black advancement by demanding that African Americans fix a variety of vaguely defined social ills before they were allowed to desegregate white schools.

Finally, like J. P. Coleman, Hodges worked hard to rein in white extremism, particularly the Ku Klux Klan. Klan activity posed a considerable problem in North Carolina, despite the state's otherwise progressive reputation. Hodges employed informers to infiltrate the organization and used state agents to intimidate Klan leaders. He also struggled with media portrayals of the Klan in an effort, much like J. P. Coleman, to project a positive image of his state. Hodges's response to the Supreme Court presents another example of just how broad and complex the ideological, political, and legal battle over desegregation could be.

To Raleigh via New York

Born on March 9, 1898, Luther Hartwell Hodges came from relatively modest origins. His father worked as a tenant farmer in Pittsylvania County, Virginia, before moving his wife and nine children to Spray, North Carolina, so he could work in the region's textile mills. Though mill life was hard, it provided Luther Hodges with considerable opportunity. He attended a company-owned school, worked as an office boy in one of the mills near his home, and later became a mill hand to help pay tuition at the University of North Carolina in Chapel Hill. After graduation, Hodges returned to the mills as a secretary at an operation in Leaksville, then owned by Marshall Field of Chicago. By the relatively young age of twenty-two, Hodges became personnel manager of all Marshall Field's mills in his home area. By thirty-six, he was promoted to production manager of all the company's mills in Leaksville, and by forty-two he became general manager of all Marshall

Field's mills in the United States. Before his forty-sixth birthday, Hodges was promoted to vice president of the entire company, a dramatic rise that took him out of the South and brought him to New York City from 1940 to 1947.[5]

Hodges's career path through North Carolina's mill world helps explain his approach to racial politics. Textile mills tended to be extremely segregated spaces, as well as economically efficient ones. Because he rose up through management ranks, Hodges was less likely to see segregation as a hindrance to economic growth and more likely to view it as a mutually beneficial arrangement, perhaps even a bar to unionism.[6] Hodges's eventual move to New York City did little to change this. During the summer of 1943, for example, Harlem erupted in some of the worst race rioting in New York history, prompted by the brutal arrest of a black serviceman by a white officer.[7] Two years later, in September 1945, "open warfare" broke out between white and black students, again in Harlem, at a local high school.[8] Such conflicts convinced Hodges that if segregation did anything, it kept the peace, even in the North.[9]

Such conflicts also convinced Hodges that the South was ultimately not that different from the North. While New York–based organizations like the CRC and NAACP were pressing for racial change in Dixie, few could have denied that Harlem and other parts of the city were segregated in the 1940s. Hodges did not mix with Bella Abzug or others spearheading calls for change in the South, but with the city's business elite, who seemed to have little problem with his southern roots and supported his rise to become president of the New York City Rotary Club. Such success helps explain Hodges's later interest in drawing northern investment to the South, coupled with his conviction that a reasonable, professional, moderate stance would be well received in the North, perhaps even allowing the South to continue its racial practices unchanged.[10]

Another experience that might have contributed to Hodges's moderation occurred after he retired from Marshall Field in 1950. Thanks to Robert M. Hanes, an influential North Carolina banker involved in the allied reconstruction of Germany, Hodges received an appointment as "chief of the industry division" of the Economic Cooperation Administration in West Germany. This job took Hodges to the ruins of Frankfurt, Munich, Stuttgart, and Berlin to oversee the dissemination of Marshall Plan money and to make sure that the Germans did not return to "any build-up of military or strategic items."[11] Though Hodges made little mention of this experience later in his career, it is certainly possible that his tour of the former Third Reich drove home to him the potential costs of racial extremism. It is also possible that he gained an appreciation for the potential largesse that might be bestowed by the federal government on a developing region, provided that it remained compliant.

When Luther Hodges finally returned to the South at the end of 1951, it was a firm belief in economic development and business investment, not racial demagoguery, that motivated his decision to run for lieutenant governor.[12] In Hodges's opinion, industrialization was the South's best chance for improving the lot of its citizens, black and white.[13] He later noted that he was particularly sensitive to the fact that North Carolina, in 1954, ranked forty-fourth of the forty-eight states in per capita income. Ameliorating this "low economic state" became his primary goal as governor, one that he pursued through an aggressive campaign of "industry hunting"that took him around the country and the world, selling the South to outside investors.[14] Part of this campaign involved telling "the North Carolina story," as he put it, of attractive corporate taxes, cheap labor, abundant resources, and progressive government.[15]

The controversial subject of racial integration, if anything, interfered with this story. To Hodges, segregation did not hinder the state's advancement; it prevented racial tension and facilitated "a friendly relationship of mutual helpfulness" between the races, one that would help it move "forward."[16] This type of thinking coincided with the manner in which North Carolina's textile mills were run, as highly efficient, segregated institutions.[17] Consequently, when he learned that his predecessor, William B. Umstead, who died in office on November 7, 1954, had already assembled an advisory committee to study the *Brown* ruling and come up with "lawful" means of evading it, Hodges agreed to continue the committee's work.[18]

Drafting a Legalist Response: The Pearsall Committee

The leading member of North Carolina's committee to evade *Brown* was a lawyer named Thomas J. Pearsall. Owner of a large plantation in Rocky Mount, North Carolina, Pearsall had served in a variety of positions in state government prior to 1954, including speaker of the State House of Representatives.[19] Sometime during the summer of 1954, he agreed to head Governor Umstead's Special Advisory Committee on Education, a body made up of nineteen members, three of them African American.[20] The African American members, in a manner that coincided with the type of biracial cooperation that emerged in Mississippi after *Brown*, were all on the state payroll and were asked to represent North Carolina's black community.[21] Yet, their ability to do so became a matter of some controversy, which became clear in August 1954 when Governor Umstead met with a group of African American leaders from across the state, all of whom demanded immediate compliance with the *Brown* ruling.[22]

Partly as a result of this black protest, the committee decided, early on, to remove its black members. "I felt like they would be a hindrance to the Committee," noted Pearsall, specifically because they lacked "objectivity."[23] Hodges agreed, and soon after he became governor, he dismissed the three African American members.[24] He later noted that this decision had to do not only with Pearsall's recommendation but also with the political pressure he felt the NAACP was putting on the committee to encourage forced, mass integration. In his opinion, the group's black members would have been forced to work "under almost impossible conditions" due to "outside pressure" from the NAACP.[25]

Hodges tended to view the NAACP just as J. P. Coleman did: an outside, meddling force that sought to impose its agenda onto an unwilling African American population.[26] In his view, African Americans in North Carolina possessed their own institutions, their own teachers, and their own pride in black schools, none of which they particularly wanted to change. In fact, instead of integration, Hodges came to believe that a silent majority of African Americans in North Carolina actually wanted compensation, more money to raise teachers' salaries and improve black schools. His belief in a black silent majority that favored continued segregation was reinforced when he occasionally found African Americans who were willing to endorse segregation.[27] On August 22, 1955, for example, Hodges alerted Thomas J. Pearsall to two potential black supporters. "We sent you the other day a memorandum of a Negro in Siler City," wrote Hodges, "by the name of T. R. Edwards, Jr. I have asked the Editor of the paper there to advise me if he is in a position to help out publicly, if needed."[28] In addition, "[p]lease note also that Dr. Nathaniel Tross (Minister and educator) of Charlotte is available," wrote Hodges. "He made a public statement on August 9, the day after my speech, supporting it strongly."[29]

Hodges's belief that black allies could be recruited in the struggle against *Brown* was indicative of his conviction that blacks generally did not support integration and that *Brown* could be handled, and segregation maintained, with relative ease. Contributing to this belief, perhaps ironically, was his belief that even the Supreme Court did not truly endorse integration and would tolerate continued racial separation so long as it was conducted in a manner that conformed, formally, to *Brown*.[30] "The average person, white and Negro," Hodges remembered, "had not really studied the court order," leading many to believe "that the court had ordered integration, which it had not."[31] Just like Coleman, Hodges thought that *Brown* could be read in different ways, some of which provided hope for Jim Crow.[32] One way it could be read, for example, was that it did not order integration so much as demand that states remove the formal requirement that blacks and whites attend different schools. Methods of assigning students to schools according to factors other than race might be considered constitutional. Similarly, leaving black and white schools intact might be constitutional, so long as students remained free to choose which schools they attended.

Such technical, legalist distinctions became matters of significant interest to the Pearsall Committee. In fact, the committee gained insight into some of the legal ambiguities of *Brown*, thanks to James Paul, a young lawyer who had served as a law clerk to Supreme Court Chief Justice Fred M. Vinson during the early stages of the *Brown* case. Vinson, who opposed integration, died abruptly on the bench on September 8, 1953, opening the way for a unanimous ruling in favor of the NAACP. Vinson's death left Paul out of a job, a situation he remedied by going to work for the University of North Carolina's Institute of Government, to which the Pearsall Committee turned for analysis. Paul's report on *Brown*'s legal implications, together with his analysis of possible responses to it, became a "guideline" for the committee, underscoring the multiple interpretations of the decision.[33]

Paul's report also convinced the Pearsall Committee to abandon any pretense of defiance against the Supreme Court, lest it invite federal court "supervision" over desegregation in North Carolina.[34] This report's anticipation of a link between defiance and federal supervision suggests that North Carolina came to understand early on that extremism might backfire on the South and actually speed integration in the region. As early as 1954, in other words, legal strategists in North Carolina, like legal strategists in Mississippi, recognized that moderation, not extremism, might provide a better method of preserving segregation.

Even though Paul warned against extremism, it was Mississippi that provided North Carolina with the legalist strategy that it would eventually use to evade *Brown*.[35] "We have to bow to Mississippi," joked Pearsall, for providing North Carolina with a scheme that promised to both preserve segregation and comply with the Supreme Court.[36] By ending placement based on race, the plan "legally struck out the requirement in North Carolina statutes for segregation" yet, rather than "permit integration," it became a way for the state to "protect [itself] from integration."[37]

Another insight to emerge from the report was a notion, based on the committee's reading of the Court's opinion in *Brown*, that desegregation could best be fought on the local level, rather than the state level. According to Paul, the less centralized the authority over segregated schools was, the harder the system would be to dismantle. "We got the feeling that implementation had to be localized," noted Pearsall, "[t]herefore, the thing for us to do was to take from the State and put back into the local school boards the authority of assignment."[38] Devolving authority to local officials, the committee hoped, might have the advantage of forcing the NAACP to file lawsuits in every school district in the state, rather than simply targeting the State Department of Education. Such a measure could increase the cost of litigation considerably, perhaps forcing the NAACP to end its crusade against segregation for lack of money.[39]

"Voluntary" Segregation

To further siphon support from the NAACP's legal campaign, the Pearsall Committee recommended that North Carolina attempt to build support among African Americans for remaining in their schools voluntarily. To do this, the committee encouraged the state to "accelerate to the fullest extent possible" a massive "school construction program" for black schools.[40] Behind this strategy was the hope that blacks would not voluntarily go to school with whites if they did not have to. According to this idea of "voluntary" segregation, as it came to be called, state officials would maintain two school systems and gamble that black parents would send their children to vastly improved black schools, not to white ones.[41]

Though the idea of voluntary segregation might have had a slightly naive ring to it, since racial segregation had historically meant dramatically inferior public schools for blacks, it is not shocking that whites hoped it might work. After all, whites and blacks had gone to separate schools for generations in the South, and as far as most whites were concerned, this arrangement was agreeable to both races. In fact, one of the most striking aspects of white reactions to the prospect of integration, not just in North Carolina but across the South, was the extent to which whites failed to comprehend the level of black dissatisfaction with Jim Crow as a system of legally enforced racial repression.[42] To whites like Luther Hodges, racial segregation was not repressive at all. If anything, it was a progressive legal arrangement that allowed African Americans and whites to coexist peacefully, even allowing state programs aimed at aiding both races to continue without losing popular support.

Much like southern moderates who lobbied for racial segregation as a solution to racial strife in the 1890s, Hodges portrayed Jim Crow as a good thing: a legal program that allowed for the continuation of state services to blacks without leading to interracial violence.[43] Hodges even identified himself with turn-of-the-century white leaders who had played a critical role in the establishment of segregated schools as part of what they perceived to be a progressive policy designed to facilitate racial uplift. During a televised address on August 8, 1955, Hodges referred admiringly to Charles B. Aycock, governor of North Carolina from 1901 to 1905. Noting that Aycock had risen to power in the aftermath of the "crushing blow" of the Civil War, Hodges argued that North Carolina would never have survived the "bitter political struggles" that followed the war, had it not been for

Aycock, the "great educational" governor of North Carolina, who began "a march of progress that has never since been halted."[44]

Aycock's "march of progress" hinged on the establishment of formal racial segregation in North Carolina. He had risen to power in North Carolina at a moment when white extremists were pushing for a return to white supremacy in the South, after almost three decades of unprecedented racial equality following the Civil War. This campaign was spearheaded by white populist leaders, bitter over the South's defeat in the war, who seemed fully prepared to endorse mass violence against blacks. Running against such leaders were individuals like Aycock, "imaginative, ingenious, often moderate men," who embraced white supremacy yet disapproved of violence, if for no other reason than that it would hinder economic development.[45] Although some such leaders advocated that blacks be cut off from state services, including public education, others like Aycock tempered their commitment to white supremacy by offering concessions to blacks, even offering to fund segregated black schools from white tax dollars.[46]

Just as white moderates faced a wave of populist racial extremism in the post-Reconstruction era, so, too, did Hodges see himself confronting a wave of populist extremism after *Brown*. Hodges perhaps saw segregation as a necessary compromise to appease extremists and, perhaps ironically, help African Americans. While acknowledging that Aycock played a key role in the "white supremacy campaign of 1900," for example, Hodges reminded black North Carolinians that segregation, for Aycock, helped preserve black education, not hinder it.[47]

Underlying Hodges's attitude toward black education was a fundamentally prejudiced view of the world, one that had arguably not changed since he was a boy growing up during Aycock's administration. Convinced that racial segregation preserved racial peace, Hodges was certain that racial segregation helped blacks—a position that completely ignored the damaging effect Jim Crow had had on black life. He seemed oblivious to the ways in which Jim Crow had condemned blacks to separate, inferior public accommodations, denied them any hope of equal education, and disenfranchised them from the political process, thereby doing much to keep them in a subordinate, castelike position for more than half a century. In a speech to black teachers at Raleigh's Shaw University, for example, Hodges again invoked Aycock, identifying him as a "sincere and true friend of the Negro" who helped create an era of "good will" between the races, one that lasted for the first half of the twentieth century.[48] To anyone who knew about the white supremacy campaigns of the 1890s, including the devastating impact that racial segregation and disenfranchisement had had on black education and political power, the characterization of this era as one of "good will" was arguably absurd. Yet, Hodges clung to it, thereby revealing a type of segregationist thinking that automatically presumed racial inequality to be a product of innate racial differences, not legal repression. Between the lines of his statements, we see an example of how a prominent white southerner, representing a substantial portion of the voting public in his state, reconciled the perpetuation of segregated schools with economic progress, peace, and the moral good, all based on a flawed perception of race. After telling black teachers that Aycock was their "friend," Hodges proceeded to claim that the Supreme Court's opinion in *Brown* advanced an alien "logic" predicated on an "abstract" notion of racial equality that simply was not true.[49] Instead of being equal, Hodges maintained, the races actually differed substantially in what he vaguely described as "culture."[50] According to him, whites possessed an "older culture" that needed to be maintained, while blacks possessed a "new and rapidly developing culture" that needed to be encouraged, but should not be integrated.[51] "[U]nless we can, through good will and pride in the integrity of our respective racial cultures and way of life," Hodges argued, "separate schools voluntarily," then much of the progress made by both cultures would be "undone."[52]

Though Hodges did not explain what, precisely, he meant by "racial cultures," it was obvious by his words that he saw whites and blacks differently, and that these differences were not simply biological. This was a relatively liberal view for a white southerner to hold at the time. In contrast, white extremists like Tom P. Brady and James O. Eastland both claimed that African Americans were biologically inferior and could advance only by intermarrying with whites. Hodges, on the other hand, joined more liberal southerners who argued that blacks could advance on their own, provided they were given the right resources.[53] Hodges even went so far as to suggest that blacks could advance better on their own, without white interference caused by integration. Only a "selfish and militant organization," argued Hodges on August 8, 1955, would try "to convince you [African Americans] that you cannot develop your own culture within your own race and therefore that you must be ashamed of your color and your history by burying it in the development of the white race."[54] Again, what Hodges meant by black "culture" was unclear, yet he seemed to be suggesting that African Americans had their own cultural identity that would be compromised if they enrolled their children in school with whites. Though he never detailed how this would happen, he seemed to be playing on an inchoate sense that blacks might have a certain amount of pride in their racial identity and did not want to see it destroyed. Much like white extremists, who argued that integration would bring whites down, Hodges seemed to argue the corollary, namely, that integration would bring blacks down as well.

Hodges's conviction that African Americans might be persuaded to engage in voluntary segregation, far-fetched as it may seem, led him to appeal directly to black parents in his August televised address. "Have any of you ever heard," Hodges asked blacks, "of any real leaders of any race who set out to raise the standards and pride of their race by encouraging its members to lose their identity in complete merger with other races?"[55] Hodges's use of the term *merger* here was significant. Far from a crude term like *amalgamation* or *mongrelization,* merger was a relatively business-like way of saying that integration might lead to either cultural syncretism or interracial sex. That he suggested miscegenation—or, as he put it, "merger"—in a portion of his speech clearly directed at blacks, however, suggests that he believed that they, too, might have had doubts about the consequences of integrated schools. Just as extremists thought that the specter of miscegenation could be used politically to rally whites, Hodges seemed to think that it could be used to mobilize blacks as well.

Perhaps not surprisingly, African Americans interested in the immediate enforcement of *Brown* protested. Cortez Puryear, writing for the Winston-Salem branch of the NAACP, penned a letter criticizing Hodges's attempt to promote "voluntary" segregation. "You have insulted all well-thinking people of both races," Puryear wrote Hodges, for having the "gall" to ask African Americans to take a "backward step" and "accept segregation and discrimination on a voluntary basis."[56] On the subject of amalgamation, Puryear assured Hodges that even in integrated conditions, blacks did not "lose their identity."[57] However, he did admit that whites posed just as much a threat to racial purity as African Americans did. "[Y]ou, Governor," he stated, "as well as everyone else in North Carolina are fully aware why Negroes are losing their darker tint."[58] Puryear closed by suggesting that Hodges stop looking for black "stooges" willing to support his plans "to circumvent the law of the land."[59]

Anticipating that black support for "voluntary" integration would not be overwhelming, Hodges followed up his pleas that blacks endorse segrega-tion willingly with subtle threats aimed at black parents worried about the impact of insisting too heavily on *Brown.* "[A]ny among you who refuse to cooperate in this effort to save our public school system," he scolded, "are not to be applauded but are to be considered as endangering the education of your children."[60] Localized white resistance could, in his opinion, mani-fest itself in mass school closures, coupled with a turn to private schools. If this happened, warned Hodges, then African Americans would, in all likelihood, "suffer most" by being denied any education whatsoever.[61]

There was an element of coercion to such words. Rather than help African Americans advance their interests, Hodges made it clear that black bids to enter white schools would backfire, leaving blacks without access to educational institutions. Desperate to rally support for voluntary segregation, Hodges tried to present segregation as absolutely vital to black goals, not a "blind spot" in progressivism, to borrow from C. Vann Wood-ward, but an outward manifestation of it.[62] Not only did segregation nurture black traditions, he argued, but also it provided African Americans with at least some access to state services.[63] Hoping that blacks might be coerced, if not convinced, into adopting this line of thinking became a central part of Hodges's response to *Brown*. In fact, the Pearsall Committee hoped that "the subtle pressure of culture and society," as one member of the University of North Carolina's Institute of Government later put it, might be enough to "make the Negroes go to Negro schools and the white go to white."[64]

Hodges and his committee, however, found black resistance to be much greater than they expected. One of the most "miserable" encounters he had with African Americans in this regard, according to his own account, occurred during a speech that he delivered at predominantly black North Carolina A&T College in Greensboro in the fall of 1955.[65] There to present the students with several brand new buildings, presumably part of a larger plan to buy their support, Hodges expected a courteous reception. Much to his disappointment, many of the students refused to stand when he entered and insisted on shuffling their feet and talking during his speech. Hodges became so upset at the students' response to what he thought was a "fair speech" that he ended his talk abruptly and left.[66]

Black opposition to his plans joined with other factors to convince Hodges that not only was voluntary segregation doomed but also it was unnecessary. On May 31, 1955, for example, the Supreme Court handed moderates like Hodges a considerable victory by granting the South an indefinite amount of time to desegregate its schools. This opinion, known as *Brown II*, rejected NAACP requests that the South begin integration immediately and instead granted the South "all deliberate speed" to reconfigure its public school systems. By the fall of 1955, as Hodges endured embarrassment at A&T, it had become obvious that *Brown II* constituted a significant victory for white southerners. It was almost as if the Supreme Court had actually done what moderate leaders like Luther Hodges and J. P. Coleman had wished, namely, allow *Brown* to stand as a symbolic gesture while issuing subsequent rulings to limit its impact.[67]

Interestingly, the Pearsall Committee came to believe that *Brown II*, though a considerable victory for the white South, also meant that at least some token integration would need to occur in the region before the federal judiciary would finally leave Dixie alone. This reading, of course, distinguished North Carolina from Mississippi. J. P. Coleman did not think that *Brown II* meant anything save a reassuring reluctance on the part of the Supreme Court to enforce *Brown I*. In his opinion, whether the South actually admitted black students to white schools was not as important as whether the South rewrote its laws to comply formally with the text of the Supreme Court's opinion. Thanks to the advice of James Paul, however, the Pearsall Committee took its reading one step further and immediately began to plan for the admission of token numbers of black students to white schools.[68]

At first glance, this was a big step. Token integration, even if it meant negligible numbers of black students, represented a fissure in the ideological fortress of Jim Crow.[69] If nothing else, it marked a concrete move away from the idea that North Carolina would insist on total racial segregation and opened the possibility that increasing numbers of black students might be admitted to white schools. Yet, the Pearsall Committee saw token integration as a concession necessary for preventing mass integration, not an initial tentative step toward it. Aware that many white voters might overlook this, the committee began to develop measures that would neutralize extremism by allowing local voters to determine for themselves whether their districts would integrate. Local elections to close school districts, the committee hoped, would provide suitable safety valves for extremist pressures in communities that did not want to send even negligible numbers of black children to white schools.[70]

Accommodating Extremism: "Safety Valves"

To some, the idea of granting local communities the option of closing their own school systems—something that quickly became known as the Pearsall Plan—marked a significant shift toward extremism on the part of Luther Hodges. Yet, the Supreme Court's *Brown II* ruling convinced Hodges and others that safety valves were necessary to appease voters who feared, reasonably, that this was only the beginning of a gradual move toward mass integration. Rather than a turn away from his original commitment to open schools, Hodges saw the Pearsall Plan as a realistic method of implementing that policy. Again and again, Hodges emphasized that his support for the Pearsall Plan was not a desire to close schools but rather to make sure that public schools remained open by limiting closures to isolated districts. Hodges even articulated a theory that the Pearsall Plan might discourage closures by placing considerable burdens on local parents, including the requirement that they build their own private schools if they wanted their children to get an education. If white voters wanted to close public schools and send their children to private schools, they could, but they would not receive money for construction, only tuition.[71] In fact, when white parents complained that "local option" could lead to the destruction of schools, Hodges did little to reassure them, suggesting that private classes could be held in the "back of a Moose hall," hardly a substitute for a well-equipped school.[72]

Extremists advocated even more radical solutions. Assistant Attorney General I. Beverly Lake, an outspoken supporter of defiance, argued that North Carolina could simply close its public schools and reopen them as private ones—thereby circumventing *Brown* completely. Whether Lake actually believed that such a plan would work is not clear. The Pearsall Committee rejected such an idea as too transparent. "One could not simply change the name above the school house door from public to private," noted Robert E. Giles, also an assistant attorney general at the time, "finance it the same way in substance, and have the Court sustain it."[73] Lake disagreed. However, it is not evident if his disagreement was an honest conviction that state-funded private schools would be held constitutional or if he had personal political motivations. That summer, for example, Lake delivered a speech in Asheboro that was so negative toward the NAACP that the organization requested Hodges to remove him from the position of assistant attorney general. The following year, Lake ran against Hodges for governor, challenging him for not being committed enough to preserving segregated schools.[74]

To counter challenges by political opportunists like Lake, Hodges included with the Pearsall Plan a relatively forthright statement of opposition to the Supreme Court. This statement coincided closely with the rise of interposition as a legal theory of constitutional defiance to the Court, which occurred dramatically in the spring of 1956. Even though Hodges endorsed a statement of opposition to the Court, he did not endorse interposition as an actual legal strategy. In fact, the Pearsall Plan was a way of circumventing the Court without resorting to interposition, a plan that hinged, ultimately, more on compliance with *Brown* than on defiance of it.

Committed to the policy of formal compliance, the Pearsall Committee struggled to finish its plan for preserving segregation and surviving federal court review. In so doing, it began to suspect that even though the Court would probably not accept an absolute shift to private schools, it might accept a more sporadic approach that provided select students with "tuition grants" to go to genuine private schools. Under such a system, public school teachers would not suddenly be called "private," nor would public school facilities suddenly be transferred to private owners. Instead, private citizens would have to build their own private schools and hire their own teachers.[75]

Managing the Legislature

As the Pearsall Committee completed work on its plan, it also developed a strategy to facilitate the passage of its program in the state legislature. Certain legislators, like those allied with Beverly Lake, the committee realized, would reject their suggestions and push for more drastic measures. Yet many, they hoped, could be talked into endorsing the Pearsall Plan, particularly if they were subjected to sufficient pressure. To accomplish this, the committee invited groups of fifteen to thirty legislators to the governor's mansion for a series of "friendly" dinners during the spring of 1956.[76] Over these meals, Hodges addressed the legislators, and Thomas Pearsall then briefed them on the committee's work thus far. Their explicit goal was to give them "a plank to run on," meaning a policy agenda to sell to their constituents that spring.[77] Part of the reason for this, Pearsall later noted, was to pressure legislators into endorsing the governor's plan and to ensure that they would not "make all sorts of wild promises" to their constituents about what they were going to do to preserve segregated schools.[78]

Once every legislator in the state had visited the governor's mansion, the committee scheduled a second round of briefings for legislators, at which they were allowed to provide input. Held in secret locations across the state, these briefings were intentionally kept private to prevent press attention that would allow the committee's work to be attacked by extremists. Another reason for secrecy was to keep the committee's true goals out of the public record, where they could be used as evidence in federal court cases challenging the plan.[79]

Once the committee gained the input and allegiance of a majority of the state's legislators, it went public. In a series of public hearings held over the summer of 1956, the Pearsall Committee took open commentary about its plan. Two notable figures attacked it. One was I. Beverly Lake, who declared that devolving power over integration to the local level was ill advised. Another detractor was Duke University Law Professor Douglas B. Maggs, who warned that the plan's approval of local school closings, coupled with its authorization of tuition grants, would be struck down by the Supreme Court. "Let us not resort to subterfuge and coercion," Maggs argued. He suggested instead that the state rely on other ideas, voluntary segregation and even segregation by sex among them.[80]

Unswayed by such critiques, the Pearsall Committee continued with its program, and a majority of the state's legislators proved surprisingly compliant. On July 27, 1956, the North Carolina legislature enacted the Pearsall Plan into law with only two votes against it. The enactment was a triumph for Hodges and for the advisory committee. It was also a testament to the manner in which the committee worked to keep its proposals out of the public eye, yet still managed to pressure state legislators into endorsing its suggestions. At least some of the credit for this success goes to Hodges for dealing strategically with lawmakers in his state, educating them, and perhaps even pressuring them into accepting a reasonable, viable plan of resistance to *Brown*.

The quality of Hodges's proactive approach to the integration problem, replete with its emphasis on formal compliance and safety valves for neutralizing local unrest, became clear only a month after the North Carolina legislature approved the Pearsall Plan. In the early fall of 1956, both Texas and Tennessee found themselves embroiled in embarrassing situations when local extremists reacted violently to the threat of integrated schools. In Texas, white mobs formed outside a public school in the small town of Mansfield, near Dallas. Governor Allan Shivers, a business conservative like Hodges, was caught off guard and had done little in the way of coming up with a viable strategy for preventing integration. He had allowed the integration of public schools in West Texas and did not anticipate the mob in Mansfield. To quell the unrest, Shivers went from tolerating token integration to forbidding it, even calling in the Texas Rangers to prevent black students from entering the white school.[81]

In Tennessee, moderate Governor Frank G. Clement found himself in a similar situation. After carelessly tolerating integration in certain counties, Clement was taken by surprise when a mob began to form outside a public school in the small town of Clinton. Matters worsened when an agitator named John Kasper began to rally the white crowd, prompting them to riot. Clement, who lacked Hodges's proactive approach to managing extremists through the imposition of safety valves and so on, called in the National Guard to restore peace.[82]

Luther Hodges saw both incidents as fiascos that could have been avoided. He reflected on these crises during a televised address that was broadcast throughout the state on September 7, 1956. The speech was scheduled for the night before voters across the state were to decide on a constitutional amendment permitting the implementation of certain components of the Pearsall Plan. "Events of the past few days," noted Hodges, "including riots and violence in Texas and Tennessee are very disturbing and we hope such things are not repeated here."[83] Hodges assured North Carolinians that if they approved the Pearsall Plan, similar conflagrations would be less likely in their state. "I have been asked in the last few days," remarked Hodges, "if I thought these other States which are having difficulty would have been in a better position if they had the protection or guarantee such as are offered in the Pearsall Plan. My answer is 'yes.'"[84] "The trouble in these states," he explained, is that they don't have safety valves for citizens who might prefer engaging in violence rather than sending their children to integrated schools.[85] The prospect of violence, in fact, rose in direct correlation to the likelihood of a federal—or, for that matter, state—order to integrate. "Under such conditions," he noted, "people are inclined to take things into their own hands," which leads to a breakdown in "law and order."[86] The Pearsall Plan, by contrast, offered North Carolinians "a legal and orderly method" of handling potential violence in the wake of even token integration.[87]

Hodges's interest in an "orderly method" of controlling white violence distinguished him from moderate governors like Frank G. Clement and Allan Shivers, who allowed events to devolve before stepping in. It also suggested that he understood how moderation actually increased the chance of violence in the South. Precisely because moderate governors attempted to comply with the Supreme Court, outbreaks like Clinton and Mansfield were more likely to occur in moderate states. Conversely, in states that took an early, defiant approach to *Brown*, radicals never felt the need to resort to vigilantism or violence, and peace, more often than not, ensued. This explains why Virginia, Georgia, and South Carolina, which embraced massive resistance early on, experienced few outbreaks of mob violence in the 1950s, while moderate-led states like Tennessee, Texas, Arkansas, and even Alabama all endured rioting.[88]

Recognizing that moderation could jeopardize domestic peace, Hodges worked hard to develop a legal mechanism that would absorb popular anger resulting from the token integration of public schools. Even though opinion polls taken in Guilford County, North Carolina, suggested that most white voters were not so opposed to integration that they would resort to violence to prevent it, Hodges focused on the more radical minority of white voters, those who risked derailing his strategic constitutionalism.[89] This overemphasis on extremism reflected a type of populism at the heart of his constitutional vision, a populism that empowered local people by enabling them to make their own constitutional choices, regardless of the Supreme Court. "Under the Pearsall Plan," Hodges noted, "it is only the people themselves who will have authority to take action on these proposals."[90] To those who might have opposed the plan, Hodges made their opposition sound like an attack on the people of North Carolina rather than an attack on the policies of his administration. "I, for one," he noted, "am willing to place my trust in the people."[91]

On September 8, 1956, Hodges's faith in the people was affirmed, as North Carolina voters approved the Pearsall Plan by a 4 to 1 margin in a statewide referendum.[92] That white North Carolinians decisively sided with Luther Hodges and his moderate approach to *Brown* at a point in time when many white voters in the South were calling for massive resistance is remarkable. Certainly, some of this support was attributable to moderate tendencies among voters in North Carolina at the time, yet Hodges's aggressive, legalist approach to *Brown* must also be credited with giving those moderate tendencies a political voice. Hodges's inclusion of a local option arrangement went beyond a legalist response to the Court and focused directly on empowering those segments of the white population that might be uncomfortable with moderate means. Pursuant to the Pearsall Plan, for example, local communities maintained at least the illusion of local control over public schools. This meant that extremists retained the power to close public schools and build their own private, segregated ones, provided they could muster majorities at the local level. While the likelihood that this might happen in any given community was small, considering the costs of setting up private schools capable of accommodating all white children, it nevertheless gave extremists the sense that they could exercise their own choice.

Once the Pearsall Plan was approved by an overwhelming majority of white voters, Hodges suddenly took a much more aggressive stance toward African Americans. As if confident that black bids to integrate public schools would now be handled at the local level, and perhaps tired of black rebukes to his bids for voluntary segregation, Hodges turned on the very black voters he had previously tried to court. Several weeks after the referendum, he delivered a scathing attack on black illegitimacy rates and related welfare abuses. Hodges began by discussing that he was "disturbed" about high numbers of black illegitimate children whose "so-called parents" collect "welfare money" and seemed to "consider this money a 'reward' for their actions."[93] "We have this problem with us, particularly as it affects the Negroes," he contended, asserting that he would let "no political group," either in "North Carolina" or in "Washington," make the state continue "encouraging illegitimacy and the abandonment of children."[94]

Hodges's sharp tone and his reference to "so-called parents" and "rewards" for illegitimacy reflected a palpable shift in his racial rhetoric. During his television address a year earlier, he had been relatively conciliatory in his posture toward African Americans. Desperate for them to engage in voluntary segregation, he had made vague allusions to their "rapidly developing culture," stressing that they should be proud of their achievements. Now, as the need for voluntary segregation dwindled in the aftermath of a successful referendum on the Pearsall Plan, Hodges took a more punitive stance.[95]

Targeting Black Illegitimacy

Though a new issue for Hodges, black illegitimacy rates were hardly a new issue in North Carolina. According to federal statistics dating back to the 1930s, illegitimacy rates for African Americans in the state had always been high, almost 25 percent of all black births, compared with 2 percent of white births.[96] While some of this statistical disparity might have been due to the lack of maternity homes for unwed black mothers in the state, the matter had still generated concern long before 1956.[97] In 1950, a state study had warned that "the prevalence of illegitimacy among the lower-class Negro population" was a matter of considerable state concern, given that unwed black mothers had "no means of support except through public assistance."[98] Four years later, Ellen Winston, superintendent of the State Board of Public Welfare, assigned an African American welfare official to devise strategies to reduce the rates.[99]

In her work on reducing black illegitimacy, Winston never adopted the kind of punitive, moralist tone that Hodges did in 1956. This might be because Winston, born in Bryson City, North Carolina, a mountain town home to more poor whites than blacks, did not see welfare, or welfare abuse for that matter, as a strictly black problem. For many natives of Bryson City, government aid had been one of the few consistent sources of income since the Great Depression.[100] Winston advocated proactive, interventionist state welfare policies for whites as well as blacks and exhibited little interest in linking welfare problems, like illegitimacy, to larger racial concerns.[101]

Hodges was different. He suddenly seemed very interested in linking black illegitimacy rates to larger claims of black irresponsibility, immorality, and even fraud. What accounted for this change? One possibility is that Hodges, a fiscal conservative, was interested in saving tax dollars and might have seen a vigorous attack on black welfare abuses as a way of building popular support for welfare cuts generally. However, this does not explain why he launched into an attack on black illegitimacy rates after two years in office. A more likely possibility is that Hodges had long harbored negative views of blacks and publicly displayed them to bolster his segregationist image. Beginning in the spring of 1956, talk of massive resistance had begun spreading across the South, threatening the very strategies of creative compliance endorsed by leaders like Hodges and Coleman. This talk intensified during the summer, as grassroots organizations like the Mississippi Citizens' Councils, the Virginia Defenders of State Sovereignty, and in North Carolina, the Patriots of North Carolina lobbied for massive resistance.[102] While Hodges and Coleman were both reluctant to cater to such extremists, they might have felt some pressure to go on the offensive—in a reasonable, moderate way, of course—against African Americans.

Evidence of this emerged on October 25, 1956, in North Carolina. That day, Curtis Flanagan, deputy chairman of the Pitt County chapter of the segregationist Patriots of North Carolina, sent Hodges a letter requesting him to do something about black illegitimacy rates in the state. "The controversy over segregation," wrote Flanagan, "has brought to light the amazing fact that 20% or more of our Pitt County negro population is illegitimate . . . this naked and unpalatable fact is a terrible indictment of the moral standards of a large segment of the population of Pitt County."[103] The precise reason that segregation had given rise to concern over illegitimacy rates was, according to Flanagan, a Congressional study conducted on integrated schools in Washington, D.C. Washington, pursuant to the orders of President Eisenhower, had undergone an integration process in 1955, before almost any other district in the country, and had consequently attracted considerable interest. Although some of this interest originated in the North, much of it came from southern segregationists looking for evidence of racial tensions in D.C. schools to build a case against *Brown*. The particular study that Flanagan referred to, which must have inspired him to investigate illegitimacy rates in North Carolina, had been initiated by John Bell Williams, the same Mississippi representative who had pressured J. P. Coleman into signing an interposition resolution in the fall of 1955.[104] Though the formal report for the study was not published until 1957, the monthly journal of the Mississippi Citizens' Council began publishing early findings from it, based on congressional hearings in the fall of 1956. The October 1956 issue of the *Citizens' Council*, for example, quoted testimony from a Washington school principal named John Paul Collins, who told Congress that "the problem of discipline was tremendous" in desegregated schools and that "many sex problems" had been reported, among them high rates of teen pregnancy and illegitimacy among blacks.[105]

That the Mississippi Citizens' Councils were disseminating material on black illegitimacy rates in the fall of 1956, and that such propaganda was reaching extremists in North Carolina that same year, can explain Hodges's decision to come out strongly against welfare abuses and unwed motherhood in black communities at that time. Yet, Hodges did not go as far as many extremists would have liked. North Carolina Patriot Curtis Flanagan recommended that Hodges propose legislation requiring sterilization for any woman with two or more illegitimate children who desired state welfare benefits.[106] Hodges refused. Instead, he joined Ellen Winston in proposing a "simplified guardianship" law that appointed welfare workers to "irresponsible" mothers to oversee their child-rearing and spending practices.[107]

Here was evidence that Hodges was not motivated simply by economic measures like cutting welfare expenditures. Welfare guardians were expensive, certainly costlier than just cutting funding to unwed mothers. Although it is possible that Hodges feared the federal government would strike down welfare cuts, his support for welfare guardians coincided with his racial rhetoric about "encouraging" the development of black culture. Perhaps he saw cracking down on welfare abuses as a means not only of appeasing white extremists but also of helping blacks in much the same way that he saw segregation as an institution that helped blacks. Evidence that this was so emerged that winter, as Hodges joined Ellen Winston in support of a guardianship law for unwed mothers in the state. During January and February 1957, Hodges also approved an expansive family court bill that would remove paternity suits from public view, making the proceedings, and records, secret.[108]

When these measures were introduced to the General Assembly in the spring of 1957, they confronted considerable opposition. One charge leveled at the family court bill was that it catered to parents of illegitimate children, particularly fathers who might be charged with abandonment, by making their paternity hearings secret.[109] Another charge was that it granted "unknown and unbridled" jurisdiction to the new family courts.[110] Both complaints suggest that Hodges, though a fiscal conservative, was willing to expand the size and also the reach of the state to deal with racial matters through the development of vaguely defined family courts and the creation of welfare "guardians." That said, the guardianship law drew other criticism as well, particularly from court clerks, who decried the added responsibility that assigning welfare guardians placed on them.[111]

As Hodges's progressive measures were cut down, more severe measures took their place. James Speight, a representative from heavily black eastern Bertie County, introduced a bill cutting welfare benefits to illegitimate children under the Aid to Dependent Children (ADC) program.[112] Hodges refused to endorse the bill, and Ellen Winston opposed it outright. Specifically, Winston argued that 78 percent of all money going to dependent children was federal, meaning that little state money would be saved by cutting it.[113] Winston also argued that since ADC had been introduced in North Carolina, illegitimacy rates had not increased in the state, which strongly suggested that welfare money was not enticing single women into becoming pregnant.[114]

Cutting welfare benefits was not the only suggestion made by state legislators. Wilbur Jolly, a state senator from Franklin, a heavily black eastern county not far from Pitt, introduced a sterilization measure not unlike the one recommended by Curtis Flanagan. Specifically, Jolly's bill recommended that women with two or more illegitimate children be declared feebleminded and then sterilized under North Carolina's eugenics law.[115] The eugenics law, enacted in 1933, emerged during an era when sterilization was viewed as a progressive method for improving the quality of the state's citizens.[116] A Eugenics Board met quarterly to decide on cases recommended for selective sterilization, focusing on "epileptics, mental defectives and feeble-minded" persons.[117] In 1947, after an inordinate number of white North Carolina draftees had been rejected from the armed services because of mental and physical disabilities, textile magnate James G. Hanes, then president of Hanes Hosiery, took an interest in expanding the law.[118] Hanes even established a private organization called the Human Betterment League that, beginning in 1947, actively lobbied for a variety of genetically conscious causes, most of them focused on whites.[119] Why whites and not blacks? The dominant thinking of the era seemed to hold that blacks were naturally feebleminded and that sterilizing them would be a waste of time.[120] Of course, not all white North Carolinians agreed with sterilizing whites either. In fact, popular support for sterilization declined significantly just as the Human Betterment League began its work, partly because of the rise of individualized notions of contraception and family planning in the late 1940s and early 1950s and the pall that Nazi racial policies cast on eugenics more generally.[121]

The ensuing decline in the popularity of sterilization made its reemergence in 1957 all the more remarkable. Though he did not mention race overtly, Jolly's anger at illegitimacy rates coincided with the dissemination of statistics on black unwed motherhood by groups like the Citizens' Councils, not to mention the politicization of such issues by the Patriots of North Carolina. That these rates were in fact substantially higher for blacks, 25 percent of all births as opposed to 2 percent, suggests that illegitimacy became a type of code for punishing blacks. Yet, punishment might not have been the only cause underlying renewed interest. Illegitimacy rates might also have provided white leaders with a concrete, statistically verifiable reason for stalling integration, evidence, in other words, of the fact that black "culture," as Hodges put it, was still "developing." This politicization of morality coincided with another belief articulated by state legislators: that African Americans were not burdened by state repression but were a burden on state resources, willingly exploiting services without paying for them. Luther Hamilton, a state senator from the coastal tobacco-producing county of Carteret, articulated a particularly venomous version of this argument on May 15, 1957. "The law now constitutes an inducement to illegitimacy," Hamilton claimed, echoing Hodges's statement almost six months earlier.[122] According to him, North Carolina was doing nothing short of "breeding a race of bastards."[123]

Talk of breeding bastards was unacceptable to most North Carolinians, leading some to propose other ideas. "Why should women take all the blame and be punished?" asked Lillian Byrum, a white woman from Raleigh. "In other crimes the accomplice shares, or is punished. The unwed mother could name the man or men and let them assume the upkeep of such children."[124] Bynum's suggestion that fathers be punished raised the possibility that there were ways other than sterilization for dealing with the problem of illegitimacy. Luther Hodges, of course, agreed. When asked whether he supported Jolly's sterilization measure, he reaffirmed his claim that "[s]omething should be done to reduce the amount of money the State is paying out for the support of illegitimate children" but advocated welfare guardians instead of mandatory sterilization.[125]

In the meantime, the sterilization bill attracted some ridicule. Senator Ed Lanier from liberal Chapel Hill countered the bill successfully in the Senate by asserting that "[w]hat's fair to the goose ought to be done to the gander," thereby inspiring a tongue-in-cheek amendment making the bill applicable to men as well.[126] This amendment, along with pointed criticism from moderates afraid that the law sounded like a Nazi plot, killed the bill for the duration of the 1957 session.[127]

Controlling the Ku Klux Klan

As battles over sterilization cooled in the state legislature, the Pearsall Plan was put to the test. In July 1957, fifty-one African American students challenged their assignments and applied to be reassigned to predominantly white schools.[128] Charlotte turned down thirty-six of its applications but accepted five. Greensboro admitted six students, and Winston-Salem admitted one. The numbers, though negligible, were still important.[129]

Even though token integration might have been just the type of concession that the South needed to offer the Supreme Court to escape federal intervention, there was still a risk that white extremists would take the law into their own hands. For precisely this reason, Hodges took proactive measures to ensure that the transition in Charlotte and Greensboro happened peacefully. He personally addressed voters across the state to assure them that violence would not be tolerated. He also placed state police on alert. When John Kasper, the same Citizens' Council leader who had incited crowds in Clinton, Tennessee, threatened to come to North Carolina in August 1957, Hodges personally ordered him to stay out. When Kasper refused and came to North Carolina anyway, Hodges had him followed by state troopers.[130]

Here, too, was a parallel between Hodges and Coleman. Though Hodges would not demand the increase in the number and scope of state troopers in North Carolina that Coleman had in Mississippi, he would similarly use state police to neutralize potential unrest at the local level. Hodges also endorsed improvements in the state's judicial apparatus, particularly reforming the justice of the peace system, like Coleman did. In particular, Hodges called for improving the state's criminal justice system by bringing JPs under the umbrella of appellate court review, thereby centralizing the lower tiers of North Carolina's judicial system and restoring "respect," as he put it, for the state's legal system.[131]

The way centralizing governmental power could be used as a way to deal with racial unrest became apparent in January 1958. On Monday, January 13, 1958, Klan members gained national attention by burning crosses on property owned by Lumbee Indians, a tribe near Maxton, North Carolina, widely reputed to include black members.[132] James "Catfish" Cole, a local Klan leader who had made a string of public, derogatory statements against the Indians, garnered even more attention by scheduling a rally in Maxton on January 18, 1958. Five hundred Lumbee Indians disrupted it, using shotguns and rifles to scare off a hundred or so Klan members, and making the front page of the *New York Times*.[133]

Hodges was not pleased. "The recent incident in Maxton," he announced, should be of "serious concern" to all citizens of North Carolina, particularly "thoughtful" ones like himself who were determined to maintain "law and order."[134] Of particular concern to Hodges was the manner in which the media had anticipated the fiasco. While recognizing "the great obligation" that the press had to report the news, he lamented the media's interest in Klan activity. "We all know that an over-zealousness in 'finding' news," he asserted, "can sometimes result in the unfortunate 'making' of news."[135] He then speculated that the Klan had gone through with the rally at least partially to capitalize on the growing "notoriety" that they hoped to gain from it.[136] It was significant, he noted, "that, according to our estimates, scores of news representatives were on the scene the night of the Maxton incident."[137]

Hodges's fear that the media was overemphasizing white extremism indicated a sensitivity toward the way the press could influence popular opinion, not to mention a strategic interest in preventing the media from skewing its stories against the white South. Like J. P. Coleman, who wrestled with Roy Wilkins to control negative publicity about his state, Hodges also feared that the press might disrupt moderate attempts to project an image of racial peace and harmony in the region. Northern coverage of southern racial affairs, the "race beat," struck both leaders as a direct threat to the type of strategic constitutionalism they were engaged in, which hinged just as much on influencing popular opinion as it did on interpreting the Constitution.[138] Though there appeared to be no direct constitutional link to the clash between Lumbee Indians and the Ku Klux Klan, for example, Hodges recognized that there was an implicit link between national coverage of such clashes and popular support for *Brown.* By projecting an extremist image of the South, northern reporters threatened to stir popular anger at white segregationists, which could eventually translate into calls for more robust federal enforcement of *Brown.* Just as civil rights activists like Roy Wilkins recognized that blacks needed to publicize racial atrocities to stir popular interest in the black struggle, so, too, did southern moderates like Hodges realize that they needed to squelch such atrocities, and the groups that sponsored them, to truly limit integration.

Because of its tendency to generate negative publicity and compromise strategic constitutionalism, the Ku Klux Klan became one of the primary targets of the Hodges administration. Hodges turned to a centralized law enforcement agency, the State Bureau of Investigation (SBI), to monitor and occasionally even harass Klan members. On July 20, 1958, for example, SBI agent L. E. Allen reported to Hodges on a Ku Klux Klan meeting in Jamestown, North Carolina, documenting specific names of Klan officials, as well as local law enforcement agents involved in Klan activity. An "[i]nformant" noted Allen, "stated that a Deputy Sheriff from Davison County, N.C. got some applications at a Klan meeting at Southmont recently and made the statement that he was going to give these applications to some people who wanted to join the U.S. Klan."[139] Of particular interest was James "Catfish"

Cole, who, according to Allen, "is now driving a 1956 Ford pick up truck" registered to "Theodore Carl Williams," and whose wife, sent into hiding after a rally in Maxton, could be reached "at telephone No. 1392" in Hamlet, North Carolina.[140]

In addition to tracing relatively specific personal data, the SBI was also interested in the KKK's future plans, particularly those that might involve violence. In January 1958, for example, Allen noted that one "Red Morgan," owner of Morgan Esso Service Station, had hidden machine guns after the same Maxton rally that Cole and his wife had attended.[141] The possibility that the Klan had access to such weapons added to Hodges's fears that the organization was planning further headline-grabbing violence in North Carolina and prompted him to issue a statement on January 30, 1958. "[T]he Klan," he warned, "will at some future date assemble an armed gathering" to "intimidate the people of this state."[142] To prevent this, the SBI moved from surveillance to harassment, visiting Klan leaders like James Garland Martin at his home to persuade him to "turn States' evidence against the KKK."[143] The SBI also began ordering police-style raids, prompting some Klan members in North Carolina to announce that "they were getting out of the Klan because it was getting too dangerous."[144]

State harassment, though it did not kill the organization, did drive the KKK even further underground than it already was, spurring it to hide its membership rolls and forbid its members from carrying anything "that would identify [them] with the KKK."[145] Aware that public identification might be the best way of crippling the secret society, Luther Hodges publicly asserted that the Klan could be controlled simply by exposing its membership. "[W]e need to throw the full light of public disclosure on all those individuals who take an active part in Klan matters," noted Hodges on January 30, 1958. "Identification of names, addresses and past records of such individuals is a salutary thing and in the public interest."[146]

Though the SBI's campaign against the Ku Klux Klan appeared to have nothing to do with constitutional law, Hodges's interest in thwarting the organization was closely tied to his larger vision of constitutional resistance to *Brown*. Convinced that northern reporters were feeding their readers with overly sensational, racist portraits of the South, Hodges realized that the Klan contributed to such distortions by providing racist fuel for media fires. If allowed to burn bright enough, such fires might turn national support against the South and push federal officials to endorse a more robust enforcement of civil rights decisions like *Brown*. Conversely, if southern states wanted to increase the likelihood that the Supreme Court would approve placement plans and other moderate subterfuges, then the South needed to build popular support for continued segregation by making reasonable appeals to the nation while projecting an image of racial peace and harmony in Dixie. For Hodges, the aggressive use of state agencies against the KKK became a critical part of projecting just such a harmonious image. By observing the SBI's interaction with the Klan in North Carolina, then, we catch a glimpse of how proactive state action fit into a much larger plan of strategic constitutionalism.

Of course, to see this constitutionalism through to fruition, North Carolina needed to control not only organizations like the KKK but also black civil rights groups like the NAACP. The NAACP, Hodges realized, could and indeed would love to derail his attempts to restrict *Brown,* particularly if it meant stirring outside media interest in the region. Just as he sought to drive muckraking civil rights reporters away from North Carolina, the NAACP sought to draw them into the region and use media coverage of racial incidents to rouse popular anger at white segregationists. This became apparent in 1958, when Hodges confronted a publicity storm ignited by a black NAACP leader in Monroe, North Carolina, named Robert F. Williams.

Confronting the NAACP . . . and International Outrage

Robert F. Williams first came to Luther Hodges's attention in September 1955, when Oscar L. Richardson, a lawyer in Monroe, alerted the governor to an FBI file on the black NAACP leader. Williams, a former U.S. Marine, had first attracted the attention of the FBI in the1940s after he became active in labor unions widely suspected of having Communist ties.[147] "I have information," wrote Robinson to Hodges, "that this Robert F. Williams has been under investigation by the F.B.I. for a considerable period of time and that they have a large dossier on him. You would have access to this information if you desire . . . it may be necessary for the State to defend our position in the future and the information would be valuable."[148]

Though Hodges did not act on the memo, Williams's name came up again in December 1958, when two African American boys were accused of kissing two white girls in a culvert near a white residential section of Monroe. Though a seemingly minor incident, it exacerbated local whites' tension about interracial contact among children. Consequently, the two boys were apprehended by local authorities and committed to the Morrison Training School, a reform school for black youth in North Carolina.[149]

To Robert F. Williams, the boys' commitment to Morrison was an outrage. Almost immediately, he began publicizing the boys' incarceration, eventually reaching Joyce Egginton, a reporter for the *London News-Chronicle* in England. Shocked to hear that black boys were being jailed for playing with white girls in the United States, Egginton flew to Monroe to meet with the NAACP leader and, on December 15, 1958, published a story on the case that created a stir in Europe. The publicity reverberated across the Atlantic when, on January 17, 1959, the New York—based *Nation* magazine ran an article retelling what was rapidly becoming known as "the kissing case."[150]

For Luther Hodges, the Monroe kissing case quickly became an even greater media headache than the aborted Klan attack on the Lumbee Indians. Unlike the Klan case, this incident involved direct state action, namely, the incarceration of the boys in a state facility. This implicated Hodges in a manner that the Lumbee Indian attack did not and forced him to come up with a viable explanation for taking the boys from their homes and placing them in juvenile detention. To Hodges's dismay, this response had to be convincing to international audiences who were suddenly interested in North Carolina's treatment of African Americans. "I am continuing to receive much mail from throughout this country and from foreign countries," Hodges wrote to George V. Allen, director of the United States Information Agency, a federal agency dedicated to disseminating information about the United States abroad. "I deeply regret that this whole incident has been so propagandized."[151]

That Hodges felt compelled to write Allen indicated that what he initially considered to be a relatively minor racial incident was taking on international importance. Tensions were already, high thanks to the Cold War between the United States and the Soviet Union, a war in which both nations used political propaganda to curry popular favor worldwide. In fact, the Soviets had begun to use southern racism as evidence of American moral bankruptcy, a move that led the U.S. government to file a brief in *Brown* endorsing desegregation as part of a larger "Cold War imperative."[152]

Cold War pressure created a second source of hope for black activists like Williams who recognized that international pressure, and the shame that went with it, could motivate federal officials to act in favor of black causes just as effectively as popular pressure at home. This, in certain ways, linked the moderate struggle against the NAACP to the much larger ideological struggle between the United States and the Soviet Union. Southern moderates had to articulate their position in terms that not just other Americans but also audiences worldwide might understand. Hodges launched into this task not by justifying North Carolina's incarceration of the boys as a type of punishment for violating long-standing racial taboos but rather as a state-sponsored move to help the youths. "Our state officials are doing everything possible (through local welfare agencies), to see that the boys are released to their homes," Hodges wrote to Allen in February 1959.[153] Before they could be released, however, Hodges noted that "[t]he home conditions" of both boys' families were "most deplorable" and had to be ameliorated before they could be set free.[154] Hodges had gained information about the boys' homes from Blaine Madison, commissioner for the Board of Correction and

Training, who confirmed that one boy's mother had been married several times and the other's had lived with "a succession of men."[155] Only when such "family conditions" improved, Madison argued, should the boys be allowed to return home.[156] Hodges, who had already begun to flag black shortcomings, agreed.[157]

The inversion of the kissing case controversy into an effort by the state of North Carolina to help the incarcerated boys, not punish them, was one of Luther Hodges's more remarkable moves as governor. Yet, it was also consistent with his larger attempt to parry black demands for integrated schools by asserting a paternalist interest in the well-being of North Carolina's black citizens. Since becoming governor, Hodges had maintained, and probably believed, that segregation was part of a reasonable legal arrangement that actually helped African Americans. Though North Carolina blacks disagreed, Hodges grew increasingly impatient with what he undoubtedly viewed as their ill-considered demands, and he articulated an even more aggressive rationale for precisely why they needed to remain separated from whites, a rationale rooted in the vague assertion that they suffered from a less developed culture and needed to be rehabilitated before integration could occur. The two defendants in the kissing case, once their shaky "home conditions" were revealed, provided more evidence of this.

Though Hodges's conception of black culture lacked rigor and could easily have been explained by factors other than race, he nevertheless attempted to articulate his position to critics, Canon L. John Phillips of St. Paul's Cathedral in London among them. Phillips wrote Hodges at the end of 1958, inquiring into why North Carolina was holding the Monroe boys and imploring Hodges to release them on the grounds of basic human dignity. Hodges took the letter as a chance to reaffirm his own commitment to improving black morality. "I deeply regret that inaccurate information has been widely publicized on this case," he replied on January 2, 1959, "apparently prompted by some rather irresponsible people on this side who are more interested in personal publicity than in the actual facts of the case."[158] In defense of the boys' commitment, Hodges turned not to fears of interracial sex but to the quality of the boys' homes. "According to my information," he wrote, "which is documented by independent reports of welfare agencies, the home and family background of the two young Negro boys in question leaves a very great deal to be desired."[159] After relying on evidence possibly accumulated by welfare guardians he himself had sponsored two years earlier, Hodges then went on to describe the positive role that the state could play in reforming the black children. "Unbelievable as it may seem to you," he wrote, "the circumstances and surroundings at the Morrison Training School to which these young boys were committed are usually far superior and more conducive to good conduct than the homes from which those committed come."[160] Whether Phillips believed this or not, his inquiry joined an avalanche of political mail that gradually convinced Hodges to release the boys, after claiming that the boys' home situations had been improved.[161]

Restricting State Welfare to Blacks

Even though the release of the boys might have been viewed as a capitulation by Hodges, he did not give up his moral crusade against black culture. In fact, the Monroe kissing case revived his interest in controlling black illegitimacy rates. "Perhaps we ought to ask our General Assembly to enact a specific statute," Hodges wrote Ellen Winston on January 6, 1959, only days after writing Canon Phillips, "to the effect that if any applicant for ADC has more than one illegitimate child welfare officials shall immediately terminate further payments until the applicant shows by overwhelming evidence that there is not some person around who can support the children."[162] Winston, who had refused to get involved in the Monroe kissing case and remained unwilling to cut welfare to anyone, including blacks, opposed such a measure, arguing that any law making "legitimacy the test of a child's entitlement" to federal ADC money would probably be considered "discriminatory" and therefore unconstitutional.[163] Instead, she proposed returning to the idea of a welfare guardian, or "personal representative" for unwed mothers.[164] Though Hodges did not publicly reject her recommendation, he communicated privately with Rachel Davis, a state legislator interested in the question of illegitimacy, hinting at a rift between himself and the state's highest welfare officer. On February 12, he wrote to Davis, "We have been in correspondence with Dr. Winston for quite some time about the question of illegitimate children and welfare payments. She is smart, but she doesn't always disclose the things she knows. I hate to bother you with a lot of reading, but you might like to look over the file I am enclosing, and return it at your convenience."[165]

The file included Hodges's private correspondence between himself and Ellen Winston disputing federal regulation of state welfare laws. Hodges suspected that Winston was using the threat of federal review as a means of saving unwed mothers from being denied welfare, even as he grew increasingly interested in cutting state funds. To circumvent this, Hodges suggested that Davis contact Wilbur Jolly, the senator who had proposed the sterilization of unwed mothers in 1957. "I was informed that Senator Jolly was having a bill prepared," wrote Hodges to Davis on February 12. "I hope that you can speak to him."[166] At his suggestion, Davis joined Jolly in cosponsoring a new sterilization measure that required mothers who had more than two illegitimate children to show cause why they should not be sterilized.[167] "It seems to me," declared Jolly in defense of the bill later that summer, that "we have placed a premium for every Negro woman to have an illegitimate child."[168] In Franklin County, he continued, the illegitimacy rate among blacks was 35 percent while for the state as a whole it constituted 20 percent. "Sterilize the women who make a habit of having illegitimate babies," he argued, "and you remove one breeding place for additional taxes."[169] Rachel Davis, who was white and an obstetrician from the eastern county of Lenoir before her political career, framed support for sterilization not as a tax-saver but part of an overall progressive vision of social uplift. "This is just another measure to protect society," she told a joint meeting of legislative committees on the bill, a sentiment that she used to back other legislation as well.[170] During the same session, for example, she proposed an omnibus crime commission to look into the problem of social deviants. According to her, the crime commission bill and the sterilization law were linked. The commission would be directed to study illegitimacy as well as juvenile delinquency, drug addiction, vagrancy, sexual delinquency, perversion, prostitution, and mental illness. The sterilization law, according to Davis, constituted an effective means of reducing social deviation.[171]

This was an even more punitive brand of progressivism than anything Luther Hodges had advocated. Though Davis certainly knew that her measure weighed more heavily on blacks than on whites, she never articulated overt racial animosity toward African Americans, nor did she much involve herself in the battle against *Brown*. Yet, her sudden interest in "protecting society" from illegitimacy-related deviance was eerily timed. It suggests that the struggle over integration was leading not only to state interest in black marriages but also to even more unsettling interests in finding facially neutral ways of controlling the black population. This certainly seemed to be reflected in Davis's draconian choice of sterilization over welfare guardians, which contradicted the recommendation of a committee she had recently served on. In 1958, North Carolina's Conference of Social Service, a relatively liberal, forward-looking group, had appointed Davis to serve on a subcommittee headed by Chapel Hill sociologist Guy B. Johnson to produce a report on illegitimacy in the state.[172] The report, *The Problem of Births Out of Wedlock*, found that differences in illegitimacy rates between the races were skewed by the fact that more than 40 percent of illegitimate white births were legitimated through adoption.[173] Blacks, the report continued, tended to care for illegitimate children within family groups.[174] In light of these findings, the report warned that punitive measures like sterilization should be avoided.[175]

Davis's decision to ignore the advice presented in her own report suggests that she was mixing politics with her progressivism. Sterilization, though ill advised, coincided with the emergence of interest in reducing black illegitimacy rates. It also resonated with concerns articulated by Governor Hodges that blacks were profiting from welfare and that black culture was less developed than white—concerns fueled by the desegregation crisis.[176]

Not surprisingly, the ensuing interest in mandatory sterilization of unwed mothers engendered a bitter black response. African Americans wrote to Governor Hodges, outraged at the sterilization bill. "[W]e one hundred per cent oppose the act of this present Legislature to pass a bill proposing to authorize the sterilization of the unwed mothers of our state," wrote the East Cedar Grove Missionary Baptist Association, representing thirty-seven black churches and a membership of roughly 17,000 people.[177] The *Carolinian*, a black newspaper, carried a full-page ad, signed by black leaders, warning, "Against God and Nature: Protest Illegitimate Bill."[178] Such protests intensified during a hearing when Wilbur Jolly told a group of black ministers who had come to protest the measure that "you ought to be for this . . . one out of four of the Negro race in North Carolina is illegitimate."[179] Outraged, the ministers jumped to their feet, shouting Jolly down with accusations that the bill was unfair and discriminatory.[180]

White interest in black illegitimacy rates seemed to coincide, uncannily, with black demands for freedom. The first wave of interest, in 1957, coincided with the rise of massive resistance and the victory of the Pearsall Plan. Meanwhile, white interest in 1959 coincided closely with Robert F. Williams's efforts to advertise the Monroe kissing case. Regardless of whether there was a direct link to these cases, the rhetoric of controlling illegitimacy coincided closely with the rhetoric of preserving segregation and maintaining white culture. At a very basic level, such rhetoric drew attention away from black demands for increased resources, increased access to schools, and the enforcement of constitutional rights and refocused it on black moral shortcomings. One might even say that it attempted to undermine the moral authority of the civil rights struggle.

Though illegitimacy appeared to have little to do with constitutional law, sexual propriety civility, respectability, and nonviolence worked together to form an interlocking set of cultural values or practices that bolstered black constitutional protest. Rather than isolated components of black—or, for that matter, southern—life, political and cultural practice were inextricably linked, part of a single social, ideological, ultimately racial formation. This formation, far from a unified whole, incorporated a series of contested sites within which blacks and whites waged political and *cultural* war. By attacking black illegitimacy rates, or what they might have viewed to be black cultural practices, white leaders in North Carolina sought leverage in the struggle not only against black demands but also against the contours of black rights as outlined by the Supreme Court.

Of course, white women also bore children out of wedlock; what about them? One reason that white illegitimacy may not have factored as greatly into public policy debates at the time is that many more opportunities existed for unwed white mothers to put their children up for adoption. If a white teenager became pregnant, she could tap into a relatively large network of maternity homes and adoption agencies in North Carolina that were more than willing to mask her illegitimate birth in exchange for her child.[181] African American mothers had fewer options; the major maternity homes in the state refused to accept black applicants until the 1960s.[182] This made it harder for unwed black mothers to access state services that might help them place illegitimate children for adoption. "While about 70 percent of white babies born out of wedlock are placed in adoptive homes," observed Ellen Winston, "only about 5 percent of Negro babies are so fortunate."[183]

Despite such a remarkable disparity, fears that punitive welfare measures might inadvertently target whites became a matter of some concern. This became apparent on April 22, 1959, when Wilbur Jolly and Rachel Davis announced a new proposal—less draconian than sterilization—demanding that unwed parents be prosecuted for child abandonment.[184] According to this proposal, Superior Court solicitors, the 1950s equivalents of state attorneys, would be provided with lists of illegitimate births and would be required to investigate the parents responsible for such births for possible violations of abandonment laws. Solicitors would also receive lists of ADC recipients and be required to investigate them for similar violations.[185] If the solicitors happened to find that unwed parents were misusing funds, they could charge them with a misdemeanor.[186] If they found that any of the individuals being investigated suffered from mental illness, they would be required to begin commitment proceedings.[187]

Although the descendent of a bill aimed primarily at blacks, the new Davis-Jolly bill aroused concern among those who dealt primarily with illegitimacy among whites.[188] On May 12, 1959, H. Galt Braxton, a member of the Board of Trustees of the Children's Home Society of Greensboro, wrote to the chair of the House Health Committee complaining that the bill made for bad policy.[189] In particular, he complained of the requirement that solicitors be supplied with the names and addresses of illegitimate children and their unwed mothers. "Such a law," argued Braxton in an editorial for Rachel Davis's hometown paper, the *Kinston Daily Free Press*, would "brand" every "innocent child born in North Carolina out of wedlock as illegitimate."[190] Rather than reduce illegitimacy rates, this "would defeat efforts that have been in progress for more than half a century to save such innocent youngsters by placing them in reputable and proper homes."[191] Not only that, the bill "would brand every young woman in the State who unfortunately becomes an unwed mother and would put up the bars permanently for such a girl or young woman to be redeemed to society and thereafter live a life worthwhile."[192]

Given how few maternity homes there were for black mothers, it is unlikely that Braxton was referring to the innocence or redemption of

African American girls. After all, the Children's Home Society in North Carolina dealt almost exclusively with white children. In their fervor to punish African Americans, Rachel Davis and Wilbur Jolly had forgotten the larger implications that their measures may have had for accidental white mothers. This marked a central problem of shifting strategies of discrimination from color to moral character, or what Hodges might have called "culture." As North Carolina moved away from color and toward behavior as a means of legitimating racial injustice and undermining civil rights, it was imperative that attempts be made to improve at least the appearance of morality among white people as well. White mothers, it was widely believed, should be allowed to escape the stigma of illegitimacy by altruistically offering their children up for adoption. Not surprisingly, the Health Committee amended the Davis-Jolly bill, inserting a provision that the names of mothers and children be kept confidential.[193] This amendment earned the approval of children's homes across the state.[194]

The new Davis-Jolly bill, replete with its refusal to publish the names of unwed mothers and their children, coincided with another statute introduced in the 1959 session by State Senator Elbert Peel, who hailed from the eastern county of Martin. According to Peel's bill, county attorneys would be required to enforce laws aimed at deserting parents.[195] Further, counties would be granted the power to bring actions under the uniform reciprocal enforcement of support acts so that deserting fathers could be made to pay support for children they abandoned.[196] Here, a measure that coincided with attacks on black illegitimacy rates actually promised to *help* many mothers in the state, because white women, like many black women, had trouble enforcing support orders.

Senator Lunsford Crew, a member of the Pearsall Committee, also got involved in legislation on illegitimacy. In May 1959, he proposed a bill that made it a misdemeanor to mother more than one illegitimate child.[197] Whether the rest of the Pearsall Committee endorsed this measure is unclear. However, it is unlikely that Crew would have proposed a bill that would cause problems for the committee's work. During a Senate debate on the bill, Crew cited statistics on black illegitimacy rates in the state and announced that his bill was designed to combat the "lax morals" threatening to destroy not just the South but all of America.[198] Jolly stated that although he had suffered attacks by minority groups for his sterilization crusade, he continued to believe that illegitimacy was a problem and that prosecuting unwed mothers represented a positive step toward addressing it.[199] Consequently, he supported Crew's bill.

Crew's bill collapsed under criticism that it would simply encourage evasion by compelling unwed mothers to leave the state, give birth, and then return.[200] The Davis-Jolly bill calling for the investigation of unwed mothers, however, passed, albeit in a slightly altered form. Initially mandating that solicitors investigate unwed parents, Senators Crew and Peel lobbied and won an amendment granting solicitors discretion over whether to investigate unwed parents and enforce laws against the misuse of ADC funds.[201]

Like the measure requiring names of unwed mothers and their children be kept secret, the decision to grant solicitors unlimited discretion over whether to investigate illegitimate births constituted a flexible approach to the racially convoluted problem of unwed motherhood. It enabled solicitors to attack illegitimacy among blacks while avoiding the necessity of investigating the problem among whites, thereby bolstering claims that unwed motherhood was a black problem. At the same time, it satisfied punitive impulses without transcending the limits of civility, thereby appeasing racial progressives in Raleigh and Chapel Hill.

For Luther Hodges, the Davis-Jolly bill was not only a positive consequence of a political alliance that he had helped forge but also a complement to his larger strategy of providing a rational, reasonable explanation for why the South did not want to push more aggressively for integrated schools. By introducing the question of black illegitimacy rates into the larger policy debate over desegregation, Hodges parried extremist demands that blacks be sterilized and shifted the nexus of the desegregation debate away from white repression and toward black shortcomings. This move became an increasingly significant part of Hodges's response to *Brown* after the enactment of the Pearsall Plan in 1956. Prior to that, Hodges tried desperately to appeal to black voters, hoping to convince African Americans to fight integration voluntarily. When this proved futile and the Pearsall Plan devolved desegregation decisions to the local level, Hodges began to mount a more negative ideological campaign aimed at undermining the moral authority of black constitutional claims by highlighting black illegitimacy rates.

Hodges intensified his campaign against black illegitimacy in the wake of the NAACP's publication of the Monroe kissing case. This suggests that just as the NAACP pushed J. P. Coleman to engage in a type of propaganda struggle over the representation of race and racial politics in his state, so, too, did the organization push Luther Hodges to do the same. Embarrassed by a deluge of negative national and even international press concerning the incarceration of the boys, Hodges claimed that the real problem confronting the children was not racial discrimination but the low morals of the boys' parents. Then, as if to make a larger point that African Americans suffered from poor morals generally, Hodges recommended cutting state benefits to mothers on ADC.

While inciting debates among different legislative factions over black illegitimacy rates, Hodges worked to present a peaceful, ultimately positive image of southern whites and to neutralize those who might have been tempted to confront the Supreme Court with defiance. To support this approach, he used state troopers to maintain calm in Greensboro and Charlotte and employed the State Bureau of Investigation to intimidate members of the Ku Klux Klan. Such measures paralleled J. P. Coleman's use of state agents to maintain peace and quiet in Mississippi.

How did both governors, who came from relatively divergent states, arrive at a relatively similar approach to *Brown?* One obvious answer is that Hodges was inspired by Coleman, particularly Coleman's endorsement of pupil placement in Mississippi. Another likely answer is that both Hodges and Coleman recognized the importance of maintaining a positive national image, something they might have gained from their time working in New York City and Washington, D.C., respectively. Further, both governors remained deeply interested in drawing northern investment to the South, which required projecting positive spin. Finally, both leaders benefited from critical study of *Brown* and thought about potential loopholes in its implementation.

Although Hodges and Coleman shared many similarities, they differed in at least one fundamental way. Hodges, unlike Coleman, spent a considerable amount of time finding legalist strategies for empowering white voters at the local level, creating safety valves for those who might not be satisfied with moderate resistance to *Brown.* Here we catch a glimpse of how Hodges saw limits to what the law could ultimately accomplish, regardless of whether he endorsed it. "When the law runs up against human nature and the popular will," he asserted on August 8, 1955, "something has got to give, and not infrequently it is the law which is changed or modified."[202] The idea that law could not change "popular will" was nothing new and had in fact been a central tenet of the Supreme Court's 1896 ruling sanctioning segregation in *Plessy v. Ferguson.* That Hodges mentioned it again in 1955 suggests that he shared a view similar to that of the nineteenth-century Court, a view in which law was limited in what it could accomplish and ultimately contingent on the vagaries of electoral politics. Of course, Hodges's allusion to popular will was also an indirect indictment of the NAACP's reading of *Brown* and a call for the Supreme Court to rethink its position, endorse pupil placement plans, and limit its own ruling.

Further evidence that at least part of Hodges's thinking remained rooted in turn-of-the-century racial ideas emerged in his allusions to Charles B. Aycock, who served as governor from 1901 to 1905. Convinced that Aycock had contributed positively to race relations in North Carolina by lobbying for biracially funded yet segregated black schools, Hodges made the remarkable move of trying to convince blacks to remain segregated voluntarily. Here we see Hodges's blind spot in assessing Jim Crow, which led him to view segregated schools as part of a larger strategy of racial uplift, when in fact their ultimate function was repressive. Hodges and Coleman converged on this issue as well. Coleman also seemed blind to segregation as a repressive legal regime and confident that once white voters in the North and West understood how segregation worked toward the benefit of both races in the South that they would come around to our "way of thinking."[203]

The next chapter examines how a third moderate governor, LeRoy Collins, also worked to buy black support, even as he made repeated arguments highlighting the need to improve black shortcomings before *Brown* could be implemented. Alert to class differences within the black community, Collins provided concessions to middle-class African Americans while building a defense of segregation rooted in concerns over the low "standards" of the black poor. Attitudes toward the most disadvantaged hardened, and sexual morality emerged as a focus of state attention at the very same time that the state's racial policies were being called into question. Rather than set Florida, North Carolina, and Mississippi apart from the rest of the nation, this brought them closer: reinforcing an old tradition of blaming the poor for their plight, while simultaneously abrogating the state of any responsibility for past racial discrimination.

3

"LAWFUL AND PEACEFUL MEANS": LEROY COLLINS LIMITS *BROWN* IN FLORIDA

Early on the morning of January 1, 1957, rocks crashed through the front window of a small house in Tallahassee, Florida, waking Reverend Charles K. Steele. An African American minister originally from Montgomery, Alabama, Steele had become well known in Tallahassee for leading a highly publicized bus boycott, which began when two black students at Florida Agricultural & Mechanical College refused to move to the back of a local bus. For six months, that protest had met a peaceful response. Now, suddenly, things seemed to change. Shortly after Steele's house was vandalized, shotgun blasts were fired at a black grocery store owned by relatives of Reverend Daniel Speed, another local civil rights activist.[1]

Though local incidents, the attacks triggered a rapid political response. Florida Governor LeRoy Collins, who normally would have had little interest in or even jurisdiction over a localized criminal incident involving the destruction of black property, moved quickly to ensure that the boycott would not trigger any more violence. Using special emergency powers granted to him by the state legislature the year before, Collins ordered all buses in Tallahassee stopped as of January 1, effectively ending the boycott.[2] Rather than side with the victims of the attacks, however, Collins justified his action by blaming the leaders of the boycott, men like Steele and Speed, for provoking the violence. "[I]rresponsible Negro leadership," declared Collins on New Year's Day, had driven "rabid pro-segregationists" into committing violence. To thwart such "irresponsible" leaders, "who seem to actually want to provoke incidents," he terminated bus service.[3]

It was a remarkable, if insensitive, response. Instead, Collins might have directed state police to investigate the crimes or provide police protection to Steele and Speed. Yet, he seemed reluctant to show any sympathy to the civil rights leaders, even insinuating that they were responsible for orchestrating the incidents. It would be almost ten years before the civil rights movement would make the provocation of white violence a centerpiece of its direct action strategies, but Collins seemed to anticipate such moves in 1957, immediately stopping the protest before it could draw any further attention.

Six hundred miles to the north, Luther Hodges took notice. He wrote to Collins, inquiring about his action. "I noticed in the paper yesterday," he wrote on January 3, "that you had used for the first time your emergency power. It seemed to have been used for a good purpose. Would you have a member of your staff mail us a copy of the statute covering these powers?"[4] The inquiry, though brief, suggested that just as Hodges took advice from J. P. Coleman in Mississippi on pupil placement, so, too, did he seek advice from LeRoy Collins in Florida on how to use executive authority to neutralize unrest. Yet, Collins was, in the minds of many at least, a far cry from J. P. Coleman. While many viewed Coleman as a resolute segregationist committed to finding pragmatic, legalist means of thwarting *Brown*, few thought of Collins as much of a strategist when it came to sabotaging civil rights. In fact, many believed that Collins's interest in preserving segregation was casual at best, and that he defended the institution, to the extent that he did, only to retain his political viability.[5]

Yet, a close survey of Collins's political correspondence and confidential files reveals that he did more than many suspected to preserve segregation and cast obstacles in the way of the civil rights movement in Florida. During his administration, Collins endorsed a variety of creative, legalist strategies for keeping black children out of white schools, undermining the moral authority of black constitutional claims, and neutralizing direct action protest—many of which paralleled moves taken by Coleman and Hodges in their states. He advocated a version of gradualism, long before the rise of massive resistance that placed the timetable for integration firmly in the hands of local white majorities. He also used the question of black standards as a rationale for convincing the Court, and the American public, that *Brown* needed to be revised. Finally, he turned to a committee of legal experts to provide innovative legal measures aimed at bolstering his plans, even as he worked with black leaders and state agents to outmaneuver the NAACP.

Although many of these methods paralleled tactics pursued by the governors of North Carolina and Mississippi, there were also differences. For one, Collins did not advertise the depth of his opposition to *Brown* until he was openly challenged by more outspoken segregationists. Though he became governor in January 1955, Collins kept much of his opposition to the Supreme Court confined to private letters until the spring of 1956, when he was attacked by rivals for being soft on segregation. Another critical difference was that Collins exhibited a remarkable interest in carving out not just a strategic response to *Brown*, but a socially responsible one. African Americans, Collins argued, did not need integrated schools so much as improved housing, higher moral standards, and more opportunities to improve their lives. Integration, in his opinion, was an ill-considered policy that only a politically motivated organization like the NAACP—which in Collins's opinion possessed little real concern for black lives—would endorse.

LeRoy Collins's opposition to integration did not mean that he abandoned all sense of social responsibility toward blacks. Although he expressed a visible dislike and distrust of civil rights "agitators," he otherwise made surprising gestures of goodwill toward the state's African American population. In 1955, for example, he commuted the death sentence of an alleged black rapist named Walter Lee Irvin.[6] In 1957, he promised Floridians that they could find "wise solutions" to the desegregation crisis if they only recognized that African Americans did not have "equal opportunities."[7] Such gestures were truly remarkable for a white southern governor in power at the height of massive resistance.

Yet as remarkable as Collins's position on race was, there was a decidedly conservative, perhaps even paternalist cast to his rhetoric of racial uplift. Many of the "wise solutions" to *Brown* he advocated involved shifting attention away from decades of white repression and onto detailed accounts of black shortcomings, or low "standards." What makes Collins particularly interesting is the precise manner in which he focused on raising blacks standards in lieu of desegregating schools. This campaign, while it resonated with Hodges's interest in lowering black illegitimacy rates, became for Collins the key to solving the desegregation crisis.

Convinced that integration was the wrong policy for the South, Collins focused on problems that he perceived as endemic to black communities—illegitimacy, poor housing, ill health, and poverty—arguing that they needed to be addressed before integration could occur. By invoking low black standards, Collins countered NAACP demands for immediate integration by arguing that considerable work needed to be done in black communities before African American children could be allowed to enter white schools. This work, which ostensibly pursued the "best interests" of black children, enabled Collins to engage in a type of stern progressivism not unlike what Luther Hodges endorsed in North Carolina. For example, to improve black housing standards, a condition that Collins blamed for poor hygiene and academic performance of black students in school, he promoted clearing slums and selling the remaining property to private investors. To improve black moral standards, which Collins claimed led to weak, single-parent families, he approved vague rules punishing illegitimacy that in 1959 alone cut 7,000 families and 30,000 children, 91 percent of them black, from Florida's welfare rolls.[8]

Whether such measures actually raised black standards never became a focal point of Collins's administration. Instead, he seemed to endorse punitive welfare proposals as part of a larger, socially conservative type of moral belt-tightening, a restriction of state aid to the unworthy that demanded African Americans focus less on integration and more on themselves, even as it advertised black problems and rationalized white reluctance to integrate public schools. His stern campaign of racial uplift became a central part of his effort to project a reasonable, rational side of Florida's segregation story to the nation, one that placed the well-being of African Americans, not their continued repression, at the center of opposition to *Brown*. If the rest of the country could only see the myriad problems that Florida faced with its black population, Collins believed, then popular support for enforcing *Brown* would decline. This led Collins to respond to extremists by promising moderation as an even more effective means of maintaining segregation than massive resistance. "I am against defiance of constituted authority," Collins stated publicly on February 2, 1956, after being attacked by a gubernatorial hopeful and racial demagogue named Sumter Lowry, claiming instead that he supported a solution to the integration crisis that possessed the "authority of law."[9] "This is the course our state has been following," he argued, "I hope we will stay on this course. If we don't, I fear we will actually lose ground in our efforts to maintain segregation and to carry Florida forward."[10] Three years later, long after Lowry had been vanquished, Collins expressed his view even more pointedly. "[T]here are those in Florida who want us to follow a course of hot words and defiance," he asserted. "But I think the people of this state certainly now understand that that course will mean that we will abandon our destiny to the NAACP."[11]

Collins's aversion to the NAACP, something that he shared with Hodges and Coleman, suggests that his moderation, as brave as it was, was not *just* a brave stand against white calls for defiance, nor was it simply a plea to help raise the standards of Florida's black population. In fact, it suggests that Collins, like Coleman and Hodges, possessed a strategic sensibility of how moderation could bolster the South's constitutional position vis-à-vis *Brown*. For example, Collins anticipated that civil rights activists would consciously attempt to use white extremism, or "defiance" as he called it, to turn national opinion against the South, while increasing the likelihood of federal intervention in the process. To prevent this, he sought to control unrest by centralizing the state's police power, coordinating law enforcement agencies, and tracking potential agitators, both white and black. Collins also recruited conservative black leaders whose careers depended on state patronage and deployed them to subvert civil rights protest. Meanwhile, he engaged in a larger, overarching strategy of focusing on black shortcomings as an excuse for not integrating and to shift national opinion in favor of continued segregation.

Collins's techniques, in particular his concern for avoiding demagoguery and finding lawful means for stalling the implementation of *Brown*, enabled him to bridge the gap between resistance to integration and moral respectability. For some historians, this adherence to moral respectability gave blacks a certain amount of leverage over Collins, something that they exploited to achieve black demands.[12] Yet, the victories he granted, such as the integration of city buses and lunch counters in Tallahassee, ultimately proved to be concessions in a much larger constitutional struggle over integrating schools.[13] Indeed, one lesson of Collins's leadership is that civility, morality, and accommodation proved to be useful in and of themselves as tools for evading the Court. For every concession Collins made, he reduced the chances that the movement would be able to use white intransigence as leverage for building national support in favor of federal intervention in Florida.

Collins further reduced the leverage that civil rights groups had against him by endorsing a strict adherence to legality or, as he put it, "lawful and peaceful" means.[14] This, combined with a conscious attempt to position himself as a principled leader with the best interests of blacks at heart, boosted his constitutional position against immediate integration, even as it accentuated his southernness.[15] Indeed, one might say that the story of Florida under Collins was an allegory of the role that southern manners and paternalism, not southern violence, played in resistance to racial equality. His politics provide a window into how accommodation and conciliation diffused resistance and subverted civil rights at the state level.

To Tallahassee via Poughkeepsie

LeRoy Collins, like Luther Hodges and J. P. Coleman, came from relatively modest beginnings. Born in Tallahassee on March 10, 1909, Collins grew up working for his father, who owned a general store. After high school, his father offered to pay half of his college expenses, a move that led the future governor to pursue a one-year business degree at Eastman Business College in Poughkeepsie, New York. Eastman, one of the first business schools in the country, was well respected in the South at the time; it was a destination for southern students eager for a glimpse of the commerce, industry, and economy of the urban North. For Collins, Eastman meant more than just a primer in northern business arts; it also meant visits to New York City and the opportunity to appear in theatrical productions at then all-female Vassar College.[16]

Whether such diversions had an impact on the young Floridian's racial views is unlikely. Many years later, for example, Collins noted that even after returning to Tallahassee from Poughkeepsie, he did not question the moral underpinnings of segregation. "I did not see, for many years," he noted in 1969, "that right and justice had anything to do with segregation."[17] Collins also claimed that he did not see much black support for dismantling Jim Crow. "Like many other privileged whites," noted Collins, "I rationalized that Negroes actually preferred it that way."[18] Ironically, Collins's time outside the South probably only convinced him that the rest of the country could be made to agree with southern racial beliefs.

Shortly after the outbreak of World War II, Collins enlisted in the U.S. Navy and received an assignment to the West Coast, first to California and then to Seattle, as a Navy lawyer. During his time in the West, Collins watched as the federal government ordered the internment of thousands of Japanese Americans, flagrantly denying their constitutional rights to equal protection and due process. Though the rationale behind the internment (and segregation) of Japanese Americans was certainly different from the rationale behind Jim Crow, the fact that California voters, not to mention Governor Earl Warren, willingly sponsored the move helps explain Collins's later conviction that reasonable defenses of segregation might be positively received nationwide.[19]

Regardless, after the war Collins returned to Tallahassee to practice law and run for political office. His interest in politics stemmed not so much from his experiences in the Navy as his time at Eastman and his memories of growing up in Florida during the Great Depression. During the 1930s, he had helped found a Junior Chamber of Commerce and something called the Catfish Club, an organization designed to bring progressive reform to Tallahassee, inspired, in part, by Franklin Delano Roosevelt's New Deal. Collins's positive view of the New Deal, augmented by his brief stint working for Roosevelt's Works Progress Administration, probably did affect his later conciliatory approach to the federal government after *Brown*. It might even have convinced him that cooperating with the federal government could lead to substantial increases in federal funding, capable of spurring economic growth.[20]

While World War II helped liberalize the American government's official position on racism, it did little to change Collins's views of segregation. "Our goodness presupposed that the Negro had his place, and that he would stay in it," wrote Collins in his memoirs, referring to his views of race in the 1940s and 1950s. "We expected Negroes to be somewhat inferior and irresponsible."[21] Collins did not begin to articulate a shift in his opinion until the 1960s, with the onset of the direct action phase of the civil rights movement. "My new view of the race problem came slowly," he wrote in 1969. "For me there was no sudden realization, no blinding vision, no seizure on the road to Damascus."[22] Although such a confession provides insight into Collins's mind-set in the 1950s, it did not distinguish him from many of his white peers. After all, most white southerners in the 1940s and 1950s did not see links between racial segregation, as they practiced it, and racial repression.[23] For example, in a lighthearted poem about growing up in Tallahassee, Collins described local attitudes toward African Americans not as a deep-seated hatred, but a type of bemused wonder at the Negroes' "funny ways of shanty living."[24] This description arguably captured the casual manner in which most white southerners perceived the black plight in the South. In their minds, black poverty was not the product of decades of systematic legal repression so much as a deficiency of talent and ambition. An opinion poll taken in Florida during the summer of 1954 suggests that 75 percent of white Floridians actually believed that most blacks were in favor of segregation.[25] To them, the idea of dismantling it was outlandish, not something that could logically come from local blacks who were accustomed to shanty living; it had to have originated with meddling, northern groups like the NAACP, who wanted nothing more than to destroy the South's racial harmony for its own ill-considered political gain.

Collins's confession that he held decidedly southern views of segregation while he was governor provides some context for understanding his response to *Brown*. It also illustrates an often-overlooked fact of the politics of the period, namely, that for most whites the struggle over desegregation was anything but a one-dimensional battle between forces of good and evil for simple justice. In fact, as Collins's memoirs reveal, the struggle against *Brown* was, in the opinions of many whites at least, a justifiable attempt to help blacks and preserve peace. Like an overwhelming majority of his white constituents, Collins possessed a peculiarly one-sided view of southern history, particularly the manner in which legal segregation had emerged in the 1890s. Though it had been aimed largely at destroying black political power, Collins believed that segregation and disenfranchisement reduced interracial tensions and encouraged good government.[26] This view, though challenged by black scholars like W. E. B. DuBois in the 1930s, was the dominant view in the nation during Collins's formative years.[27] Consequently, the idea that Jim Crow was repressive would probably have sounded alien to Collins even in 1954, as would claims that Jim Crow had played a central role in crushing a rising black middle class in the 1890s.[28] That there had even been a rising black middle class in the 1890s was not something that he learned in white schools, nor was it something that African Americans told him while he was growing up in the 1910s and 1920s. In fact, Collins's limited contact with the black community in Tallahassee probably only reinforced his faith in legal segregation. When he did have contact with blacks, it was usually with black employees, who were unlikely to risk their positions by complaining of white racism, or agents of black schools, like Florida A&M football coach Alonzo "Jake" Gaither, who stood to lose his job if schools were integrated. Insulated from more militant black leaders like Tallahassee's Reverend C. K. Steele, Collins was left, like many whites in the South, to draw conclusions about black life based on prejudice, limited information, and a historically distorted view of race.

Under these circumstances, Collins actually came to think of public school integration as a "ridiculous" objective that actually obfuscated the true needs of blacks, needs that extended to housing, jobs, moral standards, and health, all of which he believed could be better addressed through progressive social—albeit segregated—policy.[29] Collins's "progressive" view of Jim Crow helps explain why he fought to preserve it. It also helps explain how he could resist *Brown* and, at the same time, endorse causes sympathetic to blacks. For example, while in the state legislature in 1951, Collins endorsed a bill prohibiting members of the Ku Klux Klan from wearing masks during public demonstrations.[30] He also fought against efforts to retain Florida's white primary, which kept blacks from voting in primary elections, and he was the first candidate for governor to enter segregated black communities to campaign for black votes.[31]

Yet, when the Supreme Court issued its ruling in *Brown* on May 17, 1954, Collins stood firmly against it. He issued a statement asserting, in moderate terms, of course, that segregation was Florida's "custom and law" and that he would use all legal means available to him to preserve it.[32] Later, Collins confessed to believing that *Brown* was actually a "screwball opinion" and that "smart lawyers [would] figure ways to get around it."[33] This last claim, as we shall see, proved an apt summary of his response to the Court.

The Ervin Brief

One smart lawyer Collins had in mind was Florida Attorney General Richard W. Ervin. Ervin, who entered office before Collins because of a special provision in Florida law that made the governor's cabinet independently elected from the governor, would become a critical strategist in Florida's early response to *Brown*. By the time Collins was inaugurated in January 1955, Ervin had already laid the foundations for a moderate, long-term strategy of delay that Collins would, in many ways, continue through the end of his administration. The first step in this campaign was convincing the Supreme Court to provide the South with an indefinite period of time to adjust to the idea of interracial schools, before it actually had to integrate them. To accomplish this goal, Ervin commissioned a sociological study in the summer of 1954 to prove that integration would lead to violence and unrest. For Ervin, the Supreme Court's reliance on social science evidence in *Brown* suggested that a southern response, also rooted in social science evidence, might make a convincing case for delay. Consequently, he commissioned Lewis M. Killian, a sociology professor at Florida State University, to conduct a study of the potential impact that desegregation would have on white communities in the state. Killian, who still lived in the "dream world," as he later put it, of accepting segregation as a fact of life, agreed to conduct the study and took inspiration from Kenneth B. Clark, the sociologist who had testified on behalf of the NAACP in *Brown*. Relying on an observation made by Clark that the success of integration would hinge on white leadership, Killian decided to conduct a leadership survey in Florida, partly to gauge the extent to which community leaders might go to resist *Brown*.[34]

Three remarkable results emerged from the study. One was a dramatic contrast between white perceptions of segregation, on the one hand, as an acceptable institution that blacks themselves supported and, on the other hand, black beliefs that *Brown* was a moral opinion that only a minority of whites opposed. According to his findings, Killian concluded that 75 percent of African Americans believed that most whites felt the decision was right and that 75 percent of whites believed that most blacks supported segregation.[35] Such glaring interracial misunderstandings indicated that the South was headed for conflict, a conclusion reinforced by surveys of white police who feared that integration would breed violence so intense that law enforcement would not be able to control it.[36]

Killian's findings on police opposition to desegregation became a matter of particular interest to Richard Ervin. In a brief requesting that the Court allow the South an undefined period of time to adjust, Ervin cited Killian's study and hoped that the justices would deny the NAACP's request for immediate desegregation. Ervin also cited other data pointing to dramatic disparities in academic performance and moral behavior between whites and blacks. According to his survey, 59 percent of black students in Florida only scored as high as the lowest 10 percent of white students on standardized placement tests.[37] Ervin also cited black illegitimacy rates, contending that 24 percent of all black births in 1953 occurred out of wedlock, while only 1.9 percent of white births did.[38] Finally, Ervin claimed that 89 percent of all reported cases of gonorrhea came from blacks.[39] What did illegitimacy and gonorrhea have to do with integration? Like Luther Hodges in North Carolina and J. P. Coleman in Mississippi, Ervin no doubt hoped that such statistics would help convince the Supreme Court to stall integration until black problems could be solved because they would otherwise have a negative effect on white students. To further advance this thesis, which placed the burden of change firmly on black shoulders, Ervin cited an article written by Hodding Carter, a well-known newspaper editor from Mississippi, who argued that "there is a wide cultural gap between Negro and white in the South."[40] This gap, Carter elaborated, could be measured by looking at rates of "illiteracy," "communicable diseases," and "minor and major crimes."[41] Such data, in Ervin's opinion, spelled a litany of afflictions endemic to black communities that would inevitably harm white children who were placed in black schools. Perhaps ironically, this recast racial segregation from a system of legal repression to a defensive bulwark against black pathology. "The Southern mother doesn't see a vision of a clean scrubbed little Negro child about to embark on a great adventure," quoted Ervin. "She sees a symbol of the cultural lags of which she is more than just statistically aware."[42] Hopeful that the Supreme Court would take note of such lags, Ervin filed Florida's brief in October 1954 and waited patiently for the Court's response.[43]

LeRoy Collins also waited. From October 1954 until May 1955, when the Supreme Court issued its second *Brown* decision, Collins remained remarkably quiet on the question of integration. During his inaugural address in January 1955, he declined to mention *Brown* once.[44] During a public address to the state legislature in April 1955, he simply maintained that segregation was "custom and law" and that he would use "all the lawful power" that he possessed to preserve it.[45] He also warned that any state legislation seeking to limit the decision, particularly if enacted prior to the Supreme Court's ruling on the Ervin brief, would be "premature."[46] Consequently, when the state legislature enacted a pupil assignment law modeled after Mississippi's law later that spring, Collins threatened to veto it until *Brown II* was handed down.[47]

Why was Collins so hesitant? One possibility is that he may not have been particularly committed to resistance and hoped that whatever tension might have existed over *Brown* would dissipate, clearing the way for a good faith compliance with the ruling. Yet, this is not how he recalled it in his memoirs, nor is it what his correspondence indicates. Letters that Collins wrote to constituents that spring suggest that he remained reluctant to do anything, not out of a latent desire to comply with *Brown*, but out of fear that premature action might jeopardize Ervin's brief. On February 12, 1955, Collins wrote to a constituent in Miami and asserted that even "talk about segregation" might jeopardize "the unsettled state" of the Supreme Court's position.[48] In another letter, dated May 17, 1955, he expressed hope that the Court would decide in favor of Ervin's gradual approach and avoid "a forceful attempt," as he put it, "to abolish segregation." Any such attempt, which is precisely what the NAACP had requested in its brief, would incite, according to Collins, "the demagogue to place in jeopardy the peace and stability of our respective states."[49] Collins's interest in retaining peace and stability and his fear that forced integration would lead to demagoguery were both good reasons not to respond adversely to *Brown*, and can explain his relative silence during the spring of 1955. Yet, the manner in which he linked a "forceful attempt" to end segregation with demagoguery suggests something else as well. Like Luther Hodges, Collins used the threat of white extremism to justify a gradual response to the Supreme Court. While this appeared moderate, even progressive, winning him praise from around the country, Collins remained careful not to publicly emphasize just how gradual he believed the process of integration should actually be.

Hints of Collins's true thinking on gradualism emerged in his correspondence. In the same May 17 letter in which he warned against the dangers of forceful integration, he also delineated when, precisely, he felt that integration should occur. "The end of segregation, if and when it comes," he wrote, "will be a result of a basic change in the attitudes and thinking of the majority race."[50] Southern white voters, in other words, were the people that Collins felt should decide the timetable for integration, not the Supreme Court of the United States. This, in Collins's opinion, represented a fundamental principle of American constitutionalism, a tradition built on the "consent of the governed," as he put it, citing the Declaration of Independence.[51] Even if minority interests persuaded the Supreme Court that their rights should be vindicated, those interests still had to persuade white voters—that is, the majority race—that their demands were constitutionally valid. Acceptance of "non-segregation," argued Collins, must first be "developed in the hearts and minds of the people, and, in spite of the Supreme Court's great power, these hearts and minds are beyond its reach and control."[52]

Here was a fatalist view of the Supreme Court's power, not to mention a perversely democratic view of American constitutional law that the NAACP was unlikely to embrace. Here also was a much more recalcitrant position toward *Brown* than Collins's quiet, seemingly compliant response to the ruling seemed to suggest. By invoking the hearts and minds of white southerners, he articulated a vision of constitutional change rooted in the racial benevolence of southern white people, not the jurisprudence of the Supreme Court. He even called into question the Court's "power" and warned it that certain things, like popular opinion, were "beyond its reach and control."

Instead of trying to accomplish something that was beyond its reach, Collins counseled the Supreme Court to grant the South an unlimited amount of time to desegregate schools, allowing it to focus instead on improving the "standards of the Negro." "I shall continue," he promised on May 17, "to exercise leadership in any public office entrusted to me for the improvement of the standards of the Negro."[53] Though Collins did not elaborate on what precisely he meant by such Negro standards, this phrase echoed Richard Ervin's mention of black standards in Florida's *Brown II* brief. His mention of them also framed the problem of integration as a fundamentally black problem, not a symptom of white discrimination or noncompliance with constitutional rules. In fact, Collins seemed to suggest that the imposition of constitutional rules, like those articulated in *Brown*, could derail the more important project of fixing, or improving, black people. "During this process of improving the Negro's standards," he continued, for example, any attempt to "abolish" segregation would cause "many and grave problems."[54]

Collins's cryptic allusion to "grave problems" also echoed the Ervin brief. Ervin made it very clear, for example, that if integration were forced, violence could, and probably would, erupt. Here was another reason to give the South time to adjust, to raise the standards of the Negro perhaps, until their bids for constitutional rights achieved the "consent of the governed." Of course, such a position was, in a way, tantamount to rejecting the authority of the Supreme Court, not to mention the notion that African Americans might have legal rights protected by the Constitution that were independent of majority preferences. Yet, by pitching his rationale for resistance in such a dispassionate, democratic way, Collins avoided extremist arguments, acknowledged the massive unpopularity of integration among his constituents, and carefully, civilly, shifted the burden of political change onto black shoulders.[55]

By framing the problem of desegregation as one of popular consent rather than one of enforcing constitutional law, Collins embraced democracy *and* parried the need to enforce the Supreme Court's ruling in *Brown*. In fact, he shifted emphasis away from changing the law. The law did not need to be changed, he implied; rather, people's opinions needed to be changed. "[H]e who molds public sentiment goes deeper than he who enacts law or pronounces decision," Collins asserted, quoting Abraham Lincoln, "He makes laws and decisions possible or impossible to execute."[56] Collins's reluctance to accept the possibility that law might effect social change echoed the fatalism articulated by Luther Hodges in North Carolina.[57] Collins seemed to share both Hodges and Coleman's view that if anything was to change, it was the constitutional position of the Supreme Court. For example, in a letter from July 1955, almost a month and a half after the Supreme Court granted the South "all deliberate speed" to implement the *Brown* ruling, Collins indicated that the decision was a strategic victory for Florida, won through Ervin's moderate means.[58] "The latest decision of the Supreme Court," wrote Collins, "indicates Florida has proceeded properly in this matter up to this point. Neither legislative nor executive action has been rashly taken. The Court, in fact, followed the position expressed in the Florida brief by our Attorney General."[59] Collins's description of *Brown II* as a strategic victory for Florida is significant. It suggests, among other things, that he saw a shift on the Court in favor of the white South and away from the NAACP, which had requested an order demanding integration forthwith. It also suggests that Collins saw this shift as a direct response to the rational, reasonable arguments articulated by Ervin in his brief. Although the Court relied on factors other than Ervin's brief, its conclusion in *Brown II* certainly coincided with the conclusion that Ervin wanted from the Court.[60] To Collins, who saw the ruling from a state perspective, *Brown II* meant that Ervin's version of gradualism, and perhaps even his own version of gradualism, stood a chance of gaining constitutional recognition.

How reasonable was such a conclusion? Perhaps surprisingly, it was not completely unrealistic. On the same day that Collins wrote to the New York editor about the positive attributes of *Brown II*, the Fourth Circuit Court of Appeals handed down a ruling that gave southern moderates like him considerable hope. In the implementation phase of *Briggs v. Elliott*, one of the original cases consolidated under *Brown*, Circuit Judge John Parker asserted that *Brown* did not require forced integration at all, only that students be allowed, voluntarily, to choose which schools they wanted to attend.[61] This meant that dual black and white school systems were constitutional, so long as students were allowed to choose between them. This ruling did not directly affect Florida, which was in the Fifth Circuit, but it opened up the possibility that, were *Briggs* to be appealed, the Supreme Court might modify its *Brown* opinion and accept dual school systems as constitutional, provided students were allowed to change schools voluntarily.[62] In fact, the NAACP, already shaken by its defeat in *Brown II*, refrained from appealing Parker's ruling precisely out of fear that this might happen.[63]

Parker's "Briggs dictum," as it came to be called, granted a certain credibility to Collins's constitutional approach. In fact, the Fourth Circuit opinion in *Briggs* seemed to suggest that the Supreme Court might actually be willing to wait, just as Collins hoped, until white southerners truly did change their minds about blacks. This coincided, incidentally, with Collins's perception of the Supreme Court's job, which was not simply to articulate abstract constitutional rules and then demand enforcement of those rules, like the NAACP wanted, but rather to relate "enforcement" of its decisions to "local conditions."[64] Such local conditions, in Collins's opinion, ultimately determined the parameters within which constitutional law could reasonably operate. Dual, voluntary school systems—as Circuit Judge John Parker suggested—provided one way of ending formal segregation while remaining within such parameters. So, too, did pupil placement, which granted local authorities the power to choose selectively the students they wanted to integrate. Not surprisingly, even though Collins initially threatened to veto pupil placement out of fear that it would undermine the Ervin brief, once the Court endorsed the brief, he quickly endorsed an assignment plan.[65] Florida's plan drew direct inspiration from North Carolina's statute in granting local officials the power to assign students to schools based on vague considerations involving the quality of "health, safety, good order, education, and welfare."[66] Such a measure, promised

Collins on July 15, 1955, would be entirely "adequate" for preserving Florida's custom and law of segregated schools.[67]

While Collins rested behind the bulwark of pupil assignment, the triumph of the Ervin Brief, and a favorable Fourth Circuit ruling in *Briggs v. Elliott*, two things happened that would lead him, in the spring of 1956, to pursue a more outspoken, aggressive stance toward *Brown*. First, southern politics took a dramatic turn toward defiance. Beginning in the fall of 1955, Virginia newspaper editor James Jackson Kilpatrick began advocating interposition, an eighteenth-century theory that states could constitutionally reject Supreme Court rulings. By December, Kilpatrick had convinced his powerful friend, Virginia Senator Harry F. Byrd, of the validity of the doctrine, which prompted Byrd to announce nothing less than a campaign of "massive resistance" against the Court. In February 1956, Sumter Lowry, an avid proponent of massive resistance from Tampa, declared himself a candidate for governor of Florida.[68]

Lowry's campaign bid focused on attacking Collins for being soft on segregation, which Collins felt a certain amount of pressure to respond to.[69] As early as February 2, for example, he responded to an insinuation by Lowry that he had been "pussyfooting" around the desegregation question by asserting that his approach to *Brown* was actually more likely to preserve segregation than massive resistance.[70] "Thus far," asserted Collins, "no integration has occurred in our state, and our leadership has been far more effective than has been the case in many other states in which a great deal more noise and confusion have been generated."[71] Long aware that defiance might jeopardize segregation, Collins lobbied against massive resistance on strategic grounds. "Actually," he continued, "when the issue is agitated in such a manner as to arouse intense emotional feeling and furor, the State's ability effectively to maintain its position is substantially weakened. This I have sought to avoid in Florida."[72] This, in many ways, was Collins's most outspoken defense of segregation yet. Although it resonated with claims that he had made in personal letters much earlier, it diverged significantly from his earlier public statements, which tended to simply assert that segregation was Florida's "law and custom" and that he was dedicated to upholding it.

The second factor that led Collins to adopt a more publicly aggressive stance toward *Brown* was a Supreme Court ruling issued on March 12, 1956, ordering the "prompt admission" of a black applicant, Virgil Hawkins, to the University of Florida Law School.[73] Hawkins had been trying to enter the all-white law school since 1949 and, pursuant to the 1950 Supreme Court decision in *Sweatt v. Painter*, should have been allowed to.[74] Yet, even though Richard Ervin accepted the authority of *Sweatt*, he still requested, in October 1955, that the Supreme Court of Florida grant him time to conduct a study, much like the study of public attitudes regarding *Brown*, to see whether Hawkins's enrollment might produce negative effects. Believing this to be yet another attempt to stall, Hawkins appealed to the U.S. Supreme Court and gained a favorable ruling in March 1956 that ordered his "prompt admission" to the school.[75]

For Collins, who had hoped that the Supreme Court was moving away from ordering immediate desegregation, the *Hawkins* opinion came as an unpleasant surprise and "upset the basis on which Florida had been proceeding so successfully."[76] No doubt this meant that the Court had, in Collins's opinion at least, taken an abrupt turn against allowing an undefined period of adjustment for southern schools, a position that led Collins almost immediately to call a conference. The subject of the conference, scheduled for late March, was, as he put it, to "devise ways and means for maintaining our traditions and customs of segregation in the light of the decision of the United States Supreme Court rendered in the *Hawkins* case."[77] Collins organized a committee of lawyers and judges to recommend "any legally sound steps or any lawful means which may be utilized at any level of government for the maintenance of segregation in the State of Florida."[78] The committee, headed by retired state circuit judge L. L. Fabisinski, included one retired State Supreme Court justice, the reigning president of the Florida Bar, a former president of the Florida Bar, a former president of the American Bar Association, and three other distinguished lawyers.[79] Collins announced that he would wait for the committee to arrive at recommendations for dealing with the desegregation crisis and, upon receiving such recommendations, call a special legislative session to enact laws capable of staving off integration.[80] He admonished the committee to "maintain segregation and at the same time follow a lawful and peaceful course so as to avoid the inciting of hate, furor and disorder."[81]

The Fabisinski Committee

Collins's assignment of a legal committee to devise methods of preserving segregation without "furor and disorder," coupled with his outspoken rejection of the *Hawkins* opinion, struck many observers as a significant departure from his previous stance toward *Brown*. According to the *Southern School News*, the conference marked a shift in Collins's politics away from "pleas for moderation and understanding" and toward outright resistance.[82] However, they did not realize the extent to which he had actually resisted the ruling all along. The only thing that changed in March 1956 was the degree to which he made this resistance public, coupled with his termination of Attorney General Richard W. Ervin as the state's sole legal strategist. While Ervin would continue to advise on racial matters, he would never again have the autonomy he had when he wrote the *Brown II* brief.

It is unclear whether Collins felt that Ervin had bungled *Hawkins*, whether he simply wanted more legal expertise, or whether he desired more personal control over the crisis. However, Collins began to rely more and more heavily on his own committee and less on Ervin, as Florida's struggle against *Brown* progressed.

Why did a Supreme Court opinion ordering the enrollment of a law student worry Collins as much as it did? The Court had held, in 1950, that law schools could not discriminate based on race, but it had never linked graduate schools to primary and secondary schools.[83] The Court even noted in *Hawkins* that concerns surrounding integration at the lower level did not apply to schools at the graduate level.[84] Does this mean that Collins was using *Hawkins* as an excuse to appear more committed to preserving segregation in order to counter advocates of massive resistance, like Sumter Lowry? It is certainly possible. Collin's decision to make public his views on desegregation may have been a reaction to fears that the admission of Virgil Hawkins to the University of Florida would be viewed by Floridians as a betrayal of his promise to avoid integration through legal means, which could push them to vote for Lowry. Collins might have also been worried that Hawkins's admission would lead to public protest, perhaps even violence, that would embarrass his administration. Indeed, something like this had happened in neighboring Alabama only three months earlier, in February 1956, when the University of Alabama admitted Autherine Lucy to its undergraduate program. Lucy's admission, which was perfectly legal, led to rioting in Tuscaloosa and became a public embarrassment for Alabama Governor James Folsom. Collins may have wanted to avoid a similar crisis in Florida.[85]

Perhaps ironically, Collins's promise that Florida would step up its "lawful" campaign of resistance to the Supreme Court, something that might have been designed to appease white extremists, did little to scare blacks. If anything, it drove them to more radical forms of protest. In May 1956, for example, a little more than a month after Collins's *Hawkins* conference, two black undergraduates at Tallahassee's Agricultural and Mechanical College refused to move to the back of a city bus, prompting their arrest. Though city officials dropped the charges, A&M students voted to boycott city buses on May 28, and local civil rights leaders like C. K. Steele announced a general boycott of the city's bus system shortly thereafter.[86]

As the boycott gained momentum, the Fabisinski Committee, as it came to be known, delivered a four-part plan to limit *Brown* and help the governor prevent unrest. On July 16, 1956, it recommended a modification of Florida's 1955 pupil placement law that removed any mention of segregation or race and authorized the assignment of pupils to schools based on sociological and psychological factors. It recommended a law regulating the assignment of teachers, another law granting the governor power over public facilities, and an increase in the governor's emergency police powers.[87] Though relatively straightforward, the Fabisinski Committee's conclusions represented a subtle and civil response to the desegregation crisis. Without targeting race directly, they provided the state, and the governor in particular, with a set of strategies for dealing not only with the Supreme Court but also with black protest, such as the bus boycott that had gripped Tallahassee since May. For example, the pupil assignment law did not propose to further segregation by dividing students by color; it did so by shifting emphasis to "sociological, psychological and other social scientific factors as will prevent socioeconomic class consciousness among the pupils."[88] For students who did not agree with their placements, the law provided an appeals system littered with bureaucratic hurdles.[89]

The Fabisinski Committee augmented the pupil placement statutes with a dramatic centralization of the governor's police power. Collins was empowered to close public spaces, to declare emergencies wherever he saw fit, and to single-handedly direct state troopers to control them.[90] This expansion of the governor's powers worried many, even leaders prone to defiance. Farris C. Bryant, one of Collins's opponents for governor, declared that the bills gave the chief executive "powers unusual for a governor in a Democratic society."[91] To rein them in, he proposed limiting the governor's police powers to five years.[92] Prentice Pruitt, an outspoken segregationist and state representative from Jefferson County, also fought the measure on the grounds that it could be used to enforce integration just as easily as it could segregation.[93]

Blacks were not as hopeful. The NAACP called the Fabisinski report "a disgrace before God and man" and asked legislators to abandon attempts to preserve segregation and instead try to uphold the "Constitution of the United States and the principles of Christianity."[94] John Orr of Dade County, one of the few white Florida politicians who took a public stand in favor of racial equality, agreed. "I believe segregation is morally wrong," he maintained. "Despite the clever language employed" by the Fabisinski Commission, "the Supreme Court will surely see through the Fabisinski committee bills and will strike them down."[95]

Collins ignored Orr's entreaties. Instead, he requested emergency funds to hire 100 new state troopers, all of whom would be under his control.[96] As an expansion of the governor's power over local police, this action also garnered criticism. State Senator Harry O. Stratton of Callahan County, for example, opposed increasing state police forces and tried to humorously convey his misgivings about Collins's dramatic centralization of power. Increasing state forces would be superfluous, he complained. "On any given day you can drive to Duval County and see five patrolmen sitting with their feet on a desk reading a magazine."[97] Perhaps more important, increasing the power of state troopers risked friction between state and local authorities. Alluding to potential conflicts between local and state law enforcement, Stratton insisted that "[t]here is not a sheriff who gets along with the highway patrol, and there is not a patrolman who gets along with the sheriffs."[98]

Collins, like his counterpart J. P. Coleman in Mississippi, did not care. He had encountered repeated problems with local sheriffs, particularly Lake County Sheriff Willis McCall, who had tried to humiliate him in February 1956 after he commuted the death sentence of Walter Lee Irvin.[99] Irvin, a black man who had been wrongfully convicted for the kidnapping and rape of a seventeen-year-old white woman in 1949, had spent more than five years appealing his case. Following his initial conviction, which had occurred despite limited evidence and in a mob-dominated atmosphere, Irvin appealed to the U.S. Supreme Court, which overturned the verdict and ordered a new trial.[100] Before a new trial was held, however, McCall drove Irvin and another defendant to an isolated rural area and shot them both, claiming they had attacked him. Though Irvin survived, news of the shooting attracted international attention, leading Andrei Vishinsky, the chief Soviet delegate to the United Nations, to criticize Florida's criminal justice system.[101] By the time Collins received the case, he found little evidence supporting Irvin's guilt, suspected McCall of trying to murder him, and commuted Irvin's sentence.[102] Enraged, Sheriff McCall orchestrated a confrontation between the governor and the victim of the alleged rape on February 22, 1956.[103] Collins, who endured a harangue by the woman, did not forget the incident, nor did he forget McCall's egregious abuse of authority.[104]

The Irvin case reinforced Collins's aversion to extremism, as well as to the problems that could be caused by rogue sheriffs. Eager to rein in such local satraps, Collins, like Coleman, endorsed an increase in the number of state troopers at his disposal, together with the expansion of his own emergency powers as enumerated in the Fabisinki Report. To ensure legislative compliance with the report, he met with state legislators in secret and demanded that they approve his plan before going into session.[105] Much like Luther Hodges had done in North Carolina, Collins pressured state legislators into supporting his plan, even getting many to promise that they would not introduce further legislation on race.[106] "I must know that there is unanimity among the legislators on approval of this program," he declared, "and I must know that a majority of the Legislature will resist efforts to go beyond this report."[107] Such efforts, Collins announced, would only "shame the state."[108] When asked by a reporter whether the report itself was a way around the Supreme Court ruling, Collins asserted that it was "avoidance by lawful means and not evasion by subterfuge."[109] Almost immediately after issuing this statement, he called the legislature into special session.[110]

As legislators gathered in Tallahassee to decide precisely how Florida would manage the integration crisis, Collins's homework paid off. Previous opposition in the Florida Senate, particularly heavy during an earlier reapportionment session, dissolved.[111] Senators who at one point had accused Collins of trying to run a dictatorship now acquiesced graciously to his desegregation plan.[112] Only six legislators refused to limit their actions in the session to Collins's bills.[113] Collins's rival Sumter Lowry was one of them. He called for measures beyond the Fabisinski Report and advocated an interposition resolution.[114] Prentice Pruitt of Jefferson County joined him, adding that the state should outlaw the NAACP and pass an anti-boycott bill.[115]

Collins ignored such requests. Although the NAACP remained active in the state and Tallahassee continued to suffer a black-led boycott, he adhered to standards of the utmost civility. Up to that point, his plan had worked. Through the appointment of a handpicked committee of moderate lawyers and jurists, through the careful prepping of state legislators, and through a special legislative session to deal with the racial crisis, LeRoy Collins had steered Florida's response to *Brown* away from radicalism.

Just how subtle Florida's resistance could be emerged a month after the special session ended. In late August 1956, Collins wrote to Budget Director Harry Smith to request money to organize an advisory commission to assist him in dealing with racial problems in the state. "The duties which have been given to me as Governor by the Legislature," declared Collins, "are very far-reaching and should be exercised only with extreme caution and understanding. There is a very strong need," he continued, "for me to have an advisory commission thoroughly familiar with the laws and with conditions throughout the State, to advise with me in respect to the implementation of these laws."[116] Collins suggested three members for appointment to the commission: Judge Fabisinski; Doak Campbell, president of Florida State University; and J. R. E. Lee, African American business manager of Florida A&M College.[117]

Black Agents

Collins's selection of an African American to serve on his advisory commission gave it a remarkably progressive look. Yet, it was arguably a strategic move. Unlike Luther Hodges, who had dismissed all black members from the Pearsall Committee, Collins had more faith, and more success, in working with black agents.[118] One of Collins's most reliable black agents was Florida A&M football coach Jake Gaither. Gaither consistently developed excellent black football teams, which were at risk if public universities desegregated.[119] For this reason, coupled with the fact that his job relied on state funding, Gaither frequently cooperated with Collins.[120] In May 1956, Collins dispatched Gaither to Delray Beach to diffuse an attempt by African Americans to desegregate a popular white beach. While there, Gaither worked with black leaders in a local organization called the Negro Civic League to help them buy their own beach. In exchange, the leaders promised to quash any potential civil rights protest. Later, they wrote to Coach Gaither to thank him for his intervention. "We are all most grateful to you, Mr. Parks and Governor Collins," wrote Civic League member Spencer Pompey, "for opening the way to what looks like a workable solution to the problem at hand."[121] Gaither's ability to arrive at a "workable solution" shows how Collins was able to use black agents to intervene directly in local disputes, sometimes stealing momentum from civil rights groups like the NAACP. Shortly after Gaither visited Delray Beach, Bob Saunders, an NAACP official in Tampa, reported to Roy Wilkins at NAACP headquarters on Gaither's work. "[I]ntervention by the governor (his representative was Coach Bill [sic] Gaither of Florida A&M)," noted Saunders, "brought pressure on some of the leaders" who were "dissatisfied with the compromise" between the Civic League and the city to buy a black beach in lieu of desegregating.[122]

While Gaither proved helpful in certain situations, Collins found it harder to use strategies of accommodation against committed resistance. In Tallahassee, he became frustrated by the refusal of the local black community to abandon the bus boycott, even after they were offered a compromise by the City Commission.[123] Though the NAACP was not directly linked to the boycott, Collins blamed the organization for inspiring it. On July 3, 1956, he blasted the protest as a "miscarriage of ambition" brought on by the NAACP's desire for power.[124] He charged that if the civil rights group really cared about Tallahassee blacks, it "should concern itself with other conditions of far more importance than where people sit on buses."[125] Like Luther Hodges, Collins assumed that the NAACP was stirring up the local black community and should be discredited so that African Americans might reject it. Of course, the chances that blacks would reject the very organization that had advanced so many of their interests for so long was relatively low. In fact, Reverend C. K. Steele and others had founded the Inter-Civic Council (ICC), the group technically responsible for the boycott, precisely out of fear that leaders like Collins would go after the NAACP.[126]

Collins began to get a sense of local black commitment to civil rights after investigators traced Steele's roots to Alabama. "In view of the fact that Steele had come here from Montgomery," noted an investigator named R. J. Strickland, "it was decided to go there to learn anything available relating to the boycott and those running it."[127] While in Montgomery, Strickland saw a connection between the Tallahassee boycott and the Montgomery boycott, whose "lack of records and freedom of accounting," as he put it, gave it an advantage over a more "legitimate operation."[128] Upon returning to Tallahassee, Strickland interviewed Steele "under suitable pretext" and discovered that "this bus seating had a particular meaning to Negroes and that they have given it great and complete support."[129]

Thanks to Strickland's report, Collins steered clear of further indictments of the local boycott until violence broke out on January 1, 1957. Instead, he focused more attention on information gathering. In August, Collins approved the creation of a formal governmental agency, the Florida Legislative Investigation Committee (FLIC), to investigate civil rights activities in Florida.[130] Collins also encouraged his biracial commission to recruit black informants and establish "quiet liaison[s]" with black attorneys so that they could tip off the commission in the event they heard of potential NAACP lawsuits.[131]

Infiltration, coupled with investigation, became a critical component of Collins's "lawful and peaceful" response to *Brown*, just as it had become an important component of J. P. Coleman's response in Mississippi. For example, while his advisory commission was still forming, Collins corresponded with John Wigginton, a former member of the Fabisinski Committee, about the possibility of monitoring not just black civil rights groups but white agitators as well. Wigginton consequently sought advice from Tennessee and Alabama regarding halting the activities of agitators "coming into our State with the apparent purpose of stirring up racial dissent."[132] "If any overt acts on the part of agitators threaten the peace and tranquility of any section of the state," Wigginton recommended to the governor, then we should "be in position to move in Court for an injunction restraining them from further activity."[133] Specifically, Wigginton recommended that Collins encourage local officials to withhold or deny permits to use public spaces. Wigginton also suggested that the governor employ a newly created agency called the Sheriff's Bureau to inform police around the state of potential protests so that law enforcement could be deployed to prevent possible outbreaks of violence.[134]

Centralizing Law Enforcement Power

The Sheriff's Bureau, first endorsed by Collins in 1955, was not what its name suggests. Rather than an organization of local sheriffs, it was a centralized state agency designed to monitor local sheriffs. "[M]any sheriffs had developed a sense of power and jurisdictional arrogance," noted Collins, "that would not tolerate 'outside' pressures for more efficient law enforcement."[135] The bureau, which he personally presided over, helped Collins reduce the autonomy of local sheriffs, even as it enabled him to better coordinate law enforcement statewide. For example, it initiated a statewide teletype and radio network, created a centralized database of criminal records, and gave Collins the power to order criminal investigations himself.[136]

One of the bureau's first targets was John Kasper, the segregationist who had ignited the race riot in Clinton, Tennessee, over the integration of a local high school in the late summer of 1956.[137] One of Collins's assistants wrote a memo to Collins about the Clinton fiasco. "Noting the comment by Governor Clement about the use of National Guardsmen in the integration situations," wrote Joe Grotegut, "reminded me that I have been tossing over in my mind some effective way of dealing with the so-called 'outside agitators' if any similar developments occur in Florida."[138] Grotegut recommended that the Tennessee authorities be contacted to learn more about Kasper and his "methods of travel and operation."[139] Collins liked the idea. "I think our new committee should be alerted to this," he responded, "and we should get their advice."[140] In November, the governor's Bi-Racial Advisory Commission met and discussed Kasper's presence in Alabama. Judge Fabisinski relayed a report from the Alabama Highway Patrol about Kasper's involvement in the Citizens' Councils there. The commission then decided to step up efforts to acquire Kasper's license plate number and car description in case he came to Florida. Once that information was obtained, he could be tailed and, if necessary, apprehended "before he starts any trouble."[141]

Three months later, John Kasper arrived in Florida. Almost immediately, the commission began to monitor his activities, noting that when he delivered a speech in the rural town of Chiefland, he "jumped on the Jews with both feet and said that all of the Negro problems were caused by Jews."[142] Kasper then requested the right to be accompanied on stage by thirty riflemen in Miami. After denying the request, the commission suggested that requests for armed protection be used as grounds for canceling speeches and that "a transcript should be made of one of his speeches—or some of them—as grounds for securing an injunction against him."[143] It was also suggested that county commissions be used to deny permits to speakers who threatened to disturb the peace.[144]

Although the commission discussed the possibility of bringing local county governments into the fold, their primary apparatus for dealing with agitators like Kasper remained the Highway Patrol. Unlike local police, the patrol was "a little farther removed from politics" and could be ordered to act against white agitators who might otherwise have the support of local law enforcement.[145] Not surprisingly, the committee recommended that the patrol be assigned the job of tracking Kasper. However, some state agents expressed doubts about giving state troopers too much authority. John Blair, a representative for the attorney general's office, suggested that the patrol should be restricted to highway safety. Friction between state troopers and local sheriffs had already become a problem, he contended, one that interfered with law enforcement across the state. Further, local contacts could be established to deal with racial flare-ups and provide information. They didn't have to be police.[146]

Less than a week after John Kasper arrived in Florida, the commission developed a proactive fourteen-step plan for dealing with agitators, white and black. Collectively, the steps revealed an implicit understanding that white violence incited by men like Kasper, as well as civil rights protests, had to be controlled to allow the state's legalist response to the Supreme Court to proceed without inviting further federal intervention.[147] To do this, the plan advocated extensive, immediate notification of state authorities, including the commission and the governor, of any local disturbances or potential disturbances. If any local sheriff detected "any indication of public commotion, indignation meetings, possible signs of group action against criminal offenders, especially in sex cases, strikes, picketing, etc.," they were to notify the governor.[148] If the disturbance promised to get out of hand, the plan called for the Sheriff's Bureau to contact local law enforcement and inform them that they were under the control of the governor. The plan then authorized the commission to call out the Highway Patrol. "At all stages of any disturbance, local advisers shall be subject to twenty-four hour call, with means of communication clearly made known to both the Executive Secretary and the Governor's office."[149]

Between March 1956, when Collins replaced Ervin as the state's leading strategist, and March 1957, when his handpicked commission drafted a proactive plan for neutralizing civil rights unrest, quite a lot had changed. Perhaps most significantly, the centralized power of the state had increased dramatically, as Collins had coordinated law enforcement agencies, increased the number of state troopers, and augmented his own executive power. But this was far from the full extent of his plan to wage "lawful and peaceful" war against the Supreme Court.

Targeting Black "Standards"

As Collins's committee developed strategies to curtail black protest and white activism, the governor turned to justifying white resistance to integration by focusing on black standards. "The overwhelming majority of people in Florida are determined to continue their customs and traditions of racial segregation," Collins announced in November of 1956.[150] However, whites did not "oppose the advancement of colored people," Collins maintained. "On the contrary, they support such advancement and indeed require that blacks advance significantly in a variety of areas before they be enrolled in schools with whites."[151] To facilitate progress in some of these areas, Collins announced plans for "a program which I believe will aid [black] advancement very materially—a program under which their health standards and educational standards and civil opportunities and responsibilities will be greatly improved."[152] His announcement, in light of the bus boycott outside his window, bore a certain irony. African Americans in Tallahassee saw an end to segregation as a means of improving their standards. Collins believed black standards to be independent of Jim Crow, something that African Americans needed to work on themselves before integration could begin. Further, talk of raising black standards helped Collins take the initiative away from the ICC and the NAACP, precisely because it presented a strategy of racial uplift that had nothing to do with integration.

One person who objected to this plan, perhaps surprisingly, was Lewis M. Killian, the sociologist who had conducted the leadership survey for the *Brown II* brief. In a remarkable break from his prior support for Ervin, Killian argued that Collins's plea for blacks to raise themselves up to a point that they were "acceptable" to whites was "a flat rejection" of the Supreme Court's order in *Brown*.[153] Killian went on to blast such policies of "gradualism" as being "more detrimental" to hopes of full integration than "a posture of defiance."[154]

Regardless of Killian's criticism, Collins's committee submitted a list of suggested projects that included inquiries into the proportion of state taxes paid by blacks and the precise extent to which "public services" available to African Americans were truly unequal.[155] Of particular interest to the committee was housing. How, for example, did "poor housing" adversely effect "moral development" in black communities?[156] Collins received the questions positively, particularly those having to do with black moral and health standards. After reading over the research agenda, Collins had an administrative assistant draft a response focusing on "possible steps" that could be taken "to deal with the matter of slum clearance" and the "health problems common within the African American community."[157]

On their surface, questions of health problems and slum clearance pointed to substantive policy concerns that perhaps did play a role in racial inequality. Was Collins genuinely interested in solving them? Probably not. On March 26, Dr. Wilson Sowder, head of the State Board of Health, attended a meeting of the Fabisinski Committee and explained that the governor had asked him independently to find "things that are simple and easy which might be done to improve relationships between the races."[158] Simple and easy solutions were not necessarily the same as substantive ones, and Sowder's recommendations suggested as much. They included equalizing restroom facilities along highways, increasing the number of black dentists, and creating scholarships for black nurses.[159] Though positive measures, to be sure, the extent to which they might raise black moral and housing standards at a mass level were minimal. In fact, they seemed tailor-made to compensate the very African Americans who did not suffer from low standards and were relatively affluent—not bus boycotters but car owners, not illiterate parents but families considering professional school for their children. Why focus on measures to assist the very African Americans whose standards were probably not an issue? Though Collins never stated it outright, his policies seemed to be designed to accommodate the very African Americans who might have been most outraged at his rhetoric about low standards, like black undergraduates at Florida A&M, who had already proven more than willing to engage in protest to speed implementation of *Brown*.

Collins's interest in accommodating black elites while ignoring the black poor, all in the hopes of scoring points with the Supreme Court, became obvious during the spring 1957 legislative session. On April 2, Collins asked the legislature to make his Bi-Racial Advisory Commission permanent and declared that the committee needed to assume an "active leadership" role in raising the "standards of the Negro."[160] "It is as simple a matter as this," he continued, "good standards of morality, health and citizenship, the influence of which is not confined to color lines, do not develop in the child who grows up in a filthy, over-crowded shack under the guidance of illiterate parents."[161] Whether good standards developed in children whose parents might take advantage of state-sponsored scholarships to nursing school was not something that Collins brought up. Nor was the fact that black activists in Tallahassee, none of whom seemed to be particularly illiterate, were preparing to mark the one-year anniversary of the Tallahassee bus boycott as he spoke. This suggests that Collins was actively working to shift the terms of debate away from civil rights and toward black shortcomings.

Speaking directly to white voters nationwide, Collins explained his reasons for not simply pushing integration in the popular, national *Look* magazine. Giving the country a reasonable, rational assessment of "how it looks from the South," Collins made his contempt for integration crystal clear. "[T]o listen to some reformers talk," Collins wrote, "all the Negro needs" is to dismantle segregation.[162] "Nothing," he argued emphatically, "could be more ridiculous."[163] Rather than entry into white schools, "the Negro's most pressing needs are better health, education, moral and housing standards. He needs these desperately in order to have an equal chance to develop his talents and better command the respect and admiration of his fellow citizens."[164] Collins was dead serious about putting the onus on African Americans to command the respect and admiration of white southerners, the very people who had orchestrated their subjugation for the past fifty years. To him, integration was fundamentally "ridiculous" because it ignored vast disparities in racial standards. Careful not to mention the black elites who might enjoy integrated rest stops along interstate freeways, Collins chose instead to focus on the failings of the black poor and did so in a remarkably public national forum.

Collins's article was intended to provide the rest of the nation with more than just a "look" from the South, indeed, an alternative way to see the challenges posed by *Brown*. Rather than a landmark ruling destined to help African Americans overcome decades of legal discrimination, *Brown*, Collins told readers, was an unreasonable opinion that did little, if anything, for blacks. Assuming he knew what blacks in Florida needed better than they themselves did, Collins no doubt wrote with northern and western voters in mind, recasting opposition to integration in terms of standards that most white voters could at least understand, if not sympathize with. It also made him appear to be a southern leader desperately trying to help African Americans who were otherwise being exploited by the NAACP and the Supreme Court. If he could only convince the majority of voters in the North and West that southern blacks were hopelessly beset by problems that needed to be addressed before integration could begin, then he might win political support against *Brown*. And without substantive political support, it was unlikely that the Supreme Court would, or even could, effect a forceful implementation of its ruling. Reinforcing Collins's legal gamble was the fact that the Fifth Circuit Court of Appeals had recently endorsed pupil placement plans as a constitutionally viable form of compliance with *Brown*.[165] The question of whether the Supreme Court would approve such plans, an increasingly likely proposition given its utter failure to implement *Brown* in the Deep South, loomed over the region in the spring of 1958, just as Collins drafted his *Look* article.

Just as Collins brought his standards argument to a national audience, so, too, did he erase his own complicity in maintaining those low standards. Two months before the publication of his *Look* article, Collins wrote to the Tallahassee City Commission to specifically request that a black neighborhood in Tallahassee named Smoky Hollow be demolished, without providing any alternative living options for its black residents.[166] Smoky Hollow, so called for the way that smoke from wood-burning stoves would linger in a valley not far from the governor's office, was something of a shanty town with low-income rental property, juke joints, and bars.[167] That Collins lobbied for its destruction surprised certain black residents in the neighborhood, some of whom had grown accustomed to paying the Collins family rent on properties that LeRoy Collins, his father, and his brother, Marvin Jr., allegedly owned in the district.[168] Why destroy such valuable rental property? Erasing the neighborhood, and his own ties to it, might have been a sign of how *Brown* pushed Collins to shift priorities.[169] Once happy to collect rent from black ghetto dwellers, Collins suddenly felt compelled to appear as if he were helping them, if for no other reason than to stall integration. In a rare appearance on the nationally televised talk show *Meet the Press* two days before his *Look* article was published, Collins said that eliminating slums was much more important than integrating public schools. Again speaking to the American public, Collins declared that Florida was not pushing aggressively for school integration because it was struggling to eliminate slums, "one of the greatest deterrents to the Negro's progress."[170]

Much like Luther Hodges, LeRoy Collins used the rhetoric of racial uplift, or "progress," coupled with a paternalist presumption that integration was not in fact what African Americans needed, to bolster resistance to *Brown*. This position, which Collins took to national audiences through television and print media, represented a strategic constitutionalism that attempted to circumvent the Court by appealing directly to the common sense of the voting public. Just like J. P. Coleman, who invited northern editors to tour Mississippi, Collins recognized that winning the struggle against integration meant showing the nation that race relations in the South were not that bad and that southerners themselves were working to help blacks improve.

Just as Coleman and Hodges endorsed relatively punitive legal measures lift black standards, Collins followed. Not only did he demolish black homes but also he endorsed a general tightening of welfare restrictions on unwed mothers. Several months after the publication of Collins's article in *Look*, Hal Stallings, the chairman of Florida's State Welfare Board, asked the governor to appoint a committee to study the problem of illegitimacy in the state and recommend legislative solutions for solving it.[171] "This problem is a disgrace to the state," Stallings declared, "and we feel that it is of concern to all citizens."[172] He recommended that the legislature impose stronger penalties on couples living together outside the confines of marriage.[173] Collins agreed, suggesting that a citizens' committee be formed to study the problem and propose legislative resolutions to ameliorate it. "I am extremely interested in obtaining advice and recommendations from a qualified citizens group on the pressing problem of illegitimacy," wrote Collins in January 1959. "The serious economic, social, and moral implications of the problem require that some corrective measures be developed to overcome this shameful situation within our state."[174] Linking illegitimacy to pressure on the state's welfare rolls, Collins located the committee within the Department of Welfare.[175]

Collins's support for controlling illegitimacy through welfare meshed with his turn toward imposing stricter moral controls on the poor generally. In May 1959, Collins endorsed legislation tightening provisions against welfare fraud and authorizing the state welfare board to conduct investigations against private citizens for use in the criminal prosecution of welfare abuse.[176] The legislature, which proved receptive to this type of initiative, supported the law by cutting funds to children living in unsuitable homes.[177] A home's suitability was determined by a set of vague criteria, each one capable of disqualifying the recipient. For example, if children were left alone while their parents engaged in "social activities or undesirable pursuits," they could lose welfare benefits.[178] Also, if parents engaged in promiscuous conduct "either in or outside the home" or had an illegitimate child after receiving an assistance payment or otherwise failed "to demonstrate an intent to establish a stable home," they could lose support.[179]

The law, in a manner suggestive of its racial intent, disproportionately affected blacks. Of a total of 14,664 reports on unsuitable homes that were filed because of the 1959 restrictions, 91 percent of these reports were filed against black families, with the end result that 7,000 families and nearly 30,000 children lost welfare funding.[180] The primary reasons for cutting funding were the presence of illegitimate children or unacceptable sexual conduct on the part of the mother.[181] For a governor interested in raising black standards, it was a not-so-subtle way of pulling the rug out from under thousands of black families and shifting the burden of uplift onto the shoulders of the most destitute.

Collins's new welfare regulations sent a clear message that Florida henceforth would make moral behavior a heightened prerequisite for receiving state services and even enjoying constitutional rights. If blacks wanted political equality, then they would have to adhere to a particular standard of moral conduct. By pursuing such a path of punitive progressivism, LeRoy Collins cobbled together a moral response to black demands for civil rights—meanwhile shifting politics in the direction of personal responsibility to the extent that it trumped constitutional guarantees.

Collins's campaign against immorality also aligned him with proponents of racial extremism in Florida. In 1957, Senator Charley Johns, one of Collins's rivals and a proponent of massive resistance, raided the library of a Coral Gables public school, discovered "obscene" materials, and declared a statewide investigation into the relationship between morals and education.[182] This investigation culminated in a measure approved by both the Florida House and Senate to increase criminal penalties for anyone "impairing the morals of young people by publication, distribution, sale or possession of obscene literature and other salacious material."[183] While such laws on their surface had nothing to do with race, they coincided closely with LeRoy Collins's concern over moral standards and fueled the idea that Florida's youth were at risk of being corrupted in public schools.[184]

Though extremists like Johns did not pressure Collins to focus on illegitimacy in school, the governor's campaign to raise black standards may have been a way for Collins to poach votes by using the fight against moral corruption as a substitute for endorsing outright defiance of *Brown*. Even though Florida was a moderate state, Collins was pressured by extremists,

Johns included, to endorse outright defiance, thereby pushing him even harder to come up with a viable, alternate response to massive resistance. Fighting for better standards—while materially reducing support for the black poor—was just such a response.

Interposition a "Lie"

Signs that extremism might challenge Collins's approach to *Brown* emerged in the spring of 1957, when a state representative and outspoken segregationist named Prentice Pruitt introduced an interposition resolution in the state legislature.[185] Almost immediately, Collins declared interposition to be not only an inordinately extreme response to *Brown* but also a legal mistake. He suspected that it might actually spur integration by convincing federal courts that Florida's less extreme forms of resistance, like pupil placement, were part of a strategy of defiance and therefore needed to be struck down. Consequently, he called interposition a lie and asserted publicly that it would endanger the state's pupil placement law.[186] His biracial commission, not surprisingly, stood behind him. The members rejected interposition, citing Virginia's experience. A spokesman for the commission described a case recently decided in Virginia where a pupil assignment law "was knocked out" because the state had also come up with an interposition resolution, "which was an indication of bad faith on the question."[187] Other representatives agreed. Senator Brackin of Crestview moved to table Pruitt's bill because of the possibility that it might speed up integration rather than slow it down.[188]

Many of Collins's rivals did not seem to care. Sumter Lowry, who had challenged him for the governorship in 1956, endorsed interposition and asserted that adoption of such a resolution would be "a great victory for the people of our state."[189] North Florida's rural legislators, many from counties with large black populations, agreed. Why did rural representatives, along with leaders like Lowry, endorse a legal strategy that had little, if any, chance of actually working against the Supreme Court? Part of the answer may lie in the particular type of constituents that rural conservatives and Lowry were trying to attract. Collins had risen to power largely with the support of voters interested in modernizing Florida and attracting business to the state. His constituents tended to come from counties in Central and South Florida that were either suburban or urban, had relatively high levels of education, and had relatively small African American populations.[190] Collins's opponents tended to come from counties in the Panhandle that were agricultural, had large black populations, and had a higher percentage of massive resisters. To many of them, Collins appeared weak and ineffectual for not endorsing interposition.[191]

Just as J. P. Coleman confronted voters in Mississippi who doubted his commitment to Jim Crow, so, too, did Collins. Unlike Luther Hodges, who provided safety valves to such voters through local option, Collins gambled that he could appeal to reason. This was perhaps his greatest mistake. His belief that the majority of voters in Florida could see the strategic advantages of his legalist approach to *Brown* presumed a constitutional sophistication that the majority of voters in Florida, who supported segregation, simply lacked. Beyond that, his measures, for the most part, were successful. By the end of 1958, not only the Fifth Circuit but also the Supreme Court had endorsed pupil placement, and Collins had, through a shrewd use of state law enforcement, made the job of white extremists, and arguably also civil rights activists, harder.

Yet, Collins was not entirely successful in preventing racial unrest in his state. He failed to prevent the Tallahassee bus boycott, even if he acted quickly, once white violence began to materialize, to use executive power to suspend bus service, a move that sapped much of the protest's momentum.[192] Collins also failed to quell popular unrest two years later in May 1959, when four white men raped a black Florida A&M student in Tallahassee. The rape led to mass demonstrations and a widely publicized trial, both of which attracted national and even international attention.[193] Collins did little to stop this; indeed, there was little he could do. Nonetheless, his brand of moderation seemed to be spreading, as the all-white jury convicted the four white men and sent them to prison for life.[194]

The Sit-ins as "Mob Rule"

Perhaps the biggest challenge to Collins's antiprotest strategies occurred in the last year of his governorship, when black students from Florida A&M College, a consistent source of dissent, staged sit-ins in local restaurants and lunch counters. The first of these began on February 13, 1960, not long after the Greensboro sit-ins in North Carolina. Collins's network of informers, including the Sheriff's Bureau and state police, failed to predict the uprising, and Collins himself underestimated the full moral implications of the student protest. Initially, he denounced it as a violation of property rights and an attempt to spread disorder, at one point even calling the state patrol to keep black students from leaving campus.[195] Despite arrests, incarcerations, and alleged beatings, the students continued to protest, showing a remarkable level of discipline and resolve. This complicated things. Collins, who had long invoked moral justifications for stalling integration, consulted with local leaders, both liberal and conservative, including Florida State Professor Lewis Killian to arrive at an appropriate response.[196] Killian, who had blasted Collins's gradualism in the past, told the governor that he needed to address the protest's moral implications head-on, lest they continue.[197] Collins complied. "There is inherent in this lunch counter matter moral considerations that I think are impelling," announced Collins on March 20, 1960, "and should appeal to everyone's sense of fairness and justice."[198] "Very frankly," he continued, "I think that if a business includes several departments and the general public is invited in to trade, the management is not fair to discriminate against Negro customers, denying them the services of one department. . . . To me this is a matter of simple moral justice."[199] Collins concluded on an emphatic note: "[W]e can never stop Americans from struggling to be free. We can never stop Americans from hoping and praying that some day in some way this ideal that is imbedded in our Declaration of Independence is one of these truths that is inevitable that all men are created equal, that that somehow will be a reality and not just an illusory distant goal."[200] It was a bold speech. Indeed, it sounded like a speech that a civil rights activist would make, not a southern governor who had been struggling to prevent integration and cast aspersions onto black character for the past five years. Yet, his address contained within it important continuities. Collins's invocation of morality was not inconsistent with his attention to black shortcomings. All along, he had stressed the moral component of the desegregation battle, arguing that integration should be allowed when and if African Americans raised their moral standards. Now, he suggested that those standards were not as important when it came to retail shopping. This was a concession, to be sure, but it did not change his basic position that moral concerns prevailed, and that black standards needed to be raised before mass integration of public schools.

Collins also took a jab at the direct action form that the sit-ins took. "We cannot let this matter and these issues be decided by the mobs," asserted Collins, "whether they are made up of white people or whether they are made up of colored people."[201] The implication that the student sit-ins represented a type of mob rule sent a relatively clear message to the Florida A&M undergraduates that their means were illegitimate, even if their ends were not. Of course, Collins did not mention that relatively little else was left to African Americans other than direct action protest, particularly as the Supreme Court had officially endorsed pupil placement in *Shuttlesworth v. Birmingham* and otherwise given up its attempts at enforcing *Brown*. Although the full implications of Collins's distaste for direct action would not manifest themselves until events in Selma five years later, his comments following the student sit-ins were hardly as liberal as many took them to be.

Indeed, as vexing as the student sit-ins were, LeRoy Collins could look back at a remarkably successful campaign against the NAACP's demands in *Brown* in the closing months of 1960. In the five years since the

Supreme Court's landmark ruling, only 28 of 212,280 black students were actually attending school with whites in Florida.[202]

Collins, along with Luther Hodges and J. P. Coleman, stood, in many ways, victorious.[203] Even though proponents of defiance lingered in places like New Orleans, where massive resistance was flailing desperately, interposition as a formal legal strategy had failed by the end of 1960. Similarly, the NAACP's legal campaign had stalled. After the Supreme Court's approval of pupil placement in *Shuttlesworth v. Birmingham*, not to mention the anti-NAACP campaigns across the South, further litigation did not seem particularly promising. Frustration with the glacial process of change in the courts led black college students to take to the streets.

Yet, it was far from clear what the results of those protests would be. If southern leaders followed Collins in accommodating black activists, it is possible that street protest would have won minor concessions—desegregated lunch counters, for example—but would not have had an appreciable effect on larger constitutional issues, certainly not the enforcement of *Brown*. In fact, that direct action protest could bring about constitutional change at all was uncertain. Even if the movement could convince federal judges of the need for more aggressive constitutional change, it still confronted the problem of enforcement. What would it take to convince the president, or a Congress laden with southerners, to enforce federal law?

The next chapter shows how the civil rights movement became increasingly radical just as the South veered toward moderation, ultimately gambling that the few extremists left in the region could help blacks win federal legislation and constitutional enforcement of *Brown*. Although this story is well known, the role that Luther Hodges, LeRoy Collins, and J. P. Coleman played in trying to counter this move is not. That story, which extends from the 1960s into the 1980s, raises questions about the movement's achievements, the reasons for its decline, and the relationship between the South and the rest of the country during the era following the Second Reconstruction.

4

THE PROCESSES OF LAW: COLLINS, HODGES, AND COLEMAN JOIN THE FEDERAL GOVERNMENT

On April 3, 1960, two weeks after LeRoy Collins spoke out in favor of desegregating lunch counters in Tallahassee, television host David Susskind invited five guests to appear on *Open End*, a New York–based public television talk show, to discuss the implications of the student protests. The panel included Leonard Holt, a field representative for the Congress of Racial Equality (CORE); Ulysses Prince, a student activist from Atlanta University; Dr. Martin Luther King Jr., chairman of the Southern Christian Leadership Conference (SCLC); and James Jackson Kilpatrick, editor of the *Richmond News-Leader*.[1]

It was a group with impressive credentials. Dr. King had attained national prominence as a leader of the Montgomery bus boycott four years earlier. Leonard Holt had represented plaintiffs in a lawsuit challenging segregation in Portsmouth, Virginia. Ulysses Prince, a member of the NAACP, had served time on a chain gang for violating Jim Crow laws in South Carolina.[2]

James Jackson Kilpatrick, on the opposite side of the civil rights struggle, also possessed a notable resume. The editor of one of the South's most respected newspapers, he had written a series of widely read editorials promoting interposition as a constitutional strategy of resistance to *Brown* and a book on the subject, *The Sovereign States*. Thanks in large part to his efforts, a majority of southern states had approved interposition or interposition-inspired measures, transforming the theory into a centerpiece of massive resistance.[3]

Not surprisingly, Kilpatrick mounted a spirited defense of Jim Crow on *Open End*. Unfazed by the activists, he attacked the sit-ins as a violation of the "ancient law" of trespass. He denied that there was any legal "right" to the protests, other than the property rights of the owners of white restaurants.

He even insinuated that the motivation behind the protests did not come from African Americans in the South but had been "deliberately timed" by agitators linked to CORE in the North.[4]

Yet, Kilpatrick did not mention interposition once. Eager to invoke the property rights of segregationists, he seemed reluctant to mention massive resistance. Eager to impugn the direct-action methods of black student protesters, he seemed reluctant to challenge their constitutional aspirations. This became particularly obvious when CORE's Leonard Holt asked him about LeRoy Collins's recent statement on the Tallahassee sit-ins. "I would like to direct our attention away from the purely legal aspect of this," began Holt, trying to redirect Kilpatrick's attention from the illegality of the demonstrations. "I'd like to refer you, if I may, to the statement by Governor Collins, of Florida . . . that it was unreasonable to expect that you could stop Americans from seeking dignity, or longing for freedom."[5] Holt's quotation of Collins reflected the national attention the Florida governor's statement had attracted. It also reflected the larger moral question the sit-ins had raised, one that Collins had answered positively in favor of civil rights for blacks.[6]

Even Kilpatrick had a hard time refuting such a claim. "I am happy to see that emerge," he responded, "I think it's fine. It's fine." What was not fine, he countered, was the way the protests had been conducted. "You talk about non-violence," he blasted, commenting on sit-ins that he had observed in Richmond, but "what is so awfully non-violent and passive about pushing and shoving?" According to him, the student demonstrators had consciously incited a violent response from local white extremists, compromising the protest's legitimacy. What is wrong, he asked, "with the processes of law?"[7]

Kilpatrick's invocation of the processes of law, coupled with his nod to Collins, was remarkable. For five years, he had rejected moderates and advocated outright, legal interposition as the best strategy against the Supreme Court, an approach that sought to close both the legislatures and the courts to blacks. Now, he seemed reluctant to invoke defiance and eager to encourage the civil rights movement to pursue traditional legal channels. Had Kilpatrick become less committed to preserving segregation and more accepting of the black struggle? Or had he abandoned hope that massive resistance would ever actually work and turned to other means of limiting civil rights? Though he did not mention it on *Open End*, Kilpatrick indicated the latter in a note to a friend written on January 7, 1960. "I will always believe that the interposition movement of four years ago had great political value," wrote Kilpatrick, but "[t]he full power and weight of the Federal judiciary have been thrown into enforcement of the doctrines laid down generally in *Brown v. Board of Education,* and the impact of that decision can no longer be avoided." Instead of pursuing legal defiance, Kilpatrick now counseled formal compliance with *Brown* and argued for a campaign aimed at turning popular opinion against the civil rights movement. "It seems to me," he surmised, that "the task is one of propaganda, publicity, and education" aimed at pressuring Congress into limiting *Brown*, "not one of passing foolish and useless laws which could not possibly be enforced without making Virginia look ridiculous."[8]

Kilpatrick's reversal flags a critical turning point in southern resistance to *Brown* that is often obscured by the rise of student demonstrations and direct-action protest. Though massive resistance had enjoyed a remarkable degree of popular support from 1956 to 1958, by the close of 1959, formal defiance of the Supreme Court had lost much of its legal viability and was beginning to lose political support. Not only did Kilpatrick, the one person perhaps most responsible for resurrecting interposition, abandon it but also from 1960 to 1963, states like Virginia, Georgia, Arkansas, and South Carolina all began to pursue more moderate strategies of resistance, like those endorsed by Collins, Coleman, and Hodges five years earlier. Meanwhile, the federal government showed increasing signs of tolerating, if not endorsing, such a move. The Supreme Court, for example, kept a low profile following its tentative approval of pupil placement in *Shuttlesworth v. Birmingham* in 1958, allowing *Briggs* to remain the prevailing interpretation of *Brown* for the next decade. At the same time, congressional proponents of civil rights found themselves unable to override southern opposition to substantive reform, a challenge bolstered by seniority rules and parliamentary procedures that boded well for moderate resistance to desegregation in the South. Even President-elect John F. Kennedy, who articulated an interest in expanding black voting power nationally, proved reluctant to offend the southern wing of the Democratic Party, knowing that a loss of southern support could cripple his own administration.[9]

Just as massive resistance collapsed, emerging moderate forces threatened to gain national credibility and preserve segregation, more or less intact, indefinitely in the South. That massive resistance had contributed to the rise of these forces is no doubt true, as the specter of southern extremism certainly encouraged the Supreme Court to accept moderation in lieu of defiance. Yet, even if extremism had never reared its head, it is by no means certain that the federal courts would have pushed independently for mass, forced integration. Indeed, this was the promise that Collins, Coleman, and Hodges had made to their constituents early on, namely, that strategic compliance could have circumvented mass integration indefinitely precisely because the federal courts lacked sufficient commitment to the black cause. Reinforcing this claim was the reality that the Court, though theoretically free from electoral control, could not go too far beyond what the majority of white southerners, and white voters nationally, were willing to accept. If it did, it jeopardized having its opinions ignored by southern leaders, its decisions undermined by southern legislators, and its own ranks reshuffled by presidential candidates eager for southern support.[10]

The electoral underpinnings of constitutional law placed substantial restrictions on what southern blacks, a largely disenfranchised group, could expect in the way of substantive change. Southern moderates like Coleman, Collins, and Hodges arguably knew this, and for that very reason, they admonished their constituents to avoid extremism. By 1960, after the rise and fall of massive resistance, all three governors stood perched on the edge of constitutional victory. Although their commitment to moderation had created opportunities for blacks to win local concessions like they did during the Tallahassee sit-ins, it lessened the chances that such concessions would go further to winning constitutional change. Such change could be avoided precisely because moderates gave the Supreme Court easy opportunities to endorse evasive schemes like placement plans. That such schemes were spreading rapidly across the South, even in states where voters still clung to defiance, strongly suggests that moderates had prevailed over extremists in the constitutional battle against civil rights.[11]

While this might be a fitting endpoint to a discussion of moderate resistance to integration in the American South, this was, of course, not the end of the black struggle to achieve full enforcement of *Brown.* Just as moderates rose to a position of dominance in the region, black activists intensified their commitment to direct-action protest. Building on strategies developed in the 1950s, black college students drew considerable attention to southern disrespect for civil rights by entering white restaurants and sitting down at white lunch counters. In 1961, civil rights activists won national headlines by riding integrated buses through the Deep South, testing compliance with a Supreme Court order demanding the end of segregated interstate transportation facilities. Indeed, from 1960 to 1965, civil rights groups across the South staged increasingly elaborate, calculated protests, culminating in dramatic confrontations between nonviolent protesters and police in Selma, Alabama, in 1965.[12]

Although historians generally hail this direct-action phase of the civil rights movement as a success, a continued look at the role that Collins, Coleman, and Hodges played in the civil rights battles of the 1960s raises questions not only about the movement's ultimate accomplishments but also about its demise. Although President Lyndon Johnson came to endorse sweeping civil rights legislation in 1964 and 1965, so, too, did he call on Luther Hodges and LeRoy Collins to actively discourage the very direct-action protest that led to such gains. In fact, Johnson appointed Collins the director of a federal agency designed to enter local communities and negotiate peaceful compromises between civil rights leaders and whites, effectively limiting the power of direct action to create the type of dramatic confrontations that ultimately won national support for the movement.

Even as the president articulated unprecedented symbolic support for the black struggle—at one point adopting the movement slogan "we shall overcome"—so, too, did he appoint J. P. Coleman to the Fifth Circuit Court of Appeals in 1965, over the bitter protest of civil rights leaders. Coleman's appointment to the federal judiciary, from a constitutional standpoint, marked a victory for his brand of racial politics. From his position as a federal circuit judge, he would not only read increasingly restrictive interpretations of the 1964 and 1965 civil rights acts into law but also anticipate a larger convergence between southern and northern constitutionalism regarding civil rights, well into the post-*Brown* era.

How could J. P. Coleman, as a federal judge, anticipate national trends? Many of the same types of arguments that moderates like Coleman made in the 1950s began to resonate with voters nationally in the 1970s, particularly as federal courts turned their attention northward. Happy to see an end to southern brutality, northern voters proved less happy when federal courts ordered their children bused to predominantly black inner city schools. Though the movement certainly convinced white voters that racial extremism in the South needed to end, it failed to muster the type of long-term commitment to overcoming racial subordination that was arguably needed to reach true racial parity in the United States. Further, even as direct-action protest achieved federal action by provoking dramatic displays of segregationist violence, its very success at eliciting such violence pushed federal officials to find creative ways of ending such protest. And as this chapter shows, federal officials relied on southern moderates to do this. In fact, the role that moderates like Collins, Coleman, and to some extent, Hodges played in corralling direct-action protest highlights continuities between southern resistance to *Brown* in the 1950s and federal resistance to direct action in the 1960s and beyond.

The role that J. P. Coleman played as a judge on the Fifth Circuit points to even more troubling continuities between the strategic constitutionalism that southern moderates engaged in during the 1950s and national trends in constitutional jurisprudence well into the post-*Brown* era. For example, Coleman took a strong stand against direct-action protest as a menace to law enforcement, anticipating a national turn against black protest and in favor of law enforcement in the 1970s. Coleman also took a restrictive reading of school cases, employment discrimination claims, and voting rights cases, repeatedly using the principle that the Constitution is color-blind to deny black civil rights claims, while he ignored the larger contextual history of racial repression in the American South. The tendency to ignore past repression and focus narrowly on legal language was in a way what Collins, Coleman, and Hodges had argued for since the 1950s. In the 1970s, it formed a robust firewall to bids by constitutional scholars like Owen Fiss, who argued that courts should employ a "group-disadvantaging principle" aimed not just at striking down overtly racist legislation, but actively seeking to achieve just racial outcomes.[13] This position, which came to be known as "antisubordination" theory, could have led to dramatic redistributions of wealth and privilege, ending racial disparities forever.[14]

Yet, it is not what prevailed. Getting the Supreme Court to adopt a color-blind theory of constitutional jurisprudence that did not take historical context into account was a moderate agenda that took shape in the1950s and was finally achieved in the 1990s. Of course, to say that southern moderates orchestrated this goal single-handedly would overstate their role in guiding constitutional debate at the time. Yet, they did perform the important work of reconfiguring the South's position in terms that ultimately proved viable at the national level and are therefore useful in explaining the constitutional outcomes and, in particular, the civil rights setbacks of the 1970s and 1980s. While focusing on southern extremists provides a melodramatic view of civil rights history, a struggle in which forces of good overcame forces of evil in the streets, focusing on southern moderates provides a more complex portrait of legal and political reconciliation between the South and the nation. Although the civil rights movement managed to project a shocking picture of southern segregationists that engendered national outrage, that outrage was never great enough to overcome the fundamental reality that national commitment to *Brown*, and to civil rights gains for African Americans generally, was never that great. Popular support for civil rights spiked only when white southerners engaged in racist displays that shocked and shamed white voters. Once those displays ended, or were brought to an end with the help of federal agencies like the Community Relations Service, national support for enforcing racial equality waned, and constitutional politics in the North and the South converged.

This chapter shows how Collins, Coleman, and to some extent, Hodges contributed to this convergence. Although their rise to federal positions is generally not considered important, a closer look at their roles in those positions illustrates at least one thing about the civil rights movement that public, televised victories obscure. No matter how much federal officials like Presidents Kennedy and Johnson may have personally supported the black struggle, larger structural forces—many related to electoral politics—pushed them to reject direct-action protest, embrace southern moderates, and ultimately employ strategic constitutionalism themselves at the national level to limit black claims.

Though often portrayed as a struggle against racial extremism, in other words, the civil rights movement of the 1960s could just as easily be framed as a struggle against the rising alliance between national leaders and southern moderates. If anything, movement strategists used extremism to disrupt the ascension of such moderates to positions of national influence. If strategists had not done so, then blacks could have been left at the mercy of increasingly sophisticated segregationists and an increasingly close relationship between federal officials and those segregationists in the 1960s. As it was, however, the movement managed, through radical, often dangerous tactics, to temporarily crack the burgeoning political alliance between national officials and southern leaders, winning federal legislation in the process. However, the exact wording of that legislation, like that of Supreme Court decisions, became open to interpretation and even contestation once national outrage at southern extremism waned. As J. P. Coleman's jurisprudence on the Fifth Circuit shows, southern moderates continued to interpret the Constitution against blacks well into the 1980s.

Moderation Spreads

Before examining the roles that Collins, Coleman, and Hodges played at the federal level in the 1960s, it is helpful to first summarize the electoral developments that coincided with the collapse of massive resistance. The Supreme Court's invalidation of massive resistance in *Cooper v. Aaron* in 1958, coupled with its approval of pupil placement schemes a few months later, told southern states that defiance, at least constitutionally, was doomed. White parents in Arkansas and Virginia reinforced this message by protesting the closure of public school systems as a last-ditch attempt to cling to massive resistance in 1959. By the time James Jackson Kilpatrick privately acknowledged the failure of interposition in January 1960, much of the South had already begun to shift away from defiance. Virginia Governor Lindsay Almond reversed his stance mid-administration, abandoning massive resistance and adopting a policy of token integration in 1959. Arkansas Governor Orval Faubus quickly did the same, returning to his pre–Little Rock stance of moderate acceptance of token integration. In 1961, Georgia Governor Ernest Vandiver shifted away from defiance to adopt a moderate stance of token integration advocated by the Sibley Commission, a legal committee not unlike those that Collins, Hodges, and Coleman had used. Similarly, Governor Ernest F. Hollings of South Carolina, initially a proponent of massive resistance, also shifted toward a more moderate approach marked by resistance through "flexibility."[15]

Just as recalcitrant states shifted toward moderation, so, too, did most moderate states maintain their general nondefiant political trajectory. Voters in North Carolina, for example, replaced Luther Hodges with Terry Sanford, a moderate who continued many of Hodges's policies. Similarly, Texas retained a generally nondefiant stance, as was demonstrated by extremist W. Lee "Pappy" O'Daniel's defeat in the 1958 governor's race to

Price Daniel. Daniel, no proponent of integration, was also no advocate of defiance. Like Collins, Coleman, and Hodges, he promised to avoid demagoguery and use legal means to preserve segregation. Daniel's 1962 successor, John Connally, was perhaps even more moderate, making appeals to civil rights and encouraging "voluntary" integration, while endorsing local solutions to school problems, including pupil placement.[16]

Tennessee followed a similar path. Governor Frank G. Clement, a moderate on racial issues, remained in office from 1953 through 1958. Initially opposed to pupil placement, Clement eventually signed an assignment bill into law in 1957. His successor and one-time campaign manager, Buford Ellington, though more outspoken in his support for segregation, was not as outspoken as his opponent, Judge Andrew Taylor, in 1958 and also did not endorse legal defiance. Clement returned as governor in 1963.[17]

Luther Hodges Becomes Secretary of Commerce

By the end of 1962, most southern states had either assumed a legal stance of moderation toward desegregation or were approaching one. Pupil placement plans gave way, in many states, to equally moderate "freedom of choice plans" that kept black schools open but allowed parents to choose what schools they wanted their children to attend, leaving segregation up to informal social and economic pressure. Meanwhile, pro–civil rights advocates in Congress proved unable to overcome southern opposition, as witnessed by the gutting of a civil rights bill in late spring 1960 during an extended southern filibuster. Realizing the extent of southern opposition to civil rights and hoping to maintain at least some support for a second presidential bid, President-elect John F. Kennedy showed little willingness to take a bold stand in favor of southern blacks. While he campaigned for black votes in the North, Kennedy also reached out to southern Democrats, particularly moderates. One of his first cabinet appointments was Luther Hodges as secretary of Commerce. Hodges's "imagination and energy," Kennedy announced during a press conference on November 20, 1960, were impressive, as was the fact that he and Hodges both shared a "common view" of what "the functions and responsibilities of the national government are."[18]

While it is unlikely that Kennedy knew the full extent to which Hodges had gone to preserve racial segregation in his state, it is probably fair to say that he did not really care. Kennedy relied heavily on southern support for both electoral and legislative success, making it imperative that he include southerners in his administration. Hodges's racial record made him an ideal candidate, in large part because he had avoided national embarrassment and lobbied for formal compliance with the Supreme Court. That less than 1 percent of black students in North Carolina were actually attending schools with whites was probably not as important to Kennedy as the moderate, compliant image that Hodges had been able to project.[19]

Hodges's nomination points to a reality of national politics that would have a profound impact on the civil rights struggle in the 1960s and beyond. Though national leaders tended not to have a vested interest in preserving formal segregation, neither did they possess much commitment to the black struggle. Regardless of their personal beliefs on black rights, national leaders were forced to negotiate southern opposition at the polls and southern opposition in Congress, opposition capable of derailing legislative and political initiatives vital to the rest of the nation. This made moderates like Luther Hodges, LeRoy Collins, and even J. P. Coleman national assets. Because they complied formally with *Brown* and avoided racial violence or extremism, they provided national leaders with a much-needed bridge to the South. As Terry Sanford, Hodges's successor, put it, Hodges "would be a good man for any position anywhere" in Kennedy's administration.[20]

African Americans had little reason to rejoice over presidential support for leaders like Hodges. Thanks to the rise of Hodges's particular brand of moderate politics, the chances that the executive branch would step in to desegregate southern public schools were not much better in 1960 than they had been in 1954. In some ways they were worse. At least in 1954, most southern states had used overtly racist laws—laws that could easily be challenged under *Brown*—to keep blacks out of white schools. By 1960, most of these laws had been replaced with more sophisticated statutes that preserved segregation indirectly and even enjoyed constitutional approval. For example, by the end of the spring 1960 semester, more than 99 percent of black students in Florida and North Carolina were still attending entirely black schools. In Mississippi, 100 percent were. Of the eleven former Confederate states, only Texas could boast of more than 1 percent of its black students in white schools, and even then it claimed only 1.18 percent. Little had really changed in the South regarding school integration, save perhaps the rise of moderation in once-defiant states like Georgia, Virginia, and South Carolina.[21]

Of course, not all southerners abandoned massive resistance. In a bizarre, self-defeating wave of populist anger, voters in a minority of states lashed out against moderate rule in 1959 and 1960. Voters in Florida rejected moderate Doyle Carlton Jr. in 1960, a candidate who enjoyed Collins's full support, and elected a more outspoken segregationist, Farris Bryant. In Louisiana, Earl K. Long, a moderate who had actively sought to keep blacks on the state voting rolls, was replaced by an outspoken segregationist named Jimmie H. Davis in 1960. In Alabama, moderate governor James E. Folsom was replaced by an extremist named John Patterson in 1958. And in Mississippi, J. P. Coleman was replaced by a recalcitrant proponent of massive resistance, Ross Barnett, a lawyer who campaigned energetically against Coleman's delicate handling of *Brown*.[22]

The rebellion against moderates in these states was, at first glance, not entirely rational. None of these states had succumbed in any meaningful way to integration, and all of them had endorsed "multiplied means and methods" to avoid it. Further, massive resistance had lost much of its legal legitimacy by the time that Long, Davis, and Bryant were all elected. In fact, by the time Bryant and Davis were elected, the constitutional legitimacy of interposition had virtually collapsed in the South.

Perhaps the best explanation for the backlash that propelled these leaders to power was a surge of anger from many voters who did not believe their leaders had done all they could to stop civil rights. Folsom in Alabama and Long in Louisiana had both done relatively little to assuage voters that they were doing all they possibly could to fight civil rights. Folsom had criticized interposition, vetoed anti-NAACP measures, and even invited black congressman Adam Clayton Powell Jr. to the governor's mansion for a drink; Long had proven reluctant to embrace black disenfranchisement. Further, both politicians had risen to power in part by forging interracial class-based coalitions, a strategy that proved anathema to white voters in the aftermath of *Brown*. Collins and Coleman were more focused on business development, but they, too, had failed to convince voters of their commitment to maintaining segregated schools. Though he probably would have survived in most peripheral states, Coleman mocked interposition, endorsed compliance with the Supreme Court, and rejected the Citizens' Councils. Collins's resistance to interposition and insistence on formal compliance with *Brown*, coupled with his outspoken support of black aspirations in the spring of 1960, similarly did not help him in Florida. Though the generally compliant appearance of these two governors probably helped their chances of actually preserving segregation in their states, it seems to have hurt their image among voters. Herein lay the crux of the tension between the type of strategic constitutionalism that they had engaged in and the overtly racialist electoral politics that more outspoken segregationists like Barnett, Bryant, Davis, and Patterson relied on to win elections.[23]

Luther Hodges, the only moderate governor in this study who was not replaced by a more outspoken segregationist, seemed to understand this. In an interview conducted in September 1960, Hodges's chief legal advisor Thomas J. Pearsall argued that even though legal means were best suited for resisting the Supreme Court, it was still important for voters to feel as if their leaders had done everything they could to stop integration. This meant that southern politicians not only had to devise adequate legal means of circumventing the federal courts but also had to let voters know, in no uncertain terms, that they had fought bitterly to prevent integrated schools and that no other viable options for resistance existed. Though Hodges did not boast of his accomplishments, his endorsement of local option, together with his endorsement of a public protest against the Supreme Court in the spring of 1956, might have helped him win voters' trust in North Carolina. Certainly, voters and legislators seemed to believe that the Pearsall Plan would work, as witnessed by its victory in the state legislature and also in a referendum vote. Indeed, Hodges's insistence on referendums and local options probably buttressed his political position among voters, convincing them not only that moderation was superior to defiance but also that they were themselves choosing it.[24]

Collins and Coleman did not seem to leave voters in Florida and Mississippi with a similar sense of empowerment. Neither seemed to leave their constituents entirely comfortable with the strategies they had put in place. Voters in Mississippi, for example, rejected the candidacy of Lieutenant Governor Carroll Gartin in part because he was considered to be the protégé of J. P. Coleman.[25] Meanwhile, a majority of voters in Florida, including voters in South Florida who were traditionally less conservative than voters in the Panhandle, went for Bryant.[26] Of course, this might have had something to do with Bryant's ability to play both sides of the fence. Unlike Ross Barnett, Farris Bryant was hardly a fire-breathing extremist. While he looked conservative compared with Collins, in many ways the Harvard Law School graduate only furthered Collins's basic agenda. No longer the proponent of interposition in 1960 that he had been in 1956, Bryant promised Floridians, as Collins had done four years earlier, that he would resist integration through "constitutional" means.[27] He also endorsed pupil placement and tokenism, increasing the number of black students enrolled in schools with whites from 28 to a remarkably nonextremist 6,612.[28]

Ross Barnett, along with Jimmie H. Davis and John Patterson, were arguably different. All three seemed willing, if not eager, to clash openly with the federal government. In November 1960, after seizing control of public schools in New Orleans to prevent them from being integrated, Davis called a special session of the Louisiana state legislature and endorsed an interposition resolution directed at the Supreme Court. Meanwhile, Patterson dodged federal requests to protect freedom riders in 1961, even threatening federal marshals with arrest. Finally, Ross Barnett invoked interposition to prevent the integration of the University of Mississippi by a black applicant named James Meredith in 1962; he even tried to stage a theatrical confrontation between himself and federal forces before conceding defeat.[29]

Such defiant stands, which became widely publicized, had an ironic effect. Rather than bolster segregation, they tended to jeopardize it. In fact, the demagoguery that emerged in Louisiana, Mississippi, and Alabama helped the civil rights movement by pushing federal officials, often reluctantly, to intensify their support for the black cause. To take just one example, in 1961 members of CORE decided to send integrated buses through the South to test enforcement of a Supreme Court decision ordering the desegregation of interstate facilities. When the riders reached Anniston, Alabama, a white mob pursued one of the buses, set it on fire, and attacked the riders as they tried to exit the bus. Soon after, another mob met riders in Birmingham. Instead of doing something to prevent the mob from attacking the riders, however, Police Commissioner Eugene "Bull" Connor actually granted white extremists time to attack the activists before police intervened. Media coverage of the violence prompted Attorney General Robert Kennedy to contact Alabama Governor John Patterson to try to secure protection for the remaining riders. Instead of using state police to override the authority of local officials like Connor, however, Patterson used the occasion to showcase his commitment to segregation, even threatening "blood" in the streets if integration was forced on the state.[30]

Though Patterson eventually agreed to protect the riders, he failed to use state forces to follow through on his promise, leading to a third, even bloodier attack in Montgomery. Confident that the governor would not intervene, Police Commissioner L. P. Sullivan sat by as a white mob attacked a busload of riders. Due to his inaction, the mob quickly grew to almost a thousand. The following day, rioting continued, prompting John Doar, an assistant at the Civil Rights Division of the Department of Justice, to request an injunction from Federal District Judge Frank M. Johnson to authorize the federal government to intervene. Once Johnson issued the injunction, which he did in the middle of the night, Robert Kennedy sent federal marshals into Alabama to protect the protesters. Soon after, the Department of Justice secured an order from the Interstate Commerce Commission (ICC) to demand the integration of interstate bus terminals.[31]

While it is unlikely that the freedom riders expected such a dramatic response from some of the highest officials in federal government, organizer James Farmer later admitted that their primary goal was to create a "crisis."[32] Perhaps ironically, the defiant stance of Alabama authorities, not just local police like Connor and Sullivan but even Governor Patterson, helped the protesters accomplish this goal. Not only did they willingly refuse to quell the violence but also they contributed to a situation that forced the federal government to intervene, thereby generating considerable media attention for the demonstrators, vaulting pictures of burning buses and bloodied activists into newspapers around the country.[33]

If Patterson had taken a more moderate approach, it is doubtful that the freedom rides would have been as successful. Evidence of this emerged in North Carolina, one month after the Alabama fiasco. As a second wave of freedom riders approached North Carolina's northern border in June 1960, Terry Sanford, Luther Hodges's moderate successor, contacted Thomas J. Pearsall, Hodges's old advisor, and asked him for advice on how to best handle the protesters.[34] Pearsall counseled Sanford to use state police to prevent white extremists from attempting violence, while approaching the matter "quietly, informally and without public notice."[35] When buses crossed into the state, Sanford stayed in close contact with the highway patrol, ordering them to follow the demonstrators. When they stopped in Raleigh, uniformed and plainclothes police were waiting for them, keeping a protective eye out against potential attacks. "True southern hospitality," reported the *New York Times*, "greeted the group."[36]

Southern hospitality, practiced by moderate leaders like Sanford, proved to be something of an antidote to dramatic, direct-action civil rights protest. Not only did it preserve racial peace but also it pleased federal officials. While national leaders like Kennedy were eager to pick up black votes in the North, they remained committed to maintaining white support in the South. Not only did they need such support to win national elections but also they needed white congressional support to enact national legislation. So long as southern officials could neutralize direct-action protest, keeping it out of national headlines, federal officials like Kennedy felt little compunction to intervene aggressively in southern affairs.[37]

Evidence of this emerged in Albany, Georgia, one year after the freedom rides. Beginning in late 1961, civil rights activists mounted a massive nine-month campaign of demonstrations in Albany to protest, among other things, the city's failure to comply with the ICC orders won in Montgomery.[38] There, Police Chief Laurie Pritchett worked hard to prevent instances of white violence. Instead of allowing black activists to fill local jails, a maneuver that pressured local law enforcement into using violent crowd dispersal tactics, Pritchett ordered demonstrators shipped to rural jails across Southwest Georgia. Similarly, to reduce chances that demonstrators might provoke violence from local whites, like the freedom riders did in Birmingham and Montgomery, Pritchett ordered civil rights leaders like Martin Luther King Jr. protected.[39] Not surprisingly, when black activist William G. Anderson filed a class action suit in federal court protesting the city's refusal to comply with a variety of movement demands after months of relatively inconclusive protest, the district judge dismissed it. And when Anderson appealed for an emergency injunction to the Fifth Circuit, Judge Griffin Bell denied it. Though a panel led by forward-looking Circuit Judge Elbert Tuttle would finally rule in favor of the plaintiffs more than a year later, the case would still be remanded back to the district court for further review—hardly the type of immediate judicial intervention that had occurred in Montgomery.[40] This led Albany civil rights leader Slater King to note bitterly that "whites will do nothing until a holocaust breaks out."[41]

Because Albany failed to produce dramatic confrontation, civil rights gains remained limited to local concessions. For example, the Georgia demonstrators achieved the removal of certain segregation ordinances from the city's code but failed to achieve the kind of federal intervention that the freedom riders had secured. From a constitutional perspective, one might say that the movement had failed to shift popular support enough or, conversely, failed to embarrass federal officials enough to bring about federal intervention and widespread change. Even the forward-looking Fifth Circuit proved reluctant to act, particularly when local and state officials refrained from taking defiant stands. Federal aid, in many ways, remained elusive.[42]

Why did the federal government not take a more active role in enforcing civil rights in the South in the early 1960s? For one, southern states still maintained a significant amount of control over the national government. Key Senate committees, thanks to seniority rules that favored southern senators, were headed by outspoken segregationists like Mississippi's James O. Eastland. Southern senators also proved willing to block civil rights legislation in Congress through use of parliamentary methods like the filibuster. To override a southern filibuster, civil rights proponents needed a two-thirds vote in the Senate, a high number that required rallying considerable national support in favor of black rights, a cause that did not automatically resonate with most voters nationwide. Lack of national interest in civil rights, coupled with southern recalcitrance, proved a major obstacle to substantive reform, even influencing the presidency. John F. Kennedy, though sympathetic to the idea of increasing black voting power in the South, still needed white southern votes to get legislation through Congress, not to mention win reelection in 1964.[43]

Without strong executive or congressional backing, the federal judiciary lacked any real means of enforcing its civil rights opinions. Though the Supreme Court could rule that segregation in schools and interstate bus stations was unconstitutional, it lacked the power to actually enter southern communities and force change. Further, most federal judges in the South came from southern communities themselves and sympathized with, even if they did not share, the same animosity toward integration that local majorities did. This led judges who did believe in civil rights, like Fifth Circuit Judges John Minor Wisdom and Elbert Tuttle, to employ creative legal solutions to circumvent local judicial opposition. For example, beginning in 1961, Tuttle reinterpreted long-standing rules of civil procedure to create a "removal remedy," which enabled federal judges to take cases away from recalcitrant state judges. Tuttle also made innovative use of the legal injunction, a type of equitable remedy that allowed courts to order local actors to behave in a particular way. Traditionally a remedy employed by district courts, Tuttle reinterpreted the law to make it more accessible to appellate courts pending appeal, essentially empowering circuit judges to intervene directly in local affairs.[44]

As dramatic as these maneuvers were, however, they still failed to bring about the level of change that civil rights activists desperately wanted. Among other things, they failed to rouse enough national support to override southern opposition in Congress. They also failed to convince the president that he could intervene in the South and still be reelected. No matter how many cases the Fifth Circuit removed from local judges, the federal judiciary was still relatively powerless to actually force change in the region. Structural constraints inherent in the American political system supported the status quo. Not surprisingly, five years after the Supreme Court sanctioned Alabama's pupil placement law in *Shuttlesworth v. Birmingham*, evasive legalist schemes remained intact across the South, as did obstacles to voting and discrimination in hiring and promotion. Frustration at such conditions led black activists to intensify their protests, hoping not only to pressure local segregationists into offering concessions but also to push for increased federal commitment to civil rights.[45]

Evidence of how this happened emerged in 1963. Following almost a month of inconclusive demonstrations in Birmingham, civil rights leaders James Bevel, Isaac Reynolds, and others decided to recruit children from local schools, some as young as ten years old, to leave class and march against police. Knowing full well the reputation of Birmingham Police Commissioner Bull Connor for violence, Bevel and Reynolds arguably risked the safety of more than a thousand children during the course of a week in hopes of filling the city's jails and pressuring Connor into using force to control the marches. On May 3, 1963, they succeeded. As Connor ordered local officials to disperse men, women, and children with fire hoses and police dogs, media coverage of the ensuing police violence drew national attention.[46] Attorney General Robert Kennedy announced that if Alabama did not grant equal rights to blacks, "further turmoil" would ensue.[47] Five days later, Brooklyn representative Emmanuel Celler and New York Senator Jacob Javits both called for federal legislation, noting that there was "ample basis for federal intervention in the 13th, 14th and 15th Amendments to the Constitution."[48]

Though President John F. Kennedy initially opposed federal legislation, preferring instead to work with local white moderates to accommodate black demands, this changed after a series of dramatic events exploded in May and June 1963.[49] The first was a theatrical attempt by Alabama Governor George Wallace to physically block the admission of two black students to the University of Alabama.[50] The second was the murder of Mississippi NAACP leader Medgar Evers.[51] Tired of southern intransigence and hopeful that sufficient political support for civil rights legislation might be gathering, President Kennedy finally sent a robust civil rights bill to

Congress on June 19, 1963.[52] While clearly a victory for the movement, this act was a strategic attempt to get the movement off the streets as much as a push for substantive change.[53] During his speech calling for a new civil rights bill, for example, Kennedy warned that if Congress did not enact such legislation, blacks in the South would continue "to seek the vindication of [their] rights through organized direct action."[54] Such a move would, in Kennedy's opinion, increase "racial strife" and lead to a transfer of power from "reasonable and responsible men to purveyors of hate and violence."[55] What Kennedy meant by this was relatively clear. Rather than a reward for direct action, federal legislation would hopefully be a vaccination against it, something that might limit future civil rights gains by keeping power in the hands of "reasonable and responsible" southern moderates.[56]

Although Kennedy might have secretly sympathized with the movement, it was only when the movement's activities led to violence in the streets that he felt compelled, and for that matter able, to intervene. When he did intervene, he made it clear that it was not simply to help blacks but also to prevent further crisis and, by extension, further protest. Thanks to southern voting power in Congress, even a bold intervention by the president in civil rights matters was not a guarantee that national legislation would be passed or that executive enforcement of Supreme Court decisions would follow. In fact, it is unlikely that Kennedy's bill would have survived a southern filibuster had it not been for his own brutal murder five months later. Seizing on popular grief over the president's assassination, Lyndon Johnson made passage of a strong civil rights act an early priority for his administration, both as a means of securing civil rights for blacks and as an important part of fulfilling President Kennedy's legacy.

Even then, southern congressmen fought bitterly, mounting an eighty-three-day filibuster that was not broken until Johnson rallied overwhelming Republican and Democratic support in the North and West. When it was finally signed into law on July 2, 1964, the Civil Rights Act established a variety of powerful tools, all enforceable by the federal government, to help African Americans secure at least some of their constitutional rights. For example, federal funding to public schools was made contingent on the desegregation of those schools, and federal courts were empowered to issue injunctions preventing discrimination in public accommodations, including hotels, restaurants, places of amusement, and gas stations. Further, Title VII of the act created an Equal Employment Opportunity Commission and provided plaintiffs suffering from employment or other types of racial discrimination with a means of redress in the federal courts.[57]

Yet, Johnson, like Kennedy, framed the act to help African Americans win their rights, as well as to prevent them from engaging in further direct-action protest. Immediately following the signing of the 1964 bill, he gathered black civil rights leaders at the White House and explained to them "that the rights Negroes possessed could now be secured by law, making demonstrations unnecessary and possibly self-defeating."[58] The 1964 act represented an attempt to bring the process of reform back into the structured realm of normal lawmaking.

A clue to this emerged in section X of the bill, which provided for the creation of a special federal agency capable of intervening directly in local affairs and mediating civil rights disputes. This agency, called the Community Relations Service (CRS), received relatively undefined powers "to provide assistance to communities and persons therein in resolving disputes, disagreements, or difficulties relating to discriminatory practices."[59] According to William J. Randall, a Democratic representative from Missouri, the service would strive to replace "fanaticism and extremism" with "moderation" by sending "dispassionate men" into local communities to negotiate peaceful compromises without "marshals" or "troops."[60] The effect such interventions would have on direct-action protest, which had so far proven most successful precisely when confronting "extremism," were not hard to imagine.

Rather than locating the CRS in the Department of Justice, the enforcement arm of the executive branch, Congress positioned the agency in the Department of Commerce, under the control of Luther Hodges. While Hodges had done little to suggest opposition to civil rights gains at the national level, he had also done little to make the Commerce Department an ally in civil rights reform. This was remarkable only because the Constitution's commerce clause was one of the few provisions that authorized Congress to intervene directly in state affairs, placing the department, and by extension Hodges, in a uniquely powerful position to regulate all manner of racial discrimination at the state and local level.[61] For example, the authors of the Civil Rights Act justified federal intervention into southern state affairs by relying on the commerce clause.[62] Yet, Hodges refused to testify on behalf of the legislation before Congress, even though he, as secretary of Commerce, would have been an obvious choice for linking commerce to the bill.[63]

Precisely because it focused on mediation rather than enforcement, the CRS gained a surprising amount of support from southern legislators who were otherwise adamantly opposed to civil rights reform.[64] In fact, after being dropped by the House Judiciary Committee, the CRS was resurrected via an amendment by Representative Robert T. Ashmore of South Carolina, an outspoken segregationist. Secretly hoping that the Civil Rights Act would fail, Ashmore included the CRS in the hopes that if the act did somehow survive a southern filibuster, the CRS would blunt its effect.[65]

Of course, this does not explain why Lyndon Johnson, one of the most vocal proponents of civil rights in Washington, also endorsed the Community Relations Service. Johnson confronted many of the same political restraints that Kennedy did, and many of the same structural interests in preserving southern support for his administration. Even if he had not required such support, it is unreasonable to think that he would have encouraged the type of direct-action protest that Bevel and Cotton had encouraged in the streets of Birmingham. Such protest, precisely because it sought to incite violence, risked tragic consequences, even death. It also risked national embarrassment, compromising both the president's authority and the nation's image. Here was a central irony of the direct-action phase of the civil rights movement: Even as it pushed federal officials to intervene boldly in southern affairs, it spurred those very officials to undermine it.[66] The CRS provided the federal government with a mechanism for increasing its commitment to racial equality while also positioning itself to take a more active role in managing unconventional black attempts to achieve it.

Evidence that this was in fact part of the mission of the service emerged during the nomination process of its first director, Florida Governor LeRoy Collins. Johnson's decision to appoint Collins came after a recommendation from Secretary of Commerce Luther Hodges, as well as almost a decade of Johnson's personal observation of Collins's handling of racial matters in Florida.[67] In February 1959, while Johnson was still a U.S. senator, he had invited Collins to Washington at the same time that he was working on a bill to establish a conciliation service for diffusing civil rights unrest, not unlike the CRS.[68] Why did Johnson express interest in such a service long before 1964? Aspiring to run for president in 1960, Johnson knew that he needed to walk a fine line between segregationist extremism and civil rights. While evidence suggests that his support for segregation was relatively weak and his sympathy for civil rights surprisingly strong, he was acutely conscious of the need to retain southern support for his candidacy and also to keep reform grounded in the realm of conventional politics. Violence in Montgomery, Mansfield, Clinton, Tuscaloosa, and Little Rock in the 1950s threatened to disrupt reform. By 1964, signs of a conservative backlash against the extreme direct-action strategies of the movement were beginning to surface nationally. One visible proponent of such a backlash was Arizona Senator Barry Goldwater, who made a public stand against the Civil Rights Act, in part hoping to win southern support for a presidential bid against Johnson. When Goldwater won the Republican nomination for the presidency in 1964, by exploiting divisions within the liberal flank of the GOP, it put pressure on Johnson to shift right. Compounding this pressure was Alabama Governor George Wallace's decision to run for president as a Democrat in 1964, challenging Johnson in the primaries. While few believed Wallace might win, he shocked liberals and conservatives alike by gaining 34 percent of the vote in Wisconsin and 30 percent in Indiana on a platform built almost entirely on racial extremism.[69]

At least some of the growing national opposition to the civil rights movement had to do with the movement's turn away from the courts and into the streets. In April 1964, for example, strategists for CORE drew national criticism for threatening to disrupt the World's Fair in New York City by abandoning hundreds of cars on freeways leading to the fairgrounds. Though southern leaders like Fred Shuttlesworth and Dr. Martin Luther King Jr. had nothing to do with such a plan, the prospect of nonviolent protest spreading north and disrupting the lives of thousands of people did little to win sympathy for the black struggle nationwide. Nor for that matter did a wave of riots that broke out in black sections of Harlem, Rochester, Paterson, Chicago, and Philadelphia during the summer of 1964. For national leaders like Lyndon Johnson, such explosions begged for a federal response.[70]

LeRoy Collins and the Community Relations Service

LeRoy Collins, a veteran of dealing with civil rights unrest in Florida, promised to help Johnson rein in an increasingly radical civil rights movement. During a confirmation hearing held on July 7, 1964, he asserted that the CRS would not engage in civil rights enforcement but would instead seek to mediate disputes "after people are confronting each other."[71] Collins clarified precisely what this meant in response to a question posed by Senator Norris Cotton of New Hampshire, one of the few northern opponents of the 1964 Civil Rights Act.[72] When Cotton asked Collins about his position on black street protest, something that as he put it "masquerades" as "civil disobedience," Collins replied forthrightly that the CRS would do "everything in our power to avoid violence and disobedience."[73] The inclusion of the word *disobedience* was suggestive. While violence no doubt meant white violence, disobedience probably meant black protest. Such protest had been escalating in the South during the weeks immediately prior to Collins's testimony, particularly in Florida. In St. Augustine, dramatic night marches drew opposition from extremists within the local white community. On May 27, 1964, more than fifty Ku Klux Klan members confronted marchers, threatening violence. On May 28, a white mob attacked newspaper reporters trying to cover a second night march and injured two. On June 10, an even larger mob tried desperately to break through police lines and attack marchers, reaching a few.[74]

Collins indicated his approach to these confrontations during his confirmation hearing in the Senate. In response to a question from South Carolina Senator Strom Thurmond on whether the CRS would push local communities "to integrate," Collins responded no, arguing simply that the

CRS would try to keep confrontations "out of the courts" and "out of the streets."[75] Keeping the movement out of the streets probably meant bringing an end to the kind of radical direct-action protest that had been plaguing Florida over recent weeks. Keeping the movement out of the courts probably meant preventing black lawyers from using the courts to further such protest. This had also become a problem in St. Augustine, as civil rights attorneys William Kunstler and Tobias Simon had persuaded a federal district judge to allow the night marches in the name of the civil rights activists' First Amendment rights. Despite the obvious risks involved in such a proposition, Federal District Judge Bryan Simpson issued an injunction overruling a local ban on nighttime protest, thereby preventing local authorities from intervening in the rallies. This ruling resulted in violence on the night of June 9, the same day Judge Simpson issued his injunction, as well as more violence on the tenth.[76]

That LeRoy Collins opposed such violence is certain. In fact, he later asserted that if the CRS had been formed earlier, it could have prevented the violence in St. Augustine.[77] Governor Bryant borrowed from some of Collins's tactics to deal with the protest, effectively precluding St. Augustine from becoming another Birmingham. On June 10, he ordered 45 state troopers into the city, a number that he quickly increased to 150. When white extremists gathered to disrupt a peaceful black march on June 19, they were "repulsed at every turn" by state police. When black activists arrived at an all-white beach to desegregate it on June 23, police protected them from white attackers. Desperate to bring the demonstrations to a stop, Bryant invoked the same emergency power that Collins had used to end the Tallahassee bus boycott in 1957 and called an end to the night demonstrations in St. Augustine.[78]

Meanwhile, Collins joined an old ally in an effort to sell the CRS to state leaders around the country. After frightening escalations of racial violence in both the North and the South during the summer of 1964, President Johnson ordered Luther Hodges to join LeRoy Collins on a tour aimed at quietly informing state governors of the services offered by the CRS.[79] Only four governors refused to speak to Collins and Hodges: Orval Faubus of Arkansas, Paul B. Johnson of Mississippi, Donald S. Russell of South Carolina, and George Wallace of Alabama. Both Faubus and Johnson denied the team's requests to meet outright; meanwhile, Wallace invited Collins and Hodges to visit Montgomery, but only if they avoided discussion of civil rights.[80] These four rejections aside, state leaders across the country proved receptive to the idea of a federal agency dedicated to neutralizing unrest. In fact, state governors proved so receptive that after conferring with Indiana Governor Matthew E. Welsh, Luther Hodges asserted publicly that "further racial demonstrations" would be unnecessary.[81] The "Negro" asserted Hodges, "has the law to go to and doesn't need demonstration."[82]

Civil rights activists, particularly those who had helped orchestrate the demonstrations in Birmingham and St. Augustine, disagreed. Not satisfied with the 1964 Civil Rights Act, and certainly not the formation of the CRS, many of the same movement leaders who had been thwarted by Farris Bryant at St. Augustine decided to target an even smaller Alabama town, Selma. The ostensible goal of mounting demonstrations in Selma, an otherwise obscure place, was to rally national support for a voting rights act, something President Johnson told King could not be accomplished in 1965.[83] One of the biggest draws to Selma, aside from its flagrant denial of black voting rights, was the violent reputation of its sheriff, Jim Clark, together with the extremist reputations of Alabama's governor, George Wallace, and the head of the state's police force, Al Lingo.[84] Counting on such leaders to reject the moderation of Florida's Farris Bryant and North Carolina's Terry Sanford, civil rights strategists made it clear that the goal of Selma would be the instigation of violence. On February 14, 1965, for example, Andrew Young, program director for SCLC, declared that "[j]ust as the 1965 Civil Rights Bill was written in Birmingham we hope that new Federal voting legislation will be written here."[85] Ralph Abernathy, another influential civil rights leader, remembered the goal of Selma in even more sanguine terms. "With any luck we would be visibly abused," remarked Abernathy, "without being maimed or killed."[86]

On Sunday, March 7, Abernathy's goal was realized. In a remarkable display of violent force, Alabama state troopers and a county sheriffs' posse assailed more than five hundred nonviolent protesters with clubs and tear gas, beating them viciously as they attempted to march across the Edmund Pettus Bridge on the outskirts of Selma toward Montgomery. Men on horses ran down marchers, lashing them with whips. Troopers clubbed women. White crowds, watching from the sidelines, cheered. The ensuing footage captured on camera and broadcast on national television shocked audiences nationwide.[87]

Shock bred support for the movement. "Decent citizens will weep," lamented the *Washington Post*, "for the wronged and persecuted demonstrators."[88] One such citizen, Minnesota Senator Walter Mondale, announced that the travesty in Selma made "passage of legislation to guarantee Southern Negroes the right to vote an absolute imperative for Congress this year."[89] Without waiting to see whether other federal officials agreed, Martin Luther King Jr. called for a second march, across the same bridge, on Tuesday, March 9. King's announcement caused grave concern for many, including the president. "[I]t's going to go from bad to worse," Johnson told Tennessee Governor Buford Ellington, hoping that he might be able to convince Alabama Governor George Wallace to intervene and prevent a repeat of Sunday's attack.[90] When Ellington warned that such communication would in all likelihood be futile, Johnson ordered LeRoy Collins to Alabama.[91]

Collins Diffuses Selma

President Johnson's decision to send LeRoy Collins to Selma illustrates the strained relationship between the federal government and the civil rights movement in the South in the 1960s. At the same time he told King that a voting rights act could not be enacted in 1965, Johnson began working on just such a bill.[92] By January, the president encouraged King to rally popular support for black voting rights in the South. That Johnson did not bother to send federal emissaries to negotiate with King prior to March 7 might have been out of hope that a little protest would not be a bad thing and could even fuel support for his own legislative agenda. However, King's spontaneous, arguably suicidal decision to hold a second march across the Edmund Pettus Bridge, only two days after the first one ended in unprecedented violence, was too much even for Johnson to take.[93]

Consequently, Johnson ordered Collins to Selma to prevent violence and, if possible, negotiate a compromise. What transpired during the time that he was there provides an example of just how effective moderation could be at softening the impact of direct-action protest. Shortly after his arrival, Collins met with King and pleaded with him to postpone the protest, to which King responded that Collins should urge the Alabama state troopers not to deploy brutality. Collins, in a manner that resonated with his promise to keep the movement "off the streets," agreed and offered to work with Alabama authorities, but only after King promised to truncate the march. Instead of marching to Montgomery, Collins suggested that King hold a symbolic demonstration on the bridge—and then turn around. Such a demonstration could be said to defeat the purpose of holding the march in the first place, which was to provoke a violent, extremist response. However, King found it hard to reject such a proposal outright; he told Collins that he would not agree to anything in advance but that he would never order demonstrators to force themselves physically through a line of police officers.[94]

What did this mean? Was King saying that if Collins could convince the police not to attack the demonstrators that he would call off the demonstration? He probably was. Police brutality, King realized, could help the movement win sympathy. Breaking through an otherwise peaceful police line, however, could have the opposite effect. Such a move could potentially be viewed as an act of force, not nonviolence, and recast the civil rights activists as aggressors. This was the genius behind Collins's proposal. By suggesting that King make a symbolic protest, Collins was accommodating black demands and providing demonstrators like King with an opportunity to save face, much as he had done in Tallahassee in 1960. Yet, by encouraging King to abandon his plan for a march, Collins was also reducing the possibility that the protest might incite a violent response—precisely the factor that had made the first march such a success. While Collins appeared to be helping the movement by reducing the chance of violence, he was actually hurting the movement by ensuring peace. Without the shock of violence, popular support would not be mobilized behind federal legislation.[95]

Collins was not the only federal official who tried to stop violent protest in Selma. Federal District Judge Frank M. Johnson, who had authorized federal marshals in Montgomery, also tried to stop King from marching. Though sympathetic to many of the movement's goals, Judge Johnson was relatively open about his dislike for the type of direct-action strategies that had been used in Birmingham and now in Selma. That such strategies were necessary for black success did not strike Johnson as being true. He, too, believed that the movement should stay out of the streets and fight its battles in court.[96] Consequently, on the morning of the second march, Johnson issued a federal court injunction ordering King not to march. This injunction, however, was not enough to convince King to cancel the protest entirely. Even though he knew about Johnson's order, he met more than two thousand protesters at the Brown Chapel on the morning of the ninth and did not even mention the possibility that they might march to a specific point on the bridge and turn around. Of course, he might have hoped that they would march to a specific point on the bridge, stop, and then be attacked, but at this point LeRoy Collins intervened. Just as they were leaving the church, Collins approached King, handed the black minister a map for marching to the bridge and back, and then told him, "I think things will work out all right."[97] He did not explain—and probably did not have to—that he had met with Jim Clark and Al Lingo and convinced them not to attack the demonstrators.[98]

At this point, King's strategy, insofar as it was designed to provoke violence, was doomed. While he might have been willing to violate a federal injunction, he was certainly not willing to force his way through a line of peaceful police officers. Such a move, particularly if the police did not respond with violence, risked making the demonstrators look like they were advancing aggressively on law enforcement, not the other way around. Consequently, when the marchers crossed the apex of the bridge and police did nothing, King halted the march, conducted a brief prayer, and then ordered the five thousand or so demonstrators to turn around.[99] For a lot of the participants, this was an unexpected, even disappointing conclusion to the protest.

Many of the marchers had no idea just how effectively LeRoy Collins had sabotaged the demonstration. By getting the Alabama authorities to refrain from violence, Collins had taken away the chance that the demonstrators might win national sympathy by subjecting themselves to violent attack. In fact, he had opened up the possibility that the demonstrators might incite a negative national response by forcing their way through a line of respectful, nonviolent police. This was probably more of a concern to King than violating a federal injunction, something that the minister had knowingly done in Birmingham. The underlying principle of nonviolence dictated that the movement must make a symbolic protest. In fact, this is what King told Collins the morning of the march. Civil rights activists, he explained to the governor, would never break through a wall of law enforcement officials, on "the basis of the non-violent spirit and the non-violent movement."[100]

While Bloody Sunday represented the power of violence for arousing national interest in the civil rights struggle, Turnaround Tuesday, as it came to be called, represented something different. It was more of a strategic concession, a compromise that allowed a harmless exhibition of black protest, while precluding any further outrage. Though LeRoy Collins was no longer governor of Florida, he was still engaged in the process of employing lawful means to preserve peace and, ironically, derail civil rights constitutionalism.

Of course, the violence generated by Bloody Sunday did stir up national support for the movement. Almost one week after the turnaround on the bridge, on March 15, 1965, President Johnson addressed a joint session of Congress and advocated passage of a voting rights bill designed to remove obstacles to black voters in the South. In discussing the bill, the president waxed poetic, declaring Selma to be nothing less than "a turning point in man's unending search for freedom."[101] Although Johnson undoubtedly meant that Selma had been a turning point in the struggle for racial equality in the South, it was also true that LeRoy Collins, as his designated agent, had orchestrated a very different turning point on the Edmund Pettus Bridge.

Is this an unfair characterization? Johnson, perhaps more than any previous American president, had lobbied for legislation designed to secure civil rights for blacks. Collins, similarly, had distinguished himself among southern moderates for speaking out against extremism and in favor of civil rights. Does this, then, make it historically inaccurate to charge them with attempting to rein in the civil rights movement? No. King's decision to march again on March 9, like Bevel and Cotton's decision to send children up against police in Birmingham, was a desperate, potentially dangerous act. No national leader could reasonably be expected to tolerate, much less condone, such an attempt to incite violence and risk injury or death. That the movement had to resort to such radical methods to effect change was a sad commentary on the American political system's failure to ensure basic rights for racial minorities, but it did not mean that federal officials could be expected to endorse bloodshed. In fact, here was evidence of just how great the obstacles to the civil rights movement were. Even if Johnson had secretly approved of the movement's tactics in Selma, he was still subject to the same political realities as other federal officials, and those realities favored moderate resistance to civil rights.

How domestic political strategy pushed national leaders like Johnson to endorse moderate resistance became obvious during the summer of 1965. Just as Johnson prepared for the passage of the Voting Rights Act, he decided to appoint J. P. Coleman to the Fifth Circuit Court of Appeals. By that time, the Fifth Circuit, thanks to John Minor Wisdom and Elbert Tuttle, had become notorious for its pro–civil rights opinions. Judge Tuttle had even confronted allegations of corruption for assigning civil rights cases to liberal judges and keeping them out of the hands of men like Mississippi Judge Ben Cameron. In the spring of 1965, Cameron died, leaving a seat on the court open. While Johnson could theoretically have appointed anyone he wanted to the court, including a liberal on civil rights issues, he chose Coleman.

Perhaps the best explanation for his choice was electoral politics. Coleman had endorsed both Johnson and Kennedy in the 1960 presidential election. He also enjoyed the endorsement of powerful southern congressional leaders like Mississippi Senators James O. Eastland and John Stennis, both of whom were capable of threatening Johnson's initiatives in Congress. Even Robert Kennedy, who knew that Coleman had helped elect his brother, lobbied for the former Mississippi governor. Johnson, who at that point was still considering a second bid for the presidency in 1968, was reluctant to appoint a liberal to the Fifth Circuit, knowing that such a decision might jeopardize his chances of winning southern support at the polls.

Not surprisingly, Coleman's appointment, a fairly bold move given his segregationist credentials, would prove much more controversial than Collins's. During two days of hearings before a special subcommittee of the Senate Judiciary Committee, opponents to Coleman's nomination presented a litany of reasons for not appointing him to the federal judiciary. John Conyers, an African American representative from Michigan, testified against Coleman, calling him a "calculated legal technician" who had manipulated "the judicial process in order to protect a racist social order" in Mississippi.[102] John Lewis, chairman of the Student Non-Violent Coordinating Committee (SNCC), called Coleman's appointment "an affront and an insult" to African Americans. Warning that Coleman would turn the Fifth Circuit against further expansion of black civil rights, Lewis reminded the committee that Coleman had attempted to run for governor again, in 1963, on a segregationist platform.[103] Even Martin Luther King Jr., in a prepared statement in opposition to Coleman's nomination, noted that the Fifth Circuit had "been the major constitutional body to which Negroes might turn in the South." It would be "a great tragedy" to put Coleman on the Fifth Circuit, argued King, particularly given the type of politics "practiced by Gov. Coleman during his years as the architect of Mississippi's plans to circumvent the orders of the very Court to which he now seeks appointment."[104]

That Coleman had been a moderate segregationist was made relatively clear to both the Senate and the nation. Yet, Johnson showed little interest. Although this might be explained away as a capitulation to the vagaries of electoral politics, it was precisely those vagaries that promised to jeopardize the constitutional hopes of the civil rights movement. Once on the Fifth Circuit, for example, Coleman would be directly responsible for interpreting constitutional law, a role that he would use to gradually limit black claims well into the 1980s. While Johnson's endorsement of the 1965 Voting Rights Act was in all likelihood an earnest one, and while he personally may have sympathized with the movement, electoral politics pushed him to undermine its constitutional strength.

J. P. Coleman Joins the Fifth Circuit Court of Appeals

Coleman's time on the Fifth Circuit, which would span almost twenty years, provides a remarkable example of how the type of strategic constitutionalism that he, Collins, and Hodges had championed in the 1950s gained national credibility in the 1970s and beyond. As a federal circuit judge, Coleman found himself able to articulate a variety of constitutional arguments that limited the claims of civil rights plaintiffs directly, many of which prefigured legal rulings that the Supreme Court would issue well into the 1980s. Though Coleman's jurisprudence did not inspire all of these rulings, his ability to articulate anti–civil rights positions in terms that coincided with strict constructions of constitutional language contributed to a certain convergence of constitutionalism between the North and the South in the post–civil rights era.

Yet, that convergence would take some time. During his first five years on the Fifth Circuit, Coleman proved reluctant, indeed unable, to sway the dominant liberal forces on the court. Until Richard Nixon began to place conservative judges on the federal bench in 1968, Coleman took a decidedly moderate path in his civil rights opinions.[105] In a consolidation of cases decided in October 1966, for example, Coleman voted to allow civil rights activists facing trial in Mississippi state court a chance to present evidence in federal district court to the effect that their arrests had been racially motivated. If they could prove this was the case, held Coleman, then they should be released.[106] Four months later, Coleman decided two cases, one in which members of the Mississippi Freedom Democratic Party (MFDP) had been arrested for distributing leaflets in violation of an antileafleting ordinance and another in which MFDP members had been arrested for marching in violation of traffic regulations. In both cases, Coleman ruled the ordinances unconstitutionally vague, particularly for the manner in which they threatened free speech.[107] Not long thereafter, Coleman confronted an appeal by William Eaton and Collie Wilkins Jr., the two white Alabamans found guilty of murdering Viola Liuzzo, a white mother of five who had traveled south to participate in the Selma to Montgomery march.[108] Rejecting their appeal that they should have been tried in state court and not federal court, Coleman read into their crime a deprivation of Liuzzo's right to participate in federal elections, thereby securing their convictions.[109]

Such rulings were hardly the work of an extremist. They demonstrated that Coleman's early years on the Fifth Circuit were marked by a certain willingness to go along with prevailing pro–civil rights trends set by the Warren Court. However, Coleman would gradually begin to chart a less movement-friendly course, one that gained momentum as liberal members of the Warren Court were replaced by more conservative, anti–civil rights judges. Coleman's school rulings provide a good example. Beginning in March 1967, Coleman expressed reservations about a landmark opinion written by John Minor Wisdom calling for court-enforced integration of public schools and the reversal of the *Briggs* dictum. This opinion, *United States v. Jefferson County*, applied a provision in the 1964 Civil Rights Act cutting federal funding to schools that had not integrated, even when those schools were still mired in litigation. Wisdom made it clear that school districts could not get around the provision by filing appeals with sympathetic district judges. Instead, he established a set of minimum standards that all schools who wanted federal money had to abide by.[110]

This decision, in many ways, broke an almost seven-year logjam on the question of whether school systems had to actively integrate, thereby limiting the possibility that *Briggs* might be the final, authoritative interpretation of *Brown*. Though it built on two earlier rulings, also by Wisdom, *Jefferson County* was the first substantive attempt by a federal circuit court to actively strike down the types of racially neutral, moderate schemes that had spread across the South since 1959.[111] It was also evidence that the Civil Rights Acts of 1964 and 1965, and by extension the civil rights movement's direct-action campaigns, had finally influenced judicial behavior, providing southern judges like Wisdom with the tools, and perhaps the confidence, they needed to begin dismantling segregation and reinvigorating *Brown*.[112]

J. P. Coleman Fights for Local Control of Schools

In a concurring opinion that would prove both cautionary and prophetic, Coleman warned against going too far in the process of "executing," as he put it, Jim Crow's "death warrant."[113] He also questioned the feasibility of Wisdom's minimum standards plan, insinuating that it took freedom of choice away from parents at the local level—even black parents who may have wanted their children to remain in black schools. This, of course, was just the type of argument that moderates like Coleman, Hodges, and Collins had long made, namely, that blacks were ultimately willing to segregate themselves. Under freedom of choice plans, parents could choose the school they wanted their children to attend, an arrangement that many thought would preserve segregation because it retained dual school systems. Given the choice, leaders like Hodges and Coleman suspected, black and white children would be tempted to remain with their own kind, lest they face social ostracism, tacit discrimination, or worse. Coleman, who knew both the context and subtext of such rules, did not mention them in his opinion. Instead, he argued that freedom of choice maintained strong "communities" and should not be invalidated. Wisdom's opinion, argued Coleman, was not only impractical but weakened communities by placing the authority of pupil assignment in the hands of those who might only wish to make a "racial point."[114]

That the black plaintiffs in *Jefferson County* were trying to make some kind of racial point was a relatively cynical assessment of a case that many hailed as a breakthrough in the battle to desegregate public schools. Yet, in many ways, it was also a prophetic one. Coleman's concern for local communities being frustrated by judicial mandates would foreshadow a rebellion of white voters across the country against busing in the 1970s. It would also foreshadow a gradual shift on the Fifth Circuit itself, against aggressive attempts to dismantle segregation. Anticipating such a shift, Coleman himself attempted to push the court in the direction of a lenient definition of unitary schools, one rooted much more in the freedom of choice language of *Briggs* than the minimum requirements language of *Jefferson*.

Coleman began this project in a lengthy dissenting opinion filed on January 21, 1970.[115] Angered by the Supreme Court's recent reversal of a Fifth Circuit ruling allowing school districts to delay integration until the end of the school year, Coleman complained that the Supreme Court wanted "to brook no further delays" yet failed to take local conditions into account.[116] Coleman also complained that the Supreme Court failed to define, precisely, what "unitary" meant. "How are the struggling school authorities to know," queried Coleman, "at what point they shall have succeeded in dismantling a dual system or setting up a unitary system?"[117] To answer such a question, Coleman suggested that the Fifth Circuit adopt a relatively lenient definition of unitary schools, allowing as much discretion as possible to local officials. He then cited *Green v. County School Board of New Kent County*, a Supreme Court case that struck down a freedom of choice plan in Virginia, noting emphatically that time for deliberate speed had "run out."[118] Although many took this to mean that the Court was finally prepared to move aggressively in the direction of achieving integration, striking down pupil placement, freedom of choice plans, and so on,

Coleman saw it differently. According to him, even though the Supreme Court had ordered "immediate progress towards disestablishing state-imposed segregation," so, too, did it grant district courts a certain amount of discretion in determining just how much "disestablishment" needed to take place. Further, Coleman also noted that the Supreme Court had not in fact invalidated freedom of choice plans but had merely held that "adoption of a freedom of choice plan does not, by itself, satisfy a school district's mandatory responsibility to eliminate all vestiges of a dual system."[119] Indeed, the Court had held that if there were no other "reasonably available" ways of attaining unitary schools, then freedom of choice plans could stand.[120]

Coleman advanced a constitutional interpretation of unitary schools that would foreshadow Supreme Court rulings more than a decade into the future. According to him, the Supreme Court was not interested in requiring children to "walk unreasonable distances" or be "bused to strange communities" just to achieve some vague, abstract goal of "racial balance."[121] In his opinion, such measures promised little more than to destroy school districts and cause "material injury to true educational objectives."[122] Instead, the Court simply needed to end the type of blatantly segregated dual school systems that had existed in the South prior to 1954, while granting local authorities broad discretion to determine whether and when their respective school systems were suitably integrated.[123] Neighborhood schools that happened to be segregated by residential living patterns, for example, did not strike Coleman as unconstitutional, particularly if students were given the choice, through majority to minority transfers, to freely attend schools not in their neighborhood.[124] However, busing students to distant neighborhoods struck Coleman as a "highly artificial" solution that possessed "doubtful, if not harmful, value."[125]

Though the Supreme Court would initially oppose such a position and support aggressive measures like busing to achieve racial balance, it would eventually swing, following incredible popular pressure, into Coleman's camp.[126] In 1974, after violent protests against busing exploded in Pontiac, Michigan, for example, the Supreme Court overruled a circuit court opinion that the state of Michigan had "committed *de jure* segregation" by facilitating white flight from Detroit city schools to neighboring suburbs.[127] Specifically, Detroit had adopted criteria for "free choice" and "neighborhood schools," that, in the opinion of both the district and the circuit courts, was intended to "effect the maintenance of segregation."[128] The Supreme Court, sounding more like J. P. Coleman than Earl Warren, disagreed. "No single tradition in public education," noted Chief Justice Warren Burger, "is more deeply rooted than local control over the operation of schools."[129] "[L]ocal control," continued Burger, "affords citizens an opportunity to participate in decisionmaking, permits the structuring of school programs to fit local needs, and encourages 'experimentation, innovation, and a healthy competition for educational excellence.'"[130] J. P. Coleman had made almost exactly the same argument years before.

The Supreme Court's interest in local schools, and specifically in returning local control to public schools, coincided closely with a relaxation of the constitutional definition of "unitary" schools, just as J. P. Coleman had anticipated. For example, in 1991, two decades after Coleman's dissent in *Singleton*, the Supreme Court held that public schools in Oklahoma essentially had the authority to stop busing and resegregate, so long as the local district court decided that such a move was in good faith and not intentionally designed to keep blacks out of white schools. This coincided with Coleman's position in the 1960s, namely, that local district courts should be granted the authority to determine when a school system achieved unitary status. The Supreme Court even echoed Coleman's tendency to reject black demands by claiming to protect blacks, mentioning that one rationale for calling an end to busing was to alleviate "greater busing burdens on young black children."[131]

In 1992, the Supreme Court reaffirmed its commitment to a relaxed definition of unitary schools. "The term 'unitary' is not a precise concept," noted Justice Anthony Kennedy, and does not mandate local districts to go beyond what is "feasible and practical" to prevent segregation.[132] In fact, if parents left school districts to avoid integration, then there was nothing that the federal courts could do.[133]

Though J. P. Coleman played no causal role in the decision, it dovetailed with his assertion that if resistance to integration were framed in reasonable rather than extremist terms, then the South's position stood a better chance of gaining national support.[134] He had also made sure to emphasize that by focusing on a relatively legalist interpretation of *Brown*, one that placed less weight on fair outcomes than on strict constructions of judicial language, the South could minimize integration and remain within constitutional bounds. Indeed, it was Coleman's legalist defense of the status quo that would help him facilitate a reunion between North and South in the post–civil rights era.[135]

Signs of such a reunion did not emerge only in the school context. In a 1967 case brought by black citizens of Jackson, Mississippi, that protested the closure of public swimming pools, Coleman joined an opinion written by Richard Rives agreeing that a municipality could close its public pools to keep blacks from swimming in them.[136] Asserting that municipalities had no constitutional duty to provide their citizens with pools—an accurate, if strict, reading of the law—Rives and Coleman held that simply because state action might be proven to be racially motivated did not mean that it was therefore racially discriminatory.[137] Two years later, the Supreme Court agreed.[138]

A similar convergence emerged in the field of voting. In 1966, one year after the Voting Rights Act, the Mississippi state legislature split the state's largest black district, the Delta, into three pieces, attaching each piece to a larger white district, thereby reducing the number of majority black districts in the state to zero.[139] When the Mississippi Freedom Democratic Party challenged this plan for negatively affecting black voting power, a District Court panel made up of J. P. Coleman, Harold Cox, and Dan M. Russell Jr. rejected their challenge, arguing that they had failed to prove that the division of the Delta was racially motivated.[140] When the MFDP presented newspaper articles documenting the racial motivations of the state legislature, Coleman, Cox, and Russell threw out the evidence as unreliable.[141] They crafted their opinion in strict adherence to a 1964 Supreme Court ruling, *Reynolds v. Sims*, that required districts to be drawn equitably according to population percentages.[142] Looking closely at population data, meanwhile ignoring the racial impact of shattering the Delta, the three judges concluded, reasonably, that the new districts were completely proportional population-wise and were therefore constitutional.[143] The Supreme Court upheld their decision, making it exceedingly difficult for African Americans to elect a representative to Congress from the Delta, something that would not happen for the next twenty years.[144]

Coleman Rules against Black Hiring

An even more remarkable alignment between Coleman's voting record and the Supreme Court emerged on March 27, 1974, when Coleman dissented in a case ordering the affirmative, race-conscious hiring of black officers to the Mississippi Highway Patrol.[145] Although the majority found that the impact of hiring practices was discriminatory, and that affirmative action was justified, Coleman disagreed, arguing that qualifications for the patrol were fair and that blacks may simply not have been interested in becoming state troopers. To him, the fact that the patrol had hired only two blacks among the ninety-one new hires in the past two years, raising the total number of blacks to six in a total force of around five hundred, was not reason enough to prove discrimination. In fact, it was only keeping the patrol competent and free from "under-educated, sub-normally intelligent" officers.[146]

Underlying Coleman's dissent was a larger aversion to "quota hiring," as he called it, and also to the negative impact that racial preferences had on whites.[147] "[I]t is a strangely familiar message which the Court finds," noted Coleman, "for the qualified white applicant who is rejected solely because of his race."[148] Although the majority might have viewed such arguments as insensitive, perhaps even recalcitrant, Coleman's dissent prefigured Supreme Court decisions in the not-so-distant future. For example, in its 1976 ruling in *Washington v. Davis*, the Court held that recruiting tests for police officers in Washington, D.C., were constitutional, despite disparate impact, so long as they did not show discriminatory intent.[149] This opinion, which one historian has called the "sharpest reversal" of civil rights jurisprudence since *Brown,* suggests that even though Coleman found himself in a minority on the Fifth Circuit in 1974, he was actually foreshadowing larger majority trends on race-based hiring on the Supreme Court only two years later.[150]

Of course, Coleman did not always foreshadow trends. On September 26, 1975, he wrote a dissenting opinion in a case filed by African American and Jewish plaintiffs who had been denied membership to the Biscayne Bay Yacht Club in Miami, Florida. Though the lower court found a clear pattern of discrimination against both blacks and Jews, Coleman argued that such discrimination could continue so long as the club was "genuinely" private.[151] Discounting the fact that the club had been leasing property from the City of Miami for eighty-eight years, Coleman argued that the city had nothing to do with the "internal operation" or "membership policies" of the club; therefore, the plaintiffs should be barred from filing suit.[152] The majority disagreed.

Coleman Stops Civil Rights Demonstrators

Despite his failure to preserve segregated private clubs, Coleman was not always in the minority when it came to civil rights cases on the Fifth Circuit. In January 1972, he issued a majority opinion that challenged the ability of civil rights demonstrators to have their cases removed from state to federal court, thereby undermining the expanded removal remedy that Elbert Tuttle had worked hard to develop in the early 1960s.[153] Specifically, Coleman confronted an appeal from a group of student activists who had been commuting regularly to Mendenhall, Mississippi, from Jackson, the capital, in January and February 1970, to participate in marches and demonstrations.[154] One night after a demonstration, the appellants were pulled over by state troopers and arrested for reckless driving. The students were then taken to the local jail, where troopers and county police beat the leader, shaved his head, and poured moonshine on his scalp. Although considerable evidence suggested that the troopers had beaten the students to discourage further trips to Mendenhall, Coleman ignored this evidence in his opinion. According to him, the fact that the demonstrations were in one county and the arrest in another, coupled with police testimony that the driver had been veering between lanes, suggested that there was no relation between the demonstrations and the arrests, and warranted remanding the case to state court.[155]

Judge John R. Brown, in a vigorous 140-page dissent, disagreed, warning that Coleman's opinion threatened not only to limit the removal remedy but also to excuse a blatant attempt to prevent citizens from exercising their constitutional rights. Noting that the state troopers had been present at the demonstration, had taken photographs of the activists, and had later followed the van out of Mendenhall, Brown concluded that the true motivation behind the arrest was to prevent further demonstrations, not to apprehend reckless drivers. Bolstering this conclusion, argued Brown, was the torture of the leader, along with evidence that the state troopers had warned him about participating in civil rights activities in Mendenhall before, threatening that they were "not going to take anymore of this civil rights stuff."[156] All of these factors combined, concluded Brown, show that both the arrests and the state prosecution were a "classic example of the misuse of State criminal procedures for the sole purpose of intimidating the exercise of equal civil rights."[157]

Coleman, relying heavily on the testimony of the state troopers involved, disagreed. To him, the relatively obvious targeting of the activists by the police was less important than the lawlessness that the activists themselves were engaged in. Shifting attention from the police to the activists and their friends, Coleman focused on the fact that two acquaintances of the activists, both ministers, had arrived at the jail where the activists were being held with weapons in their car, pleading for their release. Though the ministers left their weapons as they entered the station, an altercation ensued between them and the police, during which a sheriff was allegedly punched in the face. To Coleman, this type of aggressive civil rights "activism" was unacceptable. "[W]e are under no duty," he wrote, "to extend some kind of left handed judicial approval to the practice of carrying an arsenal of weapons on night time visits to jails or police stations, even if the possession of such weapons is otherwise lawful."[158]

Though the visit by the two ministers to the jail was not strictly related to the viability of the constitutional claims of the arrested students, Coleman's contention reflected a new angle of attack against direct-action protest. Instead of a decision about civil rights, Coleman transformed his opinion into a defense of law enforcement. According to him, state police had not gone after civil rights activists but, rather, civil rights protesters had sent armed emissaries after the police.[159]

This was not the first time that Coleman ruled against civil rights plaintiffs and in favor of law enforcement. In May 1969, for example, Coleman wrote the majority opinion in a case brought by black demonstrators arrested for picketing in Hattiesburg, Mississippi. Specifically, the demonstrators appealed an injunction, issued by District Judge Harold Cox, an outspoken segregationist, which allowed the demonstrators to picket but limited them to six per location, demanded they remain at least five feet apart, and required them to remain absolutely silent.[160] Coleman, upon reviewing the record, determined that the picketers were attempting to provoke violence by singing "freedom songs" that included "words of a generally threatening nature."[161] Noting that the Constitution prohibited the state from silencing protesters completely, however, Coleman modified the injunction to prohibit speech "clearly calculated to provoke a breach of peace by others."[162]

While at first glance a relatively innocuous holding, Coleman's decision to sustain Cox's injunction did at least two things. First, it muted civil rights protest by sharply lowering the number of street protesters that could lawfully picket a business. Second, it granted law enforcement a relatively broad amount of discretion in determining what was and was not "calculated to provoke a breach of peace." Given that so much of civil rights movement activity had attempted to provoke breaches of the peace from 1963 through 1965, it suggests that Coleman was joining other conservative judges to discourage mass protest. While not an absolute endorsement of Cox's rather draconian order, it moved toward curtailing the demonstrators' activity.[163]

Coleman tried to curtail such protest even further in August 1970. That month, he voted against the majority in a case involving Benjamin Brown, a SNCC activist who had been shot and killed when police fired into a crowd of demonstrators in Jackson. Unsympathetic to Brown's family's claim that they should have been allowed access to the police files in the case, Coleman argued that it was a "favorite ploy" of the "law violator" to sue police on "some pretext or another."[164] Downplaying the fact that Brown had been brutally killed for what appeared to be no good reason, Coleman sided firmly with law enforcement, arguing that "fishing" expeditions into police files should not be allowed, lest they undermine the "judicial process."[165]

Two weeks later, Coleman ruled against another civil rights activist in Louisiana who was charged with battery and requested removal from state to federal court. The facts of this case were particularly remarkable. Sometime on the evening of July 28, 1966, an African American activist named Zelma Wyche led a group of more than fifty blacks, some of them armed, to a truck stop in Tallulah, Louisiana, to investigate a report that the café had denied service to a black patron.[166] Upon arriving at the café, Wyche demanded to speak with the manager. After a patron suggested that Wyche look for the manager himself, the activist retorted, "What is it to you?" and then asked, "Do you want your [ass] whipped?"[167] When the patron tried to leave, Wyche gave two shrill whistles, prompting several members of the black entourage to attack the customer. Only when another white customer produced a shotgun did the attackers desist.[168]

To Coleman, this type of aggressive civil rights vigilantism was completely unacceptable. In his dissenting opinion, which reflected a concern over the growing militance of black protest in the South, Coleman ruled that Wyche was not engaged in protected activity and should not have been allowed to remove his case to federal court. Yet, the majority disagreed, granting Wyche a hearing at the federal district level to determine whether his battery charge should have been removed to federal court under the theory that he had been engaged in constitutionally protected activity. Lamenting the ruling, Coleman noted that the majority had inflicted "a Sunday punch" on the "sagging ability of local governments to enforce their laws against crimes of violence."[169]

What was going on? Clearly, nonviolent direct-action protest was giving way to more violent, coercive means, a move prompted by the fact that many civil rights activists in remote parts of the South were growing tired of being subjected to racist intimidation. Further, violence was on the rise nationally, as urban riots rocked northern cities beginning in the summer of 1964. This shift frightened white voters nationwide, inadvertently undoing much of the ideological work accomplished by the civil rights movement in 1964 and 1965. Consequently, Coleman's interest in preventing crimes of violence, even in cases that more liberal judges chose to read as fundamentally about civil rights, signaled a larger shift on both the Fifth Circuit and the Supreme Court in favor of law enforcement. For example, even though Coleman was outvoted in *Wyche*, a relatively weak civil rights case, Coleman won a significant victory for law enforcement in the Mendenhall demonstration case, a much stronger civil rights claim, two years later. And he won relatively big. Not only did he write the majority panel opinion, over the fervent protest of John R. Brown, but also he marshaled an even larger majority at a meeting of all the Fifth Circuit judges on the same case twelve months later, over the protests of John Minor Wisdom.[170] Although Wisdom joined Brown in arguing for a broad reading of the removal remedy, the full court majority affirmed Coleman's holding that the measure did not allow the federal government to intervene when law enforcement was "lawfully carrying out" its duties.[171] Although there was substantial evidence to suggest that this was not happening, as illustrated by the torture of the Jackson civil rights leader, the majority joined Coleman in rejecting the compensatory claims of the demonstrators.[172]

Coleman's ability to marshal increasing majorities against civil rights claims brought by blacks suggests that factors beyond just chance were at work. Among these factors was undoubtedly Coleman's ability to reframe resistance to civil rights in racially neutral, constitutional terms, something that he had begun to do while governor in the 1950s. This also explains his success at limiting removal in the Mendenhall case, and in splintering what might have become the largest black voting district in the South, the Mississippi Delta.

Another factor that contributed to Coleman's increasingly successful constitutionalism was a growing conservative presence on the Fifth Circuit and on the Supreme Court.[173] Though not immediately apparent, the rise of this presence was tied to a national electoral backlash against black bids for increased political and economic power. Following the dramatic civil rights movement victories of 1964 and 1965, a variety of factors conspired to turn national opinion against aggressive black bids for racial equality and to encourage conservative appointments to the federal judiciary. One was the explosion of urban riots in cities across the country from 1964 to 1968. Another was a dramatic rise in violent crime, something that many blamed on a convergence between black lawbreaking and liberal criminal procedure rulings handed down by the Warren Court from 1963 to 1968.[174] Finally, the civil rights movement's sympathetic image as a nonviolent, peaceful struggle faltered as the federal government left much of the residual work of implementing the 1964 and 1965 Civil Rights Acts to local activists who operated in rural, remote, often hostile conditions. Constant threats of violence by local extremists led such activists to grow frustrated with nonviolence and fall back on long-standing traditions of armed self-defense in the South, not unlike what Zelma Wyche did in Louisiana.[175] Following an assassination attempt on black activist James Meredith in Mississippi, for example, SNCC leader Stokely Carmichael publicly questioned the efficacy of nonviolence and lobbied instead for a more aggressive posture of "black power."[176] By October of that year, Carmichael had helped form a militant organization that took its name from the symbol of the Lowndes County, Alabama, voter registration league: the black panther. While the membership rolls of the Black Panthers never came close to a black majority, they captured media attention, projecting a threatening image of black activism to white voters nationwide. The Panthers' call for armed self-defense, coupled with urban rioting and high crime, convinced many white voters that civil rights had gone too far and that the country needed to reestablish racial control.[177]

Collins Supports Carswell for the Supreme Court

President Richard Nixon, sensing a shift in popular opinion against the civil rights movement, made the restoration of law and order, coupled with the replacement of liberal "activist" judges, a central part of his 1968 campaign for the presidency. In so doing, he successfully cobbled together a coalition of conservative voters in the North and West, as well as the South, vaulting himself into the White House. Once there, Nixon sought to cement that coalition by making good on his promises of constitutional counterreform by appointing strict constructionists to the Fifth Circuit and to the Supreme Court. By the close of 1973, he had appointed four new justices to the Supreme Court and five judges, including Charles Clark, to the Fifth Circuit.[178]

Southern moderates provided both manpower and political support for such judicial realignments. For example, in 1969, Nixon nominated a moderate from South Carolina named Clement Haynsworth to the Supreme Court, only to have his nomination killed by senators concerned with Haynsworth's support for segregation. Nixon then turned to a second moderate from the South, Fifth Circuit Judge G. Harrold Carswell. Formerly a practicing attorney in Tallahassee, Florida, Carswell also drew considerable opposition from civil rights activists. One such activist, former NAACP lawyer Leroy D. Clark, blasted him for being "insulting and hostile" to black plaintiffs and using legal ruses to cause "unconscionable delay" in civil rights cases before him, in part by dismissing valid claims simply to force NAACP lawyers to file lengthy, time-consuming appeals.[179] Perhaps the worst example that Clark gave was a case from Leon County in which Carswell held up a desegregation challenge for three years, from 1964 to 1967, eventually approving a flagrantly evasive plan that integrated four black students of a total population of 16,000.[180]

One of the few witnesses to support Carswell's nomination was LeRoy Collins. According to Collins, who appeared before the U.S. Senate to testify on behalf of the obstructionist judge, Carswell possessed "untarnished integrity" and an "extraordinary keen mind."[181] In regard to allegations that Carswell was anti–civil rights, Collins affirmed that Carswell had in fact been a segregationist but was now a "new man," much like the American portrayed in Crevecoeur's popular eighteenth-century book, *Letters from an American Farmer*.[182] When asked about Carswell's judicial acumen, Collins testified that Carswell had worked for him in Tallahassee as a young lawyer and even recalled details about the first case that Carswell and he had argued together.[183]

Yet, when questioned about a lease that Carswell had helped arrange in 1956 to keep blacks out of the Tallahassee Country Club, a club that Collins himself had belonged to, the former governor's memory failed him. "I do know from faint recollection that I was involved," testified Collins, but "my recollection is very hazy."[184] Such selective recall suggests that Collins, too, was trying to become a "new man" and to erase his own efforts to preserve Jim Crow. While it is understandable that Collins did not want to embarrass himself by invoking his own segregationist past, his willingness to fall back on his relationship to Carswell, against the impassioned pleas of civil rights activists, nevertheless suggests that he was an agent more of continuity than change. Even if his commitment to Carswell was strictly a personal one, the fact that he would place personal ties above the constitutional hopes of African Americans for decades to come is suggestive of just how unsympathetic Collins truly was to civil rights.

Though Carswell would never reach the Supreme Court, LeRoy Collins's endorsement of him in 1970 and Coleman's jurisprudence on the Fifth

Circuit both stand as remarkable examples of the extent to which both men remained true to old patterns and resistant to new ones, even as they conformed seamlessly to national trends. Indeed, in many ways, leaders like Collins, Coleman, and even Hodges helped push national trends away from aggressive enforcement of civil rights and toward a more legalist type of passive opposition to the civil rights movement. This was evident in the attempts that all three leaders made to discourage black direct-action protest, a tactic critical to the civil rights victories of 1964 and 1965. It was also evident in the attempts by Coleman and Collins to directly influence the interpretation of constitutional law, both by endorsing strict readings of constitutional language to deny black claims and by endorsing the appointment of strict constructionists, even an outright segregationist, to the Supreme Court.

CONCLUSION: SOUTHERN MODERATES
AND THE SECOND REDEMPTION

In the fall of 1978, the *St. Petersburg Times* asked LeRoy Collins to review a book by political scientist David J. Garrow analyzing the protest on the Edmund Pettus Bridge in Selma, Alabama, thirteen years earlier. In his review, Collins assessed Garrow's argument that after failing to achieve substantive reform through conventional legal channels, the civil rights movement deliberately turned toward provoking white violence as a means of effecting change. "I am not willing to accept Mr. Garrow's interpretation," Collins asserted forthrightly, noting that the book's portrayal of the civil rights struggle in Selma was "tainted with cynicism" and that Garrow misrepresented Martin Luther King Jr. and others as "manipulators" who were "coldly calculating," not the "spiritually inspired crusaders for reform and progress" that he knew them to be.[1]

It was a remarkable conclusion by a man who had himself gone to Selma to try to neutralize Martin Luther King. Why the sudden surprise at Garrow's book? Collins presented little evidence for his critique, other than to say that Garrow's thesis was "too technical" and missed the "great drama" of the demonstration, something that could be captured better by a writer with "the talents of a Margaret Mitchell."[2] Barring the obvious irony that Mitchell was a fiction writer whose portrayal of southern race relations in *Gone with the Wind* bordered on pure fantasy, Collins's desire that a novelist take over the writing of civil rights history was suggestive of more than just a desire for a good story.[3]

To accept the argument that the civil rights movement was trying to provoke white violence at Selma, which it was, Collins would have had to confess that his ultimate role there was to thwart the demonstrators, not help them. Incidentally, this was not the way that his participation had come to be remembered. After he was photographed conversing with civil rights leaders during the final march to Montgomery, many Floridians came to believe that he was actually allied with the movement, a misconception that Collins later embraced as Selma came to represent another step in what Lyndon Johnson called "man's unending quest for freedom."[4] Through this story, Collins could join the movement in condemning violent racism, while glossing over his own role in thwarting movement gains. Indeed, Collins could sidestep the fact that the movement's real target at Selma may not have been white extremists at all but rather white moderates like him who had been relatively successful at evading the Supreme Court.

Despite the momentous Civil Rights Act of 1964, the Supreme Court had still allowed delayed implementation of desegregation during the summer of 1965.[5] Not until 1968, in the volatile aftermath of Martin Luther King Jr.'s assassination, would the Supreme Court finally bear down on the type of moderate subterfuges that LeRoy Collins, Luther Hodges, and J. P. Coleman had been advocating since the mid-1950s.[6] Even then, the Court would not strike down pupil placement or freedom of choice plans entirely, nor would it prove willing to completely end school segregation, as white families in the rural South built private academies, and white families around the country moved to predominantly white suburban school districts. Rather than counter such moves, the Supreme Court, beginning in 1974, encouraged them.[7]

In a decision that Thurgood Marshall blasted as "a giant step backward" in the struggle to eliminate segregation "root and branch" in the United States, the Supreme Court held in 1974 that intentional efforts to perpetuate segregation through the use of school district boundaries did not violate the Constitution.[8] This ruling, though in Marshall's opinion an "emasculation" of constitutional guarantees for blacks, opened the door for a wave of decisions over the next twenty years that overruled myriad attempts to end segregation resulting from white flight out of predominantly black school districts.[9] Though moderate strategies like pupil placement would fade, more passive strategies prevailed, like simply allowing whites to relocate to districts where blacks either could not afford to live or did not choose to live because of "informal societal and cultural pressures."[10]

By pushing for a dramatic, almost fictional account of civil rights—one in which nonmanipulative black leaders led a crusade against violent racists—moderate whites in the post-civil rights era could endorse the symbolic moral victory of the movement, while erasing their own role in the larger story of resistance to integration, and leave historians to focus almost exclusively on white extremists. This, in a sense, was the very strategy that moderates like Collins, Coleman, and Hodges had advocated all along, one of publicly rejecting extremism and simultaneously undermining black constitutional claims. Though Jim Crow was most certainly dead, aspects of his ghost, one might say, lived on.

Though the "epic" battle between black activists and white extremists has captured modern memory, the more important constitutional struggle at the time took place between black activists and white moderates. After all, white moderates devised legal strategies for preserving segregation that gained at least some Supreme Court approval, while white extremists invariably incurred federal wrath. White moderates employed creative means of neutralizing civil rights protest, even as they came up with a justificatory rhetoric for resistance to *Brown* that replaced vitriolic racism with less controversial notions of standards, moral values, and local control over schools. This rhetoric outlasted the civil rights gains of the 1960s, arguably creating the foundation for a new era of racial inequality in the South and the nation.[11]

Even as white extremists brought down a Second Reconstruction on the American South, white moderates helped cobble together a Second Re-demption. Like the first redemption following the Civil War, this one involved creative legislation at the state level that both reinforced racial stratification and complied with constitutional norms. How did such laws work? Clearly, the civil rights movement outmaneuvered southern attempts to preserve mass segregation. By 1978, public accommodations in the South had been desegregated and public schools, particularly in rural areas, had been fully integrated. However, southern demographics were shifting away from rural areas and toward suburban centers and, for those who could afford it, away from public accommodations and toward private ones. Here, in the new suburban Sunbelt South, Jim Crow's ghost lived on, as constitu-tional firewalls constructed by southern moderates worked to prevent fur-ther change in areas of employment discrimination, voting, schools, and even civil rights protest.[12] As J. P. Coleman's Fifth Circuit jurisprudence shows, federal courts began developing perfectly constitutional color-blind arguments to counter black voting rights claims, black employment dis-crimination claims, and even black protests against the resegregation of public schools through white migration to racially homogeneous school districts.

While the story of white flight and judicial retraction has been told by others, Collins, Coleman, and Hodges provide us with valuable insight into why such moves were made. Rather than repression, the three governors in this study acted out of aspiration, aspiration that blacks were best helped not by being forced into schools with whites, but by improvements in their own institutions, their own neighborhoods, and their own spheres. Whites, conversely, were also best-helped by segregation, freed from contact with a variety of social ills that Collins, Coleman, and Hodges all believed were endemic to the lower echelons of black life. Though such views ignored the fundamentally repressive nature of Jim Crow, none of the governors in this study saw themselves as agents of repression. This is critical to understanding their struggle against *Brown*, and arguably to understanding resistance to *Brown* nationally in the post-civil rights era. They did not necessarily want to harm blacks, but to help themselves. While leaders of massive resistance were motivated by hate, they were motivated by hope, hope that the races could live in a mutually beneficial, pluralist world where differences were respected even if some inequalities remained.

In addition to casting new light on rationales for southern resistance, LeRoy Collins, J. P. Coleman, and Luther Hodges also help us see that *Brown* served as a catalyst for relatively refined legal change. While proponents of massive resistance promoted intemperate plans of defiance simply to gain votes, Collins, Coleman, and Hodges all turned to legal experts for advice on how to comply with the Constitution yet preserve racial stratification in the region. For example, J. P. Coleman relied on a committee of legal experts, known as the Legal Education Advisory Committee, to draft measures that ended segregation based on race but allowed local officials to continue assigning students to schools based on neutral factors that were then indirectly linked to race. Such measures, which included factors like "moral background," struck Coleman as a potential avenue of resistance to integration early on; indeed, he endorsed them after traveling to Washington in 1953 and listening to oral arguments in the *Brown* case. Convinced that the Supreme Court might endorse legal measures that preserved segregation so long as they removed overt racial classifications from state law, Coleman returned to Mississippi and supported the South's first pupil assignment plan, more than a month before *Brown* was actually handed down.

Inspired by Mississippi's plan, North Carolina Governor Luther Hodges and Florida Governor LeRoy Collins endorsed similar statutes in their states. In fact, Hodges even invited one of Coleman's advisors to North Carolina to help him develop a plan likely to survive federal court review. Aiding Hodges in this process was a committee of legal experts led by a North Carolina lawyer named Thomas J. Pearsall, together with a former Supreme Court clerk who had also been party to early stages of the *Brown* case, James C. N. Paul. Paul, a former Justice Vinson clerk, warned Pearsall in 1954 that defiance would lead to increased federal "supervision" of the South, and he instead counseled a plan that decentralized decision-making power over public schools, including placement plans, to the local county level.[13]

In Florida, Governor LeRoy Collins turned to state Attorney General Richard W. Ervin to develop a legalist plan for preserving segregation that might survive Supreme Court review. Convinced that the Supreme Court might be persuaded to back away from an aggressive reading of its *Brown* decision, Ervin accumulated data on black illegitimacy, venereal disease, and crime rates to bolster a sociological study that he himself commissioned of negative white attitudes toward integration in Florida. Relying on dispassionate, statistical data, together with Mississippi newspaper editor Hodding Carter's claim that white parents had legitimate reasons to be afraid of sending their children to school with black students who suffered from "cultural lags," Ervin filed an extensive brief in the implementation phase of *Brown* in October 1954. The Supreme Court's subsequent turn away from requiring immediate integration to allowing the South "all deliberate speed" to desegregate, a holding that came to be known as *Brown II*, struck Collins as evidence that the states could in fact guide constitutional law, provided they do so in a reasonable way.

That southern states could influence the Supreme Court was a central assumption that Collins, Coleman, and Hodges all shared. It separated them from proponents of massive resistance, who rejected the Court's authority. It also distinguished them from other moderates in the South who failed to develop their comprehensive plans to modify *Brown*. Indeed, it would not be until after they left office, and massive resistance collapsed, that southern states would begin to converge around a shared policy of peaceful compliance and strategic resistance to civil rights.

Though the type of resistance sponsored by Collins, Coleman, and Hodges did not prevent federal civil rights legislation, the process of limiting Supreme Court civil rights jurisprudence that they began in the 1950s did not stop. Collins and Coleman both continued the process of convincing the Court to limit its interpretation of the Fourteenth Amendment into the 1970s. Long after leaving the governor's office, Collins testified on behalf of segregationist Supreme Court nominee G. Harrold Carswell in 1970. As chief judge of the Fifth Circuit, Coleman wrote opinions that used color-blind readings of the Constitution to limit black school claims, black employment discrimination claims, and black voting rights claims well into the 1980s. As white voters in the North and West chafed at the spread of federally sponsored initiatives like forced busing and affirmative action, Coleman's vision of symbolic endorsement, not substantive enforcement, came to dominate the Supreme Court.

Yet, southern moderates did not boast. They were never remembered as particularly committed segregationists, precisely because white voters did not realize just how intelligent they were. In some cases, they even adopted public positions that appeared favorable toward civil rights and hid the lengths they had gone to in thwarting black political gains. This is one of the great lessons that these three leaders have to teach. Just as social movements can open up new pathways for constitutional change by influencing popular opinion and increasing judicial support for minority claims, so, too, can state actors close such pathways by taking positions that appear sympathetic but undermine movement activity. Indeed, this helps to explain the movement's desperate bid to seek out extremists and provoke them into committing shocking acts of violence in 1965. Prior to that, southern states like Florida, North Carolina, and even Mississippi from 1956 to 1960 were using black informants and state agents, including state police, to minimize racial drama and rally national support for the white South. Meanwhile, southern states were also working hard to reconfigure their state laws in a manner that preserved racial stratification but complied, formally, with *Brown*. By 1963, that campaign was largely successful, as virtually every southern state had either a pupil placement plan or a freedom of choice plan to keep black students out of white schools on grounds other than race. Perhaps ironically, the few remaining white extremists left in positions of power in the region were one of the only obstacles to this moderate victory. White extremists, as historians like David J. Garrow and Michael J. Klarman have shown, actually helped the movement rouse national support and muster federal action in favor of the civil rights struggle by projecting a particularly negative image of the South, one that moderates fought bitterly to control.[14]

By looking closely at how Collins, Coleman, and Hodges tried to control racial extremism in the South in the 1950s, we gain new insight not only into strategic constitutionalism but also into the effects that *Brown* had on the southern political landscape. All three governors used popular anxiety over integration to expand their executive influence over the state legislative process. All three governors also used popular anxiety over *Brown* to centralize, and perhaps even modernize, certain aspects of their states' governmental structure. The removal of authority from local sheriffs and justices of the peace, for example, represented a critical shift in the southern criminal justice apparatus, a bid to improve police professionalism by increasing centralized state surveillance of local authorities.

That the civil rights movement would ultimately concentrate its efforts on Alabama, one of the few states where state troopers were just as extremist as local police, points out that Collins, Coleman, and Hodges all understood how undisciplined governmental bodies could influence constitutional reform in the South. This, of course, placed them in direct conflict with civil rights activists like Roy Wilkins in the 1950s and strategists for CORE and the SCLC in the 1960s. That Roy Wilkins used lapses in the South's criminal justice system, like the acquittal of Emmett Till's killers in 1955, to lobby for federal legislation helps explain how moderates anticipated the movement's more radical turn toward provoking white police for the same purpose in the 1960s.

Why did extremists not listen to such signs as well and mute their politics? What worked for constitutional politics did not always work for electoral politics. By asserting a defiant stance toward the Supreme Court, massive resisters rallied regional white voters and won elections. Yet, by projecting a stereotypical image of white southerners as violent racists, extremists also helped the civil rights movement gain national support, opening the way for a more robust interpretation of the Fourteenth Amendment by the Supreme Court. Conversely, by formally endorsing the Supreme Court's *Brown* ruling, moderates lost popular electoral support, even as they set the stage for making an end run around the movement's attempts at popular suasion.

While the civil rights movement clearly swayed significant portions of the American voting public in the 1960s, as evidenced by their ability to achieve substantial federal legislation, white commitment to the black struggle proved fleeting. Indeed, once white extremists were taken care of, voters across the country expressed profound reservations about sending their children to school with blacks, largely because of concerns like those voiced by Collins, Coleman, and Hodges in the 1950s. In fact, black illegitimacy rates, an issue that moderates like Collins, Coleman, and Hodges all focused on in the 1950s, gained national salience in 1965, following the publication of a White House report on the black family written by Undersecretary of Labor Daniel Patrick Moynihan.[15] Moynihan's report, which argued that one of the primary obstacles to black advancement was unwed motherhood, sparked considerable interest among both liberals and conservatives alike in the post–civil rights era. Indeed, the image of the unwed black mother, living comfortably off welfare, would prove particularly pernicious, emerging as a divisive symbol in Ronald Reagan's first bid for the presidency in 1976 and his subsequent bids in 1980 and 1984.[16] Even Democratic Governor William Jefferson Clinton of Arkansas would make ending welfare payments to "teen-age mothers" a focal point of his campaign to reform welfare in 1988.[17]

Meanwhile, the South's reputation as a racist backwater gradually gave way to a new image of a region steeped in conservative moral values and religious faith. This morally conservative South echoed the South that moderates like Collins, Coleman, and Hodges tried to project much more than it did the South portrayed by advocates of massive resistance. And as federal courts pushed integration northward, demanding that white children be bused to inner cities, southern calls for reining in the federal judiciary gained increasing support as well, helping to forge a "new right" founded on principles of local control, small government, and "sterner morality."[18]

Even as the civil rights movement won remarkable victories in the 1960s, opportunities for further change decreased as the South conformed to national trends. So long as the civil rights movement could shame white voters by presenting the nation with unacceptable performances of white racism, it could gain the popular support necessary for constitutional change. However, once southern moderates replaced white extremists, the movement's constitutional hopes faded. What brought an end to the civil rights movement of the 1960s was not a collapse in black leadership or a dearth of new, constitutional goals to pursue, but a change in the South. No longer extremist, the South no longer was an easy target for activists who needed to orchestrate dramatic displays of white racism to muster popular interest in the black struggle. Thanks to the ascension of moderation in the region, the South went from being a national embarrassment to becoming a bastion of conservative, moral values that many Americans came to view as a beacon of hope.[19]

By looking behind the public personas of Collins, Coleman, and Hodges, we see three southern governors who viewed the South in terms of its constitutional relationship to the rest of the country—over time. That they found themselves in power at the apex of massive resistance to integration, and hence at odds with prevailing electoral trends, makes them particularly useful as lenses through which to view moderate responses to *Brown*.[20] Unlike governors who embraced moderation after the collapse of massive resistance, such as Ernest F. Hollings of South Carolina, Lindsay J. Almond of Virginia, and Ernest Vandiver of Georgia, Collins, Coleman, and Hodges all developed their strategies in direct competition, or conversation, with massive resistance.[21] In fact, popular support for massive resistance in the latter half of the 1950s placed them under sometimes excruciating pressure to embrace defiance. Not only did their constituents look to them as symbolic leaders but also they expected them to take executive measures and introduce legislative solutions to prevent integration in their states. Though all three made concessions, at various points, to proponents of massive resistance, they were never "destroyed" by it, like many of their counterparts, nor did they ever abandon their position that defiance was a bad idea.[22] In fact, they continued to devise strategies to subvert civil rights even after massive resistance had collapsed, lending credence to Martin Luther King Jr.'s lament that it was moderates, not "Citizens' Councilors or Ku Klux Klanners" who posed the biggest "stumbling block" to racial reform in the American South.[23]

NOTES

Introduction

1. LeRoy Collins, "Can A Southerner Be Elected President?" Address to the Southern Governors' Conference, Sea Island, Georgia, Sept. 23, 1957.

2. "Southern Leader Asks Moderation: Governor Collins Gets Ovation from Colleagues—Scores Racial Furor," *New York Times*, Sept. 24, 1957, 1.

3. Ibid.

4. "Little Rock Police, Deployed at Sunrise, Press Mob Back at School Barricades," *New York Times*, Sept. 24, 1957, 1.

5. "Troops on Guard at School: Negroes Ready to Return," *New York Times*, Sept. 25, 1957, 1.

6. Though scholars agree that popular support for massive resistance spiked between 1956 and 1959, the precise extent to which southerners supported massive resistance is uncertain. Most of the support for massive resistance, for example, came from malapportioned electoral districts in rural, Black Belt areas. See Earl Black, *Southern Governors and Civil Rights: Racial Segregation as a Campaign Issue in the Second Reconstruction* (Cambridge, MA: Harvard University Press, 1976); and Numan V. Bartley, *The Rise of Massive Resistance: Race and Politics in the South during the 1950's* (1997, reprint; Baton Rouge: Louisiana State University Press, 1969). This has led some historians, like Matthew Lassiter, to conclude that massive resistance was not the result of a popular groundswell of defiance but rather outdated electoral arrangements. Because the majority of the South's population was suburban and urban, not rural, argues Lassiter, for example, there was a "silent majority" in the South that did not support massive resistance. However, Lassiter fails to explain why moderate governors like Orval Faubus, who were not subjected to disproportionate voting arrangements, felt pressure to endorse defiance. Lassiter also fails to explain why moderate governors like James E. Folsom of Alabama, LeRoy Collins of

Florida, and Earl K. Long of Louisiana were replaced by more outspoken segregationists. According to his analysis, moderate voters in urban and suburban areas should have triumphed over extremists in gubernatorial races, where malapportioned electoral districting did not apply. That they did not points to a larger weakness in Lassiter's work, which is a general tendency to read moderate "silence" too optimistically, as evidence of a latent tolerance that may not have existed.

7. Other historians who have successfully questioned the southern strategy thesis, finding indigenous moves toward moderation on racial matters, include Joseph Crespino, *In Search of Another Country: Mississippi and the Conservative Counterrevolution* (Princeton: Princeton University Press, 2007); Matthew D. Lassiter, *The Silent Majority: Suburban Politics in the Sunbelt South* (Princeton: Princeton University Press, 2006); and Kevin M. Kruse, *White Flight: Atlanta and the Making of Modern Conservatism* (Princeton: Princeton University Press, 2005).

8. Numan V. Bartley refers to Collins and Hodges as "business conservatives" in *The Rise of Massive Resistance* but calls them "business-oriented moderates" in his general history, *The New South, 1945–1980: The Story of the South's Modernization* (Baton Rouge: Louisiana State University Press, 1995), 213. Interestingly, Bartley notes that Collins and Hodges were joined by Orval Faubus as the South's most devoted suitors of industry. See Bartley, *The New South*, 215. Bartley says little of J. P. Coleman, however, even though he, too, endorsed business investment in Mississippi and refrained from the type of business-killing defiance that Faubus engaged in during the Little Rock crisis. See, for example, James C. Cobb's mention of Coleman in *The Selling of the South: The Southern Crusade for Industrial Development, 1936–1990* (2nd ed., Urbana: University of Illinois Press, 1993), 94.

9. I take "hollow hope" from Gerald Rosenberg's discussion of *Brown* in *The Hollow Hope: Can Courts Bring about Social Change?* (Chicago: University of Chicago Press, 1991).

10. I also borrow "political support" from Rosenberg's study, *The Hollow Hope:*, 31. Though political support can certainly be generated without popular support, popular support is generally synonymous with political support, hence recent emphasis on "popular constitutionalism." See, for example, Barry Friedman, "Mediated Popular Constitutionalism," 101 *Michigan Law Review* (August 2003).

11. I take my definition of *ideology* from Stuart Hall, who argues that ideologies are not simply "philosophical" systems of political ideas but also "those images, concepts and premises which provide the frameworks through which we represent, interpret, understand and 'make sense' of some aspect of social existence." Stuart Hall, "The Whites of Their Eyes: Racist Ideologies and the Media" in *Silver Linings*, G. Bridges and R. Brunt, eds. (London: Lawrence & Wishart, 1981), 31. For the notion of racial formation, I rely on Michael Omi and Howard Winant, *Racial Formation in the United States: From the 1960s to the 1990s*, 2nd ed. (New York: Routledge, 1994).

12. To borrow from the theoretical work of Stuart Hall, one might say that the southern state and, by extension, southern law were not simply "coercive" but also "educative and formative," ultimately playing a critical role in the maintenance of racial hegemony in the South. See Stuart Hall, "Gramsci's Relevance for the Study of Race and Ethnicity," 428.

13. Martin Luther King Jr., "Letter from Birmingham Jail," reprinted in *Why We Can't Wait* (New York: Signet, 2000), 73.

14. I take much of my analysis here, particularly terms like "group-salient criteria," racial "idioms," and "status-enforcing state action," from Reva Siegel, not only because she has provided perhaps the best analytic model through which to view southern constitutional responses to *Brown* so far but also because Collins, Coleman, and Hodges inform her work in particularly interesting ways. See, for example, Reva Siegel, "Discrimination in the Eyes of the Law: How 'Color Blindness' Discourse Disrupts and Rationalizes Social Stratification," 88 *California Law Review* (2000): 83; Reva Siegel, "Why Equal Protection No Longer Protects"; and Reva Siegel, "'The Rule of Love': Wife Beating as Prerogative and Privacy," 105 *Yale Law Journal* (1996): 2118.

15. For the role that moderates played in constructing the legal system of Jim Crow, see John W. Cell, *The Highest Stage of White Supremacy: The Origins of Segregation in South Africa and the American South* (Cambridge, UK: Cambridge University Press, 1982), 171–91.

16. See Earl Black, *Southern Governors and Civil Rights: Racial Segregation as a Campaign Issue in the Second Reconstruction* (Cambridge, MA: Harvard University Press, 1976), 60–61; Matthew D. Lassiter and Andrew B. Lewis define *moderates* as white southerners who "generally opposed integration but nevertheless accepted the authority of the federal courts." Mattew D. Lassiter and Andrew B. Lewis, "Massive Resistance Revisited: Virginia's Moderates and the Byrd Organization," in *The Moderates' Dilemma*, 1.

Chapter One

1. Stephen J. Whitfield, *A Death in the Delta: The Story of Emmett Till* (Baltimore: Johns Hopkins University Press, 1988); Christopher Metress, ed., *The Lynching of Emmett Till: A Documentary Narrative* (Charlottesville: University of Virginia Press, 2002); Curtis Jones's interview for *Eyes on the Prize* television series, reprinted in Henry Hampton, Steve Fayer, and Sarah Flynn, eds., *Voices of Freedom: An Oral History of the Civil Rights Movement from the 1950s to the 1980s* (New York: Bantam, 1990), 3.

2. Charles Diggs's interview for *Eyes on the Prize* television series, reprinted in Hampton et al., eds., *Voices of Freedom*, 7. Till's wake is described in "Bury Slain Boy," *Chicago Daily Tribune*, Sept. 7, 1955, 5.

3. "Designed to Inflame," *Jackson Daily News*, Sept. 2, 1955. Though Milam and Bryant were eventually acquitted, an all-white grand jury did indict them for the murder. "Indictment in Mississippi," *New York Times*, Sept. 7, 1955, 30.

4. "Murder Trial Date Set: Special Prosecutor Is Named in Mississippi Case," *New York Times*, Sept. 10, 1955, 5; "Racial Issues Stirred by Mississippi Killing," *New York Times* Sept. 18, 1955, E7; "Mississippi Vote Won by Coleman: Attorney General Is Victor in Run-Off for Governor over Paul B. Johnson," *New York Times*, Aug. 24, 1955, p. 28; "Coleman Launches Campaign Tuesday with Ringing Challenge to the People," *Webster Progress*, May 12, 1955, clipping, Coleman (J. P.) Subject File, Mississippi Department of Archives and History, Jackson, Mississippi (hereinafter MDAH). Cecil L. Summers, *The Governors of Mississippi* (Gretna, LA: Pelican, 1980), 115–16; J. P. Coleman, interview with Dr. Orley P. Caudill, Ackerman, Mississippi, November 12, 1981, Mississippi Oral History Program, University of Southern Mississippi, p. 64.

5. "Coleman Pledges Firm Stand on Segregation: Coleman Succeeds White; Vows War on Crime, Aid to Farmers and Economy," *Jackson Daily News*, Jan. 17, 1956.

6. Coleman explained the symbiotic relationship between segregation and industry in Mississippi to a New York audience in April 1957. See "Mississippi Offers 'Anything' to Industry: Gov. Coleman Heads Hunting Party of Seven Here," *New York Times*, April 19, 1957, 29. Coleman described segregation as a device for ensuring "peaceable government" in a letter to a constituent in 1958. See J. P. Coleman to C. C. Smith, April 10, 1958, Folder: "Citizens' Councils, 1957–1958," Subgroup 5, Box 12, J. P. Coleman Correspondence, MDAH.

7. "Coleman Rejects Nullification Idea: Governor-Elect Disagrees with Eastland, Williams on Plan to Fight Decree," *Jackson Daily News*, Dec. 14, 1955. For some of Coleman's earliest public comments on *Brown*, see J. P. Coleman, "Meeting the School Crisis: An Address by Attorney General J. P. Coleman of Mississippi Delivered over the facilities of TV Station WLBT, Jackson, Mississippi, Tuesday, June 1, 1954, David W. Robinson Papers, University of South Carolina School of Law, Columbia, South Carolina. See also J. P. Coleman, "Text of Governor J. P. Coleman's Inaugural Address," *State Times*, Jan. 17, 1956; "Mississippi: The Six Foot Wedge," *Time*, March 4, 1957, 25.

8. See chap. 260, Mississippi Legislative Acts, 1954 Regular Session.

9. Bartley, *Rise*, 117–19.

10. "Mississippi's Leaders 'Divided' on Proposal for Nullification," *Southern School News*, January 1956. Many years later, Coleman discussed his interest in southern, particularly Civil War, history in his interviews with Orley P. Caudill. *Time* magazine emphasized Coleman's interest in history, together with his view that the Supreme Court had allied itself with the South during Reconstruction; see "Mississippi: The Six Foot Wedge."

11. Chap. 260, Mississippi Legislative Acts, 1954 Regular Session; "Mississippi LEAC Reaffirms Stand against Desegregation 'in Any Form,'" *Southern School News*, July 6, 1955. Numan V. Bartley notes that Mississippi's law was the first to be enacted in the South; Bartley, *The Rise of Massive Resistance: Race and Politics in the South during the 1950's* (1969; reprint,

Baton Rouge: Louisiana State University Press, 1997), 78. Coleman traveled repeatedly from Jackson to Washington to listen to the oral arguments in *Brown v. Board of Education*, long before the Court issued its final ruling. J. P. Coleman interview with John Egerton, September 5, 1990, Southern Oral History Program, University of North Carolina, Chapel Hill.

12. J. P. Coleman to C. C. Smith, April 10, 1958, Folder: "Citizens' Council, 1957–1958," Subgroup 5, Box 12, J. P. Coleman Correspondence.

13. "Mississippi: The Six Foot Wedge."

14. "Coleman Sees Lessening of Desegregation Pressure," *Jackson Daily News*, Feb. 17, 1956.

15. Black, *Southern Governors and Civil Rights*, 22. *Time* magazine summarized Coleman's campaign platform in "Mississippi: The Six Foot Wedge." See also "Governor Will Be Slow in Dispensing Patronage," *Jackson Daily News*, April 2, 1956, clipping, Coleman (J. P.) Subject File, MDAH.

16. J. P. Coleman, interview with Orley Caudill.

17. Coleman expressed his support for Johnson in the 1956 presidential race in a letter. See Letter, J. P. Coleman to Senator Lyndon B. Johnson, Sept. 24, 1956, Folder: J. P. Coleman, Miss. Box 3, LBJA Famous Names, LBJ Library. For Coleman's support of Johnson in subsequent elections, and for Johnson's support of Coleman's gubernatorial bid, see J. P. Coleman, interview with Orley Caudill.

18. Chester M. Morgan, *Redneck Liberal: Theodore G. Bilbo and the New Deal* (Baton Rouge: Louisiana State University Press, 1985); Adwin W. Green, *The Man Bilbo* (Westport, Conn.: Greenwood, 1976).

19. J. P. Coleman, interview with Orley B. Caudill.

20. Coleman discussed Bilbo in his interview with Caudill. For coverage of the 1935 lynch law debates in Congress, see "Senate Holds Firm for Lynching Test: Southerners Plan to Adjourn and Thereby Sidetrack Bill," *New York Times*, April 28, 1935, 20.

21. "Congress Awaits Next Court Move: Any Attempt to Curb Tribunal May Depend on Labor and Security Rulings," *New York Times*, Jan. 24, 1937, 65.

22. For an internalist account of the Court's shift in favor of the New Deal, see Barry Cushman, *Rethinking the New Deal Court: The Structure of a Constitutional Revolution* (New York: Oxford University Press, 1998).

23. J. P. Coleman, interview with Orley B. Caudill.

24. J. P. Coleman, "Meeting the School Crisis: An Address by Attorney General J. P. Coleman," delivered over the facilities of TV Station WLBT, Jackson, Mississippi, June 1, 1954.

25. Coleman quoted these words, which were initially spoken by Judge Robert H. Thompson at a Mississippi Bar Association meeting in 1923, about the 1890 constitutional convention in an article, "The Origin of the Constitution of 1890," he wrote for the *Journal of Mississippi History* 19 (April 1957): 73. In that piece, Coleman also noted a turn to legalist evasion as a means of denying the black vote in 1890; Ibid., 87. For more on legalist evasion surrounding black voting rights, see J. Morgan Kousser, *The Shaping*

of Southern Politics: Suffrage Restriction and the Establishment of the One-Party South, 1880–1910 (New Haven, Conn.: Yale University Press, 1974).

26. Coleman, "The Origin of the Constitution of 1890."

27. Cecil L. Sumners, "James Plemon Coleman," in Summers, *The Governors of Mississippi*, 125–28.

28. For Coleman's role in the case, and before the Supreme Court, see "M'Gee Execution Stayed by Court: High Bench Will Rule on New Appeal," *New York Times*, March 16, 1951, 23; "M'Gee's Fourth Plea Fails in High Court," *New York Times*, March 27, 1951, 20; "Group Joins in Fight for Execution Stay," *New York Times*, July 20, 1950, 23; "1,000 in Times Square Rally: 'Save Willie McGee' Group Is Routed by Police," *New York Times*, July 27, 1950, 32; "Mississippi Arrests 41 at Capitol as Willie McGee Plea Is Studied," *New York Times*, May 6, 1951, 1. See also chap. 3, "Comes Now Willie McGee," in Sarah Hart Brown's *Standing against Dragons: Three Southern Lawyers in an Era of Fear* (Baton Rouge: Louisiana State University Press, 1998), 89–114.

29. J. P. Coleman to C. C. Walsh, April 10, 1958, Folder: "Citizens' Council, 1957–58," Subgroup 5, Box 12, J. P. Coleman Correspondence, MDAH.

30. Ibid.

31. J. P. Coleman interview with Orley P. Caudill; "Mississippi Offers 'Anything' to Industry"; John Dittmer provides evidence substantiating Coleman's suspicion that the NAACP pressured black leaders to endorse integration the night before they were scheduled to meet Governor Hugh White and the Legal Education Advisory Committee, of which Coleman was a member in July 1954. See John Dittmer, *Local People: The Struggle for Civil Rights in Mississippi* (Urbana: University of Illinois Press, 1994), 38–39.

32. Coleman reflected on his opposition to the councils in a letter to a constituent in 1958. See J. P. Coleman to C. C. Smith, April 10, 1958, Folder: "Citizens' Council, 1957–1958," Subgroup 5, Box 12, J .P. Coleman Correspondence, MDAH.

33. "Mississippi: The Six-Foot Wedge."

34. J. P. Coleman, "Meeting the School Crisis."

35. Ibid.

36. Ibid.

37. Ibid.

38. Tom P. Brady, *Black Monday* (Winona, MS: Association of Citizens' Councils, 1955).

39. James Graham Cook provides a firsthand description of Brady in his book *The Segregationists* (New York: Appleton-Century-Crofts, 1962), 13–33. For an academic study of the Citizens' Councils, see Neil R. McMillen, *The Citizens' Council: Organized Resistance to the Second Reconstruction, 1954–64* (Urbana: University of Illinois Press, 1971). For a discussion of the ideological interplay between sex and segregation, see Jane Dailey, "The Theology of Massive Resistance: Sex, Segregation, and the Sacred after *Brown*, " in

Massive Resistance: Southern Opposition to the Second Reconstruction, Clive Webb, ed. (New York: Oxford University Press, 2005).

40. While Kilpatrick popularized interposition in a series of editorials in the Richmond *News Leader* in November 1955, he was not the first southerner to endorse it as a response to *Brown*. That credit probably goes to a Virginia attorney, William Old, who published a pamphlet outlining it in August 1955. See Bartley, *Rise*, 129. Some confused interposition and nullification. See "Mississippi's Leaders 'Divided' on Proposal for Nullification," *Southern School News*, January 1956, 6.

41. J. P. Coleman, "Meeting the School Crisis."

42. Ibid.

43. "Joint Statement of United States Senator James O. Eastland, Judge Tom P. Brady, and Congressman John Bell Williams," Jackson, Mississippi, Dec. 12, 1955, Special Collections, Alderman Library, University of Virginia, Charlottesville.

44. J. P. Coleman to the Members of the Mississippi Legislature, form letter, Dec. 15, 1955, Coleman (J. P.) Papers, Subgroup 5, Correspondence, Box 17, Folder 32 "Legislative Correspondence, 1955–60," MDAH.

45. Ibid. To J. P. Coleman, the resolution was "legal poppycock." See "Coleman Rejects Nullification Idea: Governor-Elect Disagrees with Eastland, Williams on Plan to Fight Decree," *Jackson Daily News*, Dec. 14, 1955, clipping, Coleman (J. P.) Subject File, MDAH. Hodding Carter III, *The South Strikes Back* (Garden City, N.Y.: Doubleday, 1959), 56–57.

46. Brady confirmed rumors that he was interested in running for governor to James Graham Cook. See Cook, *The Segregationists*, 27.

47. "Coleman Rejects Nullification Idea." House Speaker Walter Sillers authorized the creation of the Legal Education Advisory Committee (LEAC) in April 1954, specifically to devise strategies for circumventing integration.

48. "Coleman Rejects Nullification Idea."

49. Barron Drewry to Coleman (J. P.), Dec. 15, 1955, Coleman (J. P.) Papers, Correspondence (Spec.) Box 6, Folder 19, MDAH.

50. Kilpatrick discussed Coleman's involvement in the interposition fiasco in a letter: Letter, James Jackson Kilpatrick to Paul S. Keyes, Jan. 11, 1956, Box 15, Folder "K," Accession # 6626-b, James Jackson Kilpatrick Papers, Small Special Collections Library, University of Virginia, Charlottesville.

51. Chap. 254, *General Laws of Mississippi*, 1956, 303.

52. *The Southern School News*, otherwise a reliable source of reporting on civil rights in the South, confused Coleman's faith in legalist evasion with interposition. See "Mississippi Sets Up 'Watch-Dog' Group on Race Problems," *Southern School News*, April 1956, 10.

53. Aaron Henry describes Lee's murder in his memoir, *The Fire Ever Burning* (Jackson: University Press of Mississippi, 2000), 93–94. The murder is also described in the NAACP pamphlet *M Is for Mississippi and Murder*, Papers of the NAACP, Part 3, Microfilm, Reel 2, Library of Congress, Washington, D.C.

54. Wilkins's quote was printed in the *Memphis Commercial Appeal*, September 1, 1955. See also *M is for Mississippi and Murder*.

55. Roy Wilkins to Branch Officers, Jan. 6, 1956, Papers of the NAACP, Part 20, "White Resistance and Reprisals," Microfilm, Reel 1, Library of Congress.

56. Martin Luther King Jr., who may have received one of Wilkins's letters regarding the Till murder, recognized this early on as well. Even southern whites would awaken to the moral worth of the black struggle, argued King, once they were "splattered with the blood," of their black brothers. Martin Luther King Jr., *Stride toward Freedom: The Montgomery Story* (New York: Harper & Row, 1958), 216. Of course, provoking violence would later become a movement objective. See Garrow, *Protest at Selma*, 220–27.

57. "Mississippi," *Southern School News*, June 8, 1955, 18.

58. Ibid.

59. William Bradford Huie, "Approved Killing in Mississippi," *Look*, Jan. 1956. Wilkins recognized that the Till murder could be used expressly to draw federal intervention into the region. He wrote this in a letter; see Roy Wilkins to Branch Officers, Jan. 6, 1956, Papers of the NAACP, Part 20 "White Resistance and Reprisals," Microfilm, Reel 1, Library of Congress.

60. Roy Wilkins to J. P. Coleman, Western Union telegram, Jan. 9, 1956, Papers of the NAACP, Part 20 "White Resistance and Reprisals," Microfilm, Reel 1, Library of Congress.

61. Ibid.

62. J. P. Coleman, "Text of Governor J. P. Coleman's Inaugural Address," *State Times*, Jan. 17, 1956.

63. Ibid. Coleman's speech was, just as he suspected, covered by major newspapers like the *New York Times* and *Chicago Daily Tribune*; "Vows to Retain Segregation in Mississippi, but without Violence Governor Says," *Chicago Daily Tribune*, Jan. 18, 1956, A8; "Gov. Coleman Takes Post in Mississippi," *New York Times*, Jan. 18, 1956, 14.

64. J. P. Coleman, "Text of Governor J. P. Coleman's Inaugural Address."

65. Roy Wilkins to J. P. Coleman, March 5, 1956, Papers of the NAACP, Part 20, "White Resistance and Reprisals," Reel 1, Microfilm, Library of Congress.

66. Ibid.

67. *Mississippi Council on Human Relations Bulletin*, May 1956, Papers of the NAACP, Part 3, Microfilm, Reel 5, Library of Congress; "Governor Cools Negro Leadership Meeting," *Jackson Advocate*, April 28, 1956.

68. "Gov. Coleman Asks Negro Congressman Adam Clayton Powell to Indefinitely Postpone His Coming to Miss," *Jackson Advocate*, April 28, 1956, 1.

69. Ibid.

70. "Governor Cools Negro Leadership Meeting." Coleman probably did not know that tension existed between the RCNL and the NAACP. For evidence, see Medgar W. Evers to Roy Wilkins, April 10, 1956, Papers of

the NAACP, Part 20, "White Resistance and Reprisals," Reel 2, microfilm, Library of Congress.

71. "Governor Cools Negro Leadership Meeting." Medgar Evers believed that Powell had actually confirmed attendance at the RCNL meeting. See Medgar W. Evers to Roy Wilkins, April 10, 1956, Papers of the NAACP, Part 20, Microfilm Reel 2, "White Resistance and Reprisals, 1956–1965," Library of Congress.

72. Bulletin, May 1956, Mississippi Council of Human Relations, Papers of the NAACP, Part 3, Microfilm, Reel 5, Library of Congress.

73. "Text of J. P. Coleman's Inaugural Address," *State Times*, Jan., 17, 1955, clipping, Coleman (J. P.) Subject File, MDAH.

74. Ibid.

75. Ibid.

76. "Miss. Legislature Meets with Segregation as Major Issue," *Atlanta Daily Journal*, January 4, 1956, A-1; "New Law in Effect: Recall Bill Signed by Governor Coleman," *Jackson Daily News*, Jan. 20, 1956, clipping, Coleman (J. P.) Subject File, MDAH.

77. During a speech before the legislature in 1958, Coleman called for fixing fees chargeable by JPs: "I hope you will pass a statute clearly fixing the fees of the justice-of-the-peace," the governor asked the legislature, "and putting a stop to the cost racket which has given us so much unfavorable and undeserved publicity"; see "JP Fines Curbed by House Action: Measure Boosted by Coleman Aims to Kill Off Speed Traps," *Jackson Daily News*, April 1, 1958, 1.

78. "Coleman Says New Constitution Needed in State," *Jackson Daily News*, Nov. 27, 1956, clipping, Coleman (J. P.) Subject File, MDAH.

79. Form letter, J. P. Coleman to unknown, Feb. 20, 1956, Subgroup 5, Box 17, Folder 32 "Legislators Corr.," J. P. Coleman Correspondence, MDAH.

80. Ibid.

81. J. P. Coleman, interview with Orley P. Caudill; "Governor Will Be Slow in Dispensing Patronage," *Jackson Daily News*, April 2, 1956, clipping, Coleman (J. P.) Subject File, MDAH; J. P. Coleman to Mississippi Legislature, form letter, Feb. 20, 1956, Coleman (J. P.) Papers, Correspondence, Subgroup 5, Box 17, Folder 32 "Legislators Correspondence, 1955–60," MDAH.

82. Weldon Cooper, "The State Police Movement in the South," *Journal of Politics* 1 (Nov. 1939), 414–33.

83. For a more on law enforcement in Mississippi in the 1950s, see Robert B. Highsaw and Charles N. Fortenberry, *The Government and Administration of Mississippi* (New York: Thomas Y. Crowell, 1954), 16–24; V. O. Key relates the precise tension between sheriffs and state troopers to bootlegging and corruption in *Southern Politics in State and Nation* (New York: Vintage, 1949), 235.

84. For a more detailed analysis of *Brown*'s impact on executive power in the South, see Coleman B. Ransone Jr., "Political Leadership in the Governor's Office," *Journal of Politics* 26 (Feb. 1964), 197–220; "Mississippi:

Bills with a Label Pass Automatically," *New York Times*, March 13, 1956, 21–22.

85. "Mississippi Sets Up 'Watch-Dog' Group on Race Problems," *Southern School News*, April 1956, 10.

86. Chap. 365, *General Laws of the State of Mississippi*, 1956.

87. Chap. 365, *General Laws of the State of Mississippi*, 1956. Coleman called for "an appropriate State Sovereignty bill to enable the state during the next two years to maintain a successful fight for preserving separation of the races." "Painful Warning: Coleman Tells Legislature State Budget Out of Line," *Jackson Daily News*, March 20, 1956, Coleman (J. P.) Papers, Subject File, clipping, MDAH. For an institutional history of the Mississippi State Sovereignty Commission, see Yasuhiro Katagiri's *The Mississippi State Sovereignty Commission: Civil Rights and States' Rights* (Jackson: University Press of Mississippi, 2001).

88. Jack J. Van Landingham to Director, State Sovereignty Commission, May 18, 1959, Mississippi State Sovereignty Commission Papers, MDAH.

89. Ibid.

90. Ibid.

91. Ibid.

92. Ibid. See also "J. P. Accused of Blocking Arrests," *Jackson Daily News*, May 19, 1959.

93. "Subject: Medgar Evers, Race Agitator," State Sovereignty Commission Memo, Mississippi State Sovereignty Commission Files, Nov. 25, 1958, MDAH.

94. "Mississippi Police Seize Negro Seeking to Enroll at University," *New York Times*, June 6, 1958, 25.

95. "Negro Committed for Mental Tests," *New York Times*, June 7, 1958, 10.

96. "I had an experience when Clennon King tried to be admitted to Ole Miss while I was Governor," explained Coleman later, "and we sealed it off then. A rabbit couldn't have gotten on the campus and didn't. There wasn't any violence and there wasn't any uproar and there wasn't any commotion." Dr. Orley B. Caudill interview with J. P. Coleman, Part 2, February 6, 1982.

97. "Segregation Unit Votes Spy Set-Up: Mississippi Will Hire Secret Agents to Report Moves in Integration Camp," *New York Times*, May 16, 1956, 28.

98. Ibid.

99. Hal DeCell to Governor Coleman, "Clarksdale Meeting of Regional Council of Negro Leadership," Dec. 10, 1957, Coleman (J. P.) Papers, Box 21, Folder 37, "Sovereignty Commission 1957–59," MDAH. Both John Dittmer and Charles Payne discuss the Regional Council of Negro Leadership, or RCNL. See John Dittmer, *Local People*, 32–33; Charles Payne, *I've Got the Light of Freedom: The Organizing Tradition and the Mississippi Freedom Struggle* (Berkeley: University of California Press, 1995), 31–32. Aaron Henry called the organization a "homegrown NAACP"; see Dittmer, *Local People*, 33.

100. William Liston, Confidential Report to Governor J. P. Coleman, Aug. 1–2, 1956, Governor J. P. Coleman Correspondence, Subgroup 5, Box 21, Folder 36, "1956 Sovereignty Commission Reports," MDAH.

101. Ibid.

102. David L. Chappell, *Inside Agitators: White Southerners in the Civil Rights Movement* (Baltimore: Johns Hopkins Press, 1994), 214.

103. William Liston, Sovereignty Commission Investigator, Confidential Report to Governor J. P. Coleman, August 7–8, 1956, Governor J. P. Coleman Correspondence, Subgroup 5, Box 21, Folder 36, "1956 Sovereignty Commission Reports," MDAH.

104. Ibid.

105. Roy Wilkins, "Mississippians Urged to Solve Race Issue through Honest Discussion," *News from NAACP*, June 3, 1956, Papers of the NAACP, Part 20, "White Resistance and Reprisals," Microfilm, Reel 2, Library of Congress.

106. Ibid.

107. Gus Courts to Roy Wilkins, April 18, 1957, Part 20, Reel 1, Papers of the NAACP, Library of Congress.

108. See Roy Wilkins to Gus Courts, April 26, 1957, Part 20, Reel 1, Papers of the NAACP, Library of Congress.

109. A. M. Mackel to Roy Wilkins, April 29, 1956, Part 3, Microfilm, Reel 5, Papers of the NAACP, Library of Congress.

110. Ibid.

111. Zack J. Van Landingham to J. P. Coleman, Jan. 12, 1959, Sovereignty Commission Memorandum, Subject: B. L. Bell, Informant, Coleman (J. P.) Papers, "Sovereignty Commission 1957–59," MDAH.

112. Some other black leaders who joined Bell were W. A. Higgins, a Negro schoolteacher at Clarksdale; B. F. McLaurin, principal of a Negro junior college, Clarksdale; Dr. J. H. White of Itta Bena; Prof. N. H. Burger, principal of the Negro school at Hattiesburg; Dr. Lee Owens, a medical doctor, Vicksburg; E. S. Bishop, prof. of a Negro school at Corinth; and Fred Miller, of Mound Bayou. Zack J. Van Landingham to J. P. Coleman, Jan. 12 1959, Sovereignty Commission Memorandum, Subject: B. L. Bell, Informant, Coleman (J. P.) Papers, "Sovereignty Commission 1957–59," MDAH.

113. Ibid.

114. Ibid.

115. Charles Payne mentions Kennard's case as one of the most frustrating that Medgar Evers faced in Mississippi; see *I've Got the Light of Freedom*, 55.

116. "Clyde Kennard: Integration Agitator; Attempt to Integrate Mississippi Southern College, File 1–21," Dec. 17, 1958, Coleman (J. P.) Papers, Box 21, Folder 37, "Sovereignty Commission 1957–59," MDAH. "Subject is living with mother and stepfather. (Mother and stepfather may be common law man and wife since extensive investigation revealed no marriage license issued to Silas L. Smith or Leonia Kennard or Kinnard), Route 1, (Eatonville, Hattiesburg, Mississippi)."

117. "All of these Negroes agreed that this was a desirable solution and they expressed confidence that they would be able to handle the situation and persuade Kennard to refrain from any further action or attempt to enter Mississippi Southern College." Ibid.

118. Ibid.

119. Ibid. Incidentally, the extensive use of black informers like White did not go unnoticed by civil rights activists. In 1959, Medgar Evers told an audience in Los Angeles that blacks were profiting off "segregation and human misery" in Mississippi by accepting payment from the Sovereignty Commission. Zack J. Van Landingham to File 1–23, Subject: Medgar Evers, 24, July 1959, State Sovereignty Commission Papers, MDAH.

120. "Kennard Guilty in Forrest Court," *Jackson Daily News*, Sept. 29, 1959.

121. Roy Wilkins, testimony, "Hearings before the Subcommittee on Constitutional Rights of the Committee on the Judiciary," U.S. Senate, Eighty-Fifth Congress, First Session, Feb. 19, 1957 (Washington, D.C.: United States Government Printing Office, 1957), 300.

122. Ibid.

123. J. P. Coleman, testimony, "Hearings before the Subcommittee on Constitutional Rights of the Committee on the Judiciary," U.S. Senate, Eighty-Fifth Congress, First Session, March 5, 1957 (Washington, D.C.: United States Government Printing Office, 1957), 741.

124. Ibid.

125. Ibid.

126. Ibid.

127. Ibid.

128. For coverage of the journalists' tour of Mississippi, see "Editors to Study Bias: New England Group Arrives in Mississippi by Invitation," *New York Times*, Oct. 7, 1956, 70. See also "Odds 'n Ends from the News Desk," reprinted in the *Peterborough Transcript*, Oct. 18, 1956, kept on file by the NAACP, Part 20, Reel 2, Papers of the NAACP, Library of Congress. Bartley discusses some of the Sovereignty Commission's public relations efforts in *The Rise of Massive Resistance*, 180–81. See also Katagiri, *The Mississippi State Sovereignty Commission*, 12.

129. Roy Wilkins to: Lewis H. Shattuck, Editor & Publisher, *Hardwick Gazette*, Hardwick, Vermont; William B. Roetch, Publisher & Editor, *The Cabinet*, Milford, New Hampshire; Roswell S. Bosworth, President, Rhode Island Press Association, Briston, Rhode Island; Doliver S. White, Publisher, *The Reporter*, Fixboro, Massachusetts; Richard P. Lewis, Editor, *Journal-Transcript*, Franklin, New Hampshire; William F. Wright, *Sanford Maine Tribune*, Sanford, Maine; Albert Rowbotham, Publisher & Editor, *Rumford Falls Times*, Rumford, Maine, Oct. 2, 1956, Papers of the NAACP, Part 20, Reel 2, Library of Congress.

130. Ibid.

131. Memorandum to Roy Wilkins from Henry Lee Moon, Oct. 1, 1956, Papers of the NAACP, Part 20, "White Resistance and Reprisals," Microfilm, Reel 2.

132. Katagiri, *The Mississippi State Sovereignty Commission*, 12.

133. Ibid.

134. Ibid.

135. Ibid. And see also "Sovereignty Commission Report to the Members of the Senate and House of Representatives of the State of Mississippi, 1957," Coleman (J. P.) Papers, MDAH.

136. *Cooper v. Aaron*, 358 U.S. 1, 17 (1958).

137. Coleman discussed some of his thoughts on Little Rock with Orley Caudill; see Caudill interview with J. P. Coleman, Part 2, Feb. 6, 1982.

138. *Cooper*, 358 U.S. 1, at 17.

139. *Shuttlesworth v. Birmingham*, 358 U.S. 101 (1958), affirming *Shuttlesworth v. Birmingham*, 162 F. Supp. 372 (N.D. AL. 1958).

140. *Cooper*, 358 U.S. 1, at 17.

141. *Shuttlesworth*, 358 U.S. 101.

142. Klarman, *From Jim Crow*, 331.

143. Chap. 260, Mississippi Legislative Acts, 1954 Regular Session. "Mississippi LEAC Reaffirms Stand against Desegregation 'in Any Form,'" *Southern School News*, July 6, 1955.

144. "Mississippi LEAC Reaffirms Stand." Laws of the State of Mississippi, 1954, Regular Session, 585–87.

145. Ibid.

146. "Coleman Pledges Firm Stand on Segregation," *Jackson Daily News*, Jan. 17, 1956, clipping, Coleman (J. P.) Subject File, MDAH.

147. "Coleman Sees Lessening of Desegregation Pressure," *Jackson Daily News*, Feb. 17, 1956, clipping, Coleman (J. P.) Subject File, MDAH.

148. Daniel J. Meador, "The Constitution and the Assignment of Students to Public Schools," *Virginia Law Review* 45 (1959): 517.

149. "Mississippi LEAC Reaffirms Stand."

150. Approved by the LEAC and signed into law on April 5, 1956, Mississippi's common law marriage bill asserted that "[n]o marriages contracted after the effective date of this act shall be valid unless the contracting parties shall have obtained a marriage license as otherwise required by law." Senate Bill No. 1954, chap. 239, *General Laws of the State of Mississippi*, 1956, April 5, 1956. Coleman recommended the invalidation of common law marriage as part of a larger, seven part plan to bolster segregation in the state. This seven-point plan included (1) the abolition of common law marriage, (2) the repeal of compulsory school attendance laws, (3) the prevention of barratry, or filing of frivolous lawsuits, (4) the outlawing of obscene or insulting language on the telephone, (5) the punishment of anyone interfering with the laws of Mississippi, (6) the requirement that teachers provide lists of all organizations that they belong to, and (7) the establishment of the Sovereignty Commission; "L.E.A.C. Recommendations," *Southern School News*, January 1956, 6.

151. *Sims v. Sims*, 85 So. 73 (1920).

152. *Butler's Estate v. McQuarters*, 48 So.2d 617 (1950).

153. "Editor Calls for Positive Thinking in Mississippi Crisis," *Southern School News*, March 1956.

154. "Common Law Marriage Ban Sent to Coleman," *Morning Advocate* (Baton Rouge), April 1, 1956, 1.

155. Ibid. "Moving swiftly through the final hours, the two houses passed: The governor endorsed bill outlawing common-law marriages, the last of a block of bills designed to throw up a bulwark around the state's segregation laws. The theory of the bill was to set up unfavorable moral background as a basis for segregation." See "Legislators in Mississippi End Session," *Morning Advocate* (Baton Rouge), April 1, 1956, 10-D. See also "State Common-Law Marriages Banned by Senate's Action: Coleman Secures Passage of Bill to Aid Segregation, *Clarion-Ledger*, March 31, 1956, 1.

156. The *Southern School News* suggested that the bill's purpose was to boost black illegitimacy rates in an article, "Editor Calls for 'Positive Thinking' in Mississippi Crisis," *Southern School News*, March 1956, 3.

157. According to the 1955 *Vital Statistics of the United States*, there were a total of 7,557 illegitimate black births in Mississippi in 1955: "Table 29, Illegitimate Live Births by Age of Mother and Color," *Vital Statistics of the United States, 1955*. In 1958, there were 7,138, a slight drop. Does this mean that whites overestimated the extent to which blacks engaged in common law marriages? Probably; one Mississippi state senator warned, for example, that the bill would "make 10,000 illegitimate children and make 10,000 women live in adultery," something that federal data on illegitimacy rates in Mississippi clearly show did not happen. "State Common-Law Marriages Banned by Senate's Action: Coleman Secures Passage of Bill to Aid Segregation, *Clarion-Ledger*, March 31, 1956, 1. Interestingly, however, the number of white illegitimate births did increase slightly, following the invalidation of common law marriage. For example, in 1955, the total number of white illegitimate births was 286. In 1958, it was 326: "Table 38: Illegitimate Live Births by Age of Mother and Color for Urban and Rural Areas and Specified Urban Places: 35 Reporting States, 1958," *Vital Statistics of the United States*.

158. "Table 29, Illegitimate Live Births by Age of Mother and Color," *Vital Statistics of the United States, 1955*.

159. The total number of recorded black births in Mississippi in 1955 was 35,553. The total number of recorded white births in Mississippi in 1955 was 27,675. "Table 26B: Live Births by Age of Mother, Live-Birth Order, Race, and Nativity of White Mother: Each State 1955," *Vital Statistics of the United States 1955*.

160. "Table 29, Illegitimate Live Births by Age of Mother and Color," *Vital Statistics of the United States, 1955*.

161. "There is no earthly reason for allowing Negroes, and a few white people, to continue to live together openly outside the rules of matrimony," the governor asserted in a memo to judges and law enforcement agents

across the state. J. P. Coleman, "Memorandum to All Circuit Judges, County Judges, District Attorneys, County Attorneys, and Sheriffs in the State of Mississippi," March 7, 1956, Coleman (J. P.) Papers, Box 17, F 32, "Legislative Correspondence, 1955–60," MDAH.

162. Daniel J. Meador, "The Constitution and the Assignment of Pupils"; Note, "The Federal Courts and Integration of Southern Schools: Troubled Status of the Pupil Placement Acts," 62 *Columbia Law Review* 1448 (1962).

163. Patrick E. McCauley, "Be It Enacted," in *With All Deliberate Speed: Segregation-Desegregation in Southern Schools*, Don Shoemaker, ed. (New York: Harper & Brothers, 1957), 137.

164. A crudely drawn Louisiana placement plan was struck down in *Bush v. Orleans Parish School Bd.*, 138 F. Supp. 337 (E.D. La. 1956, aff'd, 242 F.2d 156 (5th Cir.), *cert. denied*, 354 U.S. 921 (1957). Virginia's placement law was struck down by the Fourth Circuit in 1957. *School Bd. Of Newport News v. Atkins*, 246 F.2d 325 (4th Cir. 1957), *cert. denied*, 26 U.S.L. Week (U.S. Oct. 21, 1957). A more carefully crafted Alabama plan was upheld in *Shuttlesworth v. Birmingham*, 162 F. Supp. 372 (N.D. Ala.), *aff'd per curiam*, 358 U.S. 101 (1958). For a general discussion of pupil placement, see Robert B. McKay, "'With All Deliberate Speed': Legislative Reaction and Judicial Development, 1956–1957," 43 *Virginia Law Review* (1957): 1205.

165. Coleman was not fazed by the invalidation of Louisiana's placement statute, which relied on the state's police power. He took heart from a 1956 Fourth Circuit ruling upholding North Carolina's placement law. See "Editor Calls for 'Positive Thinking' in Mississippi Crisis," *Southern School News*, March 1956, 3.

166. King, *Stride toward Freedom*, 223.

167. Ibid., 224.

168. Walter Sillers discussed this measure to Coleman in a letter dated June 19, 1957, Walter Sillers Papers, Box 60, Folder 8, Delta State University Archives, Cleveland, Mississippi.

169. J. P. Coleman to Walter Sillers, Aug. 2, 1957, Walter Sillers Papers, Box 60, Folder 8, Delta State University Archives, Cleveland, Mississippi.

170. Ibid.

171. *Carson v. Warlick*, 238 F.2d 724 (4th Cir. 1956).

172. J. P. Coleman to Walter Sillers, Aug. 2, 1957, Walter Sillers Papers, Box 60, Folder 8, Delta State University Archives, Cleveland, Mississippi.

173. Ibid.

174. Ibid.

175. "J. P. Accused of Blocking Arrests," *Jackson Daily News*, May 19, 1959; "Miss. Citizens Council Hears Barnett Address," *Times Picayune* (New Orleans), Sept. 9, 1959.

176. Dr. Orley B. Caudill interview with J. P. Coleman, Part 2, February 6, 1982.

177. The Supreme Court declared interposition invalid in *Cooper v. Aaron*, 358 U.S. 1 (1958). It sanctioned Alabama's pupil placement law in *Shuttlesworth v. Birmingham*, 358 U.S. 101 (1958).

178. J. P. Coleman to Honorable John Patterson, governor of Alabama, copies to all governors of the Southern Governors Conference, May 6, 1959, Coleman (J. P.) Papers, Subgroup 5, Box 21, Folder 28, MDAH.

179. Governor Lindsay J. Almond to Governor J. P. Coleman, May 8, 1959, Coleman (J. P.) Papers, Subgroup 5, Box 21, Folder 28, MDAH.

180. Governor Ernest F. Hollings to Governor J. P. Coleman, May 8, 1959, Coleman (J. P.) Papers, Subgroup 5, Box 21, Folder 28, MDAH.

181. Ibid.

182. Black, *Southern Governors*, 80.

183. John A. Carroll, testimony, "Hearings before the Subcommittee on Constitutional Rights of the Committee on the Judiciary," U.S. Senate, Eighty-Sixth Congress, First Session, May 28, 1959.

184. Ibid.

Chapter Two

1. Governor Luther Hodges to Governor Hugh White, December 14, 1954, Segregation: Special Committee Folder, Box 41, Luther Hodges Papers, North Carolina State Archives (hereafter NCSA).

2. Governor Hugh White to Governor Luther Hodges, December 16, 1954, Segregation: Special Committee Folder, Box 41, Luther Hodges Papers, NCSA.

3. Luther H. Hodges, *Businessman*, 80–81; "North Carolina Placement Law," Chap. 366, *1955 North Carolina Session Laws*, March 30, 1955; reprinted in *Race Relations Law Reporter*, 1, 240–41.

4. Thomas J. Pearsall issued the formal invitation to Mississippi Sovereignty Commission Director Ney Gore requesting his help in the implementation of North Carolina's pupil assignment plan. Thomas J. Pearsall to Members of the Advisory Committee on Education, Letter No. 3, July 22, 1955, Segregation: Letters to Advisory Committee Folder, Box 39, Luther Hodges Papers, NCSA. Pearsall, a native of Rocky Mount, North Carolina, and former speaker of the House, had assisted Hodges's predecessor, William Umstead, in studying possible ways to circumvent Brown without flagrantly violating federal law. Hodges, *Businessman*, 80, 82.

5. For more background, see Luther Hodges, *Businessman*, 5–10.

6. Jacquelyn Dowd Hall et al., *Like A Family: The Making of a Southern Cotton Mill World* (Chapel Hill: University of North Carolina Press, 1987), 104; Robert Rodgers Korstad, *Civil Rights Unionism: Tobacco Workers and the Struggle for Democracy in the Mid-Twentieth-Century South* (Chapel Hill: University of North Carolina Press, 2003), 57.

7. "Harlem Is Orderly with Heavy Guard Ready for Trouble: Rioting of Sunday Night Tapers Off—8,000 State Troops Are Held in Their Armories," *New York Times*, Aug. 3, 1943, 1; "Injured Reach 600—Theatres Closed, Liquor Sales Banned, as U.S. Sends Armored Cars," *New York Times*, June 22, 1943, 1.

8. "Student 'Strikes' Flare into Riots in Harlem Schools—Negro Students Put aboard Buses and Sent Out of Area," *New York Times*, Sept. 29, 1945, 1.

9. Ibid.

10. Howard E. Covington Jr. and Marion A. Ellis make precisely this argument about Hodges in their biography of Hodges's successor, Terry Sanford: *Terry Sanford: Politics, Progress, and Outrageous Ambitions* (Durham, N.C.: Duke University Press, 1999), 177.

11. Hodges, *Businessman*, 9–10.

12. By this I mean that Hodges did not see the racial crisis as a vehicle for promoting his own political career. On the contrary, the racial crisis became an obstacle in his career. William Chafe describes Hodges's commitment to industrial development in *Civilities and Civil Rights: Greensboro, North Carolina, and the Black Struggle for Freedom* (New York: Oxford University Press, 1980), 67–80; Timothy Tyson does so as well in *Radio Free Dixie: Robert F. Williams and the Roots of Black Power* (Chapel Hill: University of North Carolina Press, 1999), 74–76; See also Osha Davidson Gray, *The Best of Enemies: Race and Redemption in the New South* (New York: Scribner's, 1996). All three authors support the argument in this book that Hodges supported not only industry but also the circumvention of *Brown*. According to Gray, for example, instead of dramatically standing in the schoolhouse door like George Wallace, Luther Hodges "would quietly appoint a Committee to deliberate for eternity over exactly which door, and of what dimensions, would best facilitate the ingress and egress of all students" (*Best of Enemies*, 83–85). Tyson, in support of Gray's thesis, adds that "the sophistication that Hodges brought to the struggle against desegregation made him far more effective than most proponents of massive resistance" (*Radio Free Dixie*, 74).

13. Luther Hodges, *Businessman*, 29–56.

14. Ibid., 32.

15. "The North Carolina Story," *News & Observer* (Raleigh), June 21, 1959.

16. Luther H. Hodges, "Address by Governor Luther H. Hodges of North Carolina on State-wide Radio-Television Network," August 8, 1955, Box 39, Folder: Segregation Advisory Committee on Integration, Luther Hodges Papers, NCSA.

17. Hall, *Like a Family*, 66–67.

18. William Chafe finds Hodges personally responsible for pursuing an overly obstructionist policy to *Brown*. Had it not been for Hodges, suggests Chafe, the state could have integrated faster and more easily than it did. According to him, for example, state leaders greeted *Brown* with "grudging acceptance, and in some cases warm approval." Chafe, *Civilities*, 48. Opinion polls conducted in Guilford County, which includes Greensboro, in 1956, reinforce Chafe's thesis, suggesting that even though more than 70 percent of the population endorsed segregation, only a little over half were actually willing to take action to prevent it. Melvin M. Tumin, *Desegregation: Resistance and Readiness* (Princeton, N.J.: Princeton University Press, 1958), 43.

19. Elizabeth Pearsall, interview with Walter Campbell, May 25, 1988, Southern Oral History Program, Southern Historical Collection, University of North Carolina, Chapel Hill.

20. Governor Luther H. Hodges, Thomas J. Pearsall, Paul A. Johnson, Robert E. Giles, and E. L. Rankin Jr., "Transcription [of] Session on History of the Integration Situation in North Carolina," September 3, 1960, Governor's Office, State Capitol, Raleigh. Southern Oral History Program, Southern Historical Collection, University of North Carolina, Chapel Hill (hereafter cited as "Transcribed Session").

21. The members were Dr. F. D. Bluford, president of North Carolina A&T College in Greensboro, Dr. J. W. Seabrook, president of Fayetteville Teachers College; and Hazel Parker, a state employee from Edgecombe County. For more on the black members, see Chafe, *Civilities*, 50; Luther H. Hodges, *Businessman*, 83; and Covington and Ellis, *Terry Sanford*, 148.

22. Pearsall, "Transcribed Session."

23. Ibid.

24. The remaining members were Thomas J. Pearsall of Rocky Mount, William T. Joyner of Raleigh, R. O. Huffman of Morganton, State Senator Lunsford Crew of Roanoke Rapids, State Senator William Medford of Waynesville, State Representative Edward F. Yarborough of Louisburg, and State Representative H. Cloyd Philpott of Lexington. Hodges, *Businessman*, 82.

25. Hodges, *Businessman*, 83.

26. For evidence of black support for the NAACP and for the manner that Hodges actually, unwittingly, increased that support, see Chafe, *Civilities*, 60–64.

27. While it is important not to overstate this point, it is certainly true that many of the African Americans closest to the white leadership in the South were much more accustomed to a politics of accommodation than to outright confrontation. It is also true that the white leadership tended to surround itself with, and also be surrounded by, African Americans who were either employed by them directly or on the state payroll and therefore unlikely to endanger their own jobs by making defiant stands in favor of black rights. For more, see Chafe, *Civilities*, 45–46. Further, there was a tradition of black education that many African Americans themselves supported. See David S. Cecelski, *Along Freedom Road: Hyde County, North Carolina and the Fate of Black Schools in the South* (Chapel Hill: University of North Carolina Press, 1994).

28. Luther Hodges to Messrs. Pearsall, Taylor & Johnson, memorandum, August 22, 1955, Box 39, Folder: "Segregation, General, Luther Hodges Papers," NCSA.

29. Ibid. On September 2, 1955, William F. Bailey, of Raleigh, sent Hodges a letter concerning Dr. Murray B. Davis, "a High Point Negro." Bailey suggested that Hodges consider contacting Davis in the future, as an informer or ally. "Dr Davis is a Negro citizen of fine leadership," Bailey explained to Hodges, "and the thought occurred to me that you might utilize his services at some future date." William F. Bailey to Luther Hodges,

September 2, 1955, Box 39, Folder: Segregation Advisory Committee on Education, Luther Hodges Papers, NCSA. Hodges, in a return letter, thanked Bailey for the information, noting that he had "previously received reference to him" but would "pass on to the Advisory Committee on Education Dr. Davis name." Luther Hodges to William F. Bailey, September 8, 1955, Box 39, Folder: Segregation Advisory Committee on Education, Luther Hodges Papers, NCSA.

30. For black support of integration in Greensboro, independent of the NAACP's influence, see Chafe, *Civilities*. For black support of integration in Durham, see Christina Greene, *Our Separate Ways: Women and the Black Freedom Movement in Durham, North Carolina* (Chapel Hill: University of North Carolina Press, 2005). For black support of integration in Charlotte, see Davison M. Douglas, *Reading, Writing and Race: The Desegregation of the Charlotte Schools* (Chapel Hill: University of North Carolina Press, 1995). For black support of integration in Monroe, North Carolina, see Tyson, *Radio Free Dixie*, 74; but see Cecelski, *Freedom Road*, 59.

31. Hodges, *Businessman*, 83.

32. Pearsall, "Transcribed Session."

33. James Paul and Albert Coates, *The School Segregation Decision* (Chapel Hill: University of North Carolina Press, 1954). For more on the study, see Douglas, *Reading, Writing, and Race*, 27. Pearsall, "Transcribed Session."

34. Pearsall, "Transcribed Session." See also James C. N. Paul, *The School Segregation Decision: A Report to the Governor of North Carolina on the Decision of the Supreme Court of the United States on the 17th of May 1954* (Chapel Hill, N.C.: Institute of Government, 1954), 118–19.

35. The committee later gave credit to Mississippi for the statute. See "Transcription Session."

36. Ibid.

37. Robert E. Giles, "Transcribed Session."

38. Pearsall, "Transcribed Session."

39. Some historians confuse North Carolina's placement, or assignment, plan with the Pearsall Plan. See Timothy Tyson, *Radio Free Dixie*, 75; Christina Greene, *Our Separate Ways*, 52. Yet, the two were different. Pupil placement was enacted in 1955. The Pearsall Plan, however, was enacted in 1956. Its central tenet was the devolution of power over schools to the district level, the authorization of local school boards to close public schools pursuant to popular vote, and the transfer of state funds to children who needed tuition to attend private schools.

40. Pearsall, "Transcribed Session."

41. Paul A. Johnston, "Transcribed Session."

42. For a survey of white attitudes toward integration in Guilford County, North Carolina, in 1957, see Tumin, *Desegregation*.

43. For the argument that Jim Crow was a moderate legalist strategy, see Cell, *The Highest Stage of White Supremacy*, 233. C. Vann Woodward confirmed Cell's conclusions in a review, "The Edifice of Domination," *New Republic* (Dec. 27, 1982): 33–35.

44. Luther H. Hodges, "Address by Governor Luther H. Hodges of North Carolina on State-wide Radio-Television Network," August 8, 1955, Box 39, Folder: Segregation Advisory Committee on Integration," Luther Hodges Papers, NCSA.

45. Cell, *The Highest Stage of White Supremacy*, 233, 176–77.

46. James L. Leloudis, *Schooling the New South: Pedagogy, Self, and Society in North Carolina, 1880–1920* (Chapel Hill: University of North Carolina Press, 1996), 177–78; Glenda E. Gilmore, *Gender and Jim Crow: Women and the Politics of White Supremacy in North Carolina, 1896–1920* (Chapel Hill: University of North Carolina Press, 1996), 158.

47. Luther H. Hodges, "Address by Governor Luther H. Hodges of North Carolina on State-wide Radio-Television Network," August 8, 1955, Box 39, Folder: Segregation Advisory Committee on Integration," Luther Hodges Papers, NCSA.

48. Luther H. Hodges, "Address by Governor Luther H. Hodges before the North Carolina Teachers' Association," Shaw University, August 26, 1955, Box 39, Folder, Segregation: General, NCSA.

49. Ibid.

50. Luther H. Hodges, "Address by Governor Luther H. Hodges of North Carolina on State-wide Radio-Television Network," August 8, 1955, Box 39, Folder: Segregation Advisory Committee on Integration," Luther Hodges Papers, NCSA.

51. Ibid.

52. Ibid.

53. Morton Sosna, *In Search of the Silent South: Southern Liberals and the Race Issue* (New York: Columbia University Press, 1977), 44–45.

54. Luther H. Hodges, "Address by Governor Luther H. Hodges of North Carolina on State-Wide Radio-Television Network," August 8, 1955, Box 39, Folder: Segregation Advisory Committee on Integration, Luther Hodges Papers, NCSA.

55. Ibid.

56. Cortez Puryear to Luther Hodges, August 15, 1955, Box 39; Folder: Segregation, General, Luther Hodges Papers, NCSA.

57. Ibid.

58. Ibid.

59. Ibid.

60. Luther H. Hodges, "Address by Governor Luther H. Hodges of North Carolina on State-wide Radio-Television Network," August 8, 1955, Box 39, Folder: Segregation Advisory Committee on Integration," Luther Hodges Papers, NCSA.

61. Ibid. For further evidence of Hodges's attempts to coerce blacks in North Carolina, see Chafe, *Civilities*, 52.

62. Woodward, *Strange Career*, 91.

63. Hodges, *Businessman*, 89.

64. Paul A. Johnston, "Transcribed Session." But see Charles Eagles, who argues that Jonathan Daniels believed voluntary segregation and its

descendant, freedom of choice, to have been positive steps toward gradual integration (*Jonathan Daniels*, 179).

65. Luther H. Hodges, "Transcription Session."

66. Hodges's negative reception hinged not only on his message but also on the manner in which he delivered it. According to accounts in the black *Carolina Times*, the reason for Hodges's negative reception was his mispronunciation of "Negro," making it sound like "nirrer." See "The A. and T. Affair," *Carolina Times*, Nov. 12, 1955; according to William Chafe and Timothy Tyson, Hodges mistakenly referred to blacks as "nigras." See *Civilities*, 61, and *Radio Free Dixie*, 107, respectively. Luther H. Hodges, "Transcribed Session."

67. *Brown v. Board of Education*, 349 U.S. 294 (1955), commonly referred to as *Brown II*.

68. "Transcribed Session."

69. According to Matthew Lassiter, it "shattered the psychological, political, and legal barriers of the Solid South"; see Matthew D. Lassiter, *The Silent Majority: Suburban Politics in the Sunbelt South* (Princeton, N.J.: Princeton University Press, 2006), 40.

70. Ibid.

71. Davison Douglas sees Hodges's endorsement of the school closing provision in the Pearsall Plan as a significant shift toward extremism. Prior to the enactment of the Pearsall Plan, for example, Davison contends that Hodges was committed to keeping schools open rather than empowering local districts to close them. Yet, Douglas fails to note that Hodges continued to emphasize open schools, even after endorsing the Pearsall Plan. In fact, according to him, the Pearsall Plan coincided with his interest in open schools partly by placing a burden on parents who chose to go such a route yet also limiting the damage to local communities and not the entire state, as I. Beverly Lake arguably wanted. See Douglas, *Reading, Writing and Race*, 36.

72. "Operation or Closing Is Made Local Option," *Durham Morning Herald*, July 15, 1956, 1.

73. Robert E. Giles, "Transcribed Session."

74. It is unlikely that Lake actually believed the Supreme Court would endorse publicly funded private schools. Lake personally did much of the work on a brief submitted to the Court by North Carolina for the implementation phase of the *Brown* ruling. He even argued the brief before the Supreme Court, conceding that North Carolina law provided for the admission of African American students to white schools. As he began to contemplate running for governor, however, he began to distance himself from such arguments, and even from arguing segregation cases. This led members of Hodges's administration to doubt Lake's commitment to realistic legal solutions and to suspect him of political opportunism. "Transcribed Session"; Hodges, *Businessman*, 98, 100.

75. Johnston, "Transcribed Session."

76. Pearsall, "Transcribed Session."

77. Ibid.

78. Ibid.

79. Johnston, "Transcribed Session."

80. "Powerful Solons Back Measure Proposed by Lake," *Durham Morning Herald*, July 25, 1956. "Pearsall Plan Invalid, Duke Law Prof Says," *Durham Morning Herald*, July 25, 1956.

81. Bartley, *Rise*, 146–47.

82. Ibid., 148.

83. Luther H. Hodges, "Address by Governor Luther H. Hodges," Sept. 7, 1956, Box 120, Folder: Public School Amendment, Luther Hodges Papers, NCSA, 3.

84. Ibid. See also "Pearsall Plan Attacks Questioned: Hodges Hits Press Segments," *Durham Morning Herald*, Sept. 5, 1956, 1.

85. Ibid.

86. Ibid. William H. Chafe discredits Hodges's fears of white violence, positing that Hodges used such fears to advance his own political agenda, which was to set the terms of the desegregation debate in favor of a legalist strategy of noncompliance. While this is a compelling thesis, it fails to take into consideration the fact that white violence did result in other, arguably peripheral states, like Tennessee, Texas, and Arkansas. Though this does not mean that Chafe is wrong, necessarily, it does suggest that a proactive approach, like the one Hodges took in North Carolina, might have prevented violence, and better preserved segregation, in these states. See Chafe, *Civilities*, 58–69.

87. Luther H. Hodges, "Address by Governor Luther H. Hodges," Sept. 7, 1956, Box 120, Folder: Public School Amendment, Luther Hodges Papers, NCSA.

88. The moderate "leaders" in question were Tennessee Governor Frank Clement, Texas Governor Allan Shivers, Alabama Governor James Folsom, and Arkansas Governor Orval Faubus (before he embraced massive resistance). See Black, *Southern Governors*.

89. The survey was conducted in Guilford County by Melvin Tumin and Princeton graduate students in 1957; see Tumin, *Desegregation*.

90. Luther H. Hodges, "Address by Governor Luther H. Hodges," Sept. 7, 1956, Box 120, Folder: Public School Amendment, Luther Hodges Papers, NCSA, 4.

91. Ibid.

92. "Southern Chiefs Meet for Parley," *New York Times*, Sept. 10, 1956, 17.

93. Luther Hodges, "Problems of Illegitimacy," *Greensboro Record*, Oct. 5, 1956, Luther Hodges Papers, Box 128, Folder: Welfare, Illegitimacy," NCSA.

94. Ibid.

95. For example, Hodges's worst fear, at least as he articulated it to blacks, was over. No longer did he confront the threat that black intransigence might lead to massive statewide school closures but, thanks to the

safety valves in the Pearsall Plan, any school closures would be limited to local districts.

96. "Table 29, Illegitimate Live Births by Age of Mother and Color," *Vital Statistics of the United States, 1955.*

97. The fact that there were no licensed maternity homes for unwed black mothers became a matter of some concern to the State Board of Public Welfare in 1955. "Minutes of Administrative Conference with County Superintendents of Public Welfare," May 24–26, 1955, NCSA.

98. Moya Woodside, *Sterilization in North Carolina: A Sociological and Psychological Study* (Chapel Hill: University of North Carolina Press, 1950), 157.

99. In 1954, North Carolina Welfare Commissioner Ellen Winston ordered African American welfare officer John R. Larkins to take proactive steps to reduce rates of unwed pregnancy in black communities. Larkins responded by meeting with African American leaders in heavily black Northampton County and, with their help, establishing a pilot program to address the problem. His program included setting up an educational program aimed at teenagers, talking to police and courts, removing home sanctions against unwed mothers, and helping support unwed mothers during pregnancy. See Joseph L. Morrison, "Illegitimacy, Sterilization and Racism: A North Carolina Case History," *Social Service Review* (March 1965): 4.

100. Stephen Wallace Taylor provides insight into the economic and political climate of western North Carolina, and Bryson City in particular, in *The New South's New Frontier: A Social History of Economic Development in Southwestern North Carolina* (Gainesville: University Press of Florida, 2001).

101. "Dr. Winston Opposes Speight Bill," *News & Observer* (Raleigh), April 2, 1957; "Court Clerks Claim Welfare Bill Saddles Them with Extra Work," *News & Observer* (Raleigh), March 6, 1957.

102. Bartley, *Rise*, 94–96.

103. Curtis Flanagan to Luther Hodges, October 25, 1956. Box 128s, Folder, Welfare: Illegitimacy, Luther Hodges Papers, NCSA.

104. "Investigation of Public School Conditions," Report of the Subcommittee to Investigate Public School Standards and Conditions and Juvenile Delinquency in the District of Columbia of the Committee on the District of Columbia, House of Representatives, 84th Congress, Second Session (Washington, D.C.: United States Government Printing Office, 1957), 45. Call number: H1388.

105. "Sordld Facts Revealed by D.C. Probe," *Citizens' Council*, October 1956, 3.

106. Curtis Flanagan to Luther Hodges, October 25, 1956. Box 128s, Folder, Welfare: Illegitimacy, Luther Hodges Papers, NCSA.

107. "New Welfare Law Is Urged," clipping attached to letter, James H. Cummings to Luther Hodges, Oct. 8, 1956, Box 128, Folder, Welfare: Illegitimacy, Luther Hodges Papers, NCSA; "Court Clerks Claim."

108. "State System of Family Courts Is Proposed," *News & Observer* (Raleigh), March 14, 1957.

109. "Bill to Promote Delinquency," *News & Observer* (Raleigh), March 22, 1957.

110. "Family Court Bill Heads toward Legislative Grave," *News & Observer* (Raleigh), March 29, 1957.

111. "Court Clerks Claim."

112. For racial breakdowns by county in North Carolina, see V. O. Key, *Southern Politics*, 216.

113. Dr. Winston Opposes Speight Bill," *News & Observer* (Raleigh), April 2, 1957.

114. Ibid.

115. "Jolly's Bill Is Approved," *News & Observer* (Raleigh), May 1, 1957, 3.

116. Johanna Schoen, *Choice & Coercion: Birth Control, Sterilization, and Abortion in Public Health and Welfare* (Chapel Hill: University of North Carolina Press, 2005).

117. "The Human Betterment League of North Carolina: 20th Anniversary," brochure issued by the Human Betterment League of North Carolina, Winston-Salem, 1967, Box 993, 1958–59 Minutes Folder, Guion Johnson Papers, UNC–CH.

118. Ibid.

119. Ibid.

120. Historian Edward J. Larson shows that sterilization was not initially viewed as punishment but a type of state-sponsored, progressive project to uplift whites. Edward J. Larson, *Sex, Race, and Science: Eugenics in the Deep South* (Baltimore: Johns Hopkins University Press, 1995).

121. Johanna Schoen, *Choice & Coercion*. Some of it had to do with the women's movement and, in particular, demands that women be empowered to make their own reproductive choices, free from interference by the state. Johanna Schoen discusses the interaction between discourses of the women's rights movement, post–World War II era anti-Nazism, and race in *A Great Thing for Poor Folks: Birth Control, Sterilization and Abortion in Public Health and Welfare in the Twentieth Century*, unpublished dissertation, UNC Chapel Hill Department of History, 1995. Schoen notes, for example, that "[s]tate-supported sterilization in North Carolina began its decline in the early 1960s, when the civil rights and women's rights movements contributed to a new understanding of an individual's personal rights" (53). For a general history of eugenics, see Daniel J. Kevles, *In the Name of Eugenics: Eugenics and the Uses of Human Heredity* (New York: Alfred A. Knopf, 1985).

122. "Senators Reject Sterilization as the Answer to Illegitimacy," *News & Observer* (Raleigh), May 15, 1957, 1.

123. Ibid.

124. "More on Sterilization," *News & Observer* (Raleigh), April 11, 1957, 4.

125. "Hodges Favors Tighter Control over Funds for Unwed Mothers," *News & Observer* (Raleigh), May 14, 1957, 3.

126. "Senators Reject Sterilization as the Answer to Illegitimacy," *News & Observer* (Raleigh), May 15, 1957.

127. Ibid.

128. "Seek Enlarged Integration in North Carolina Schools," *News from NAACP,* July 25, 1957, NAACP Papers, Part III, Series D. Reel 8, Library of Congress, Washington, D.C.

129. Ibid.

130. Hodges, *Businessman,* 121.

131. For more discussion, see Anders Walker, "Raising the Bar: *Brown* and the Transformation of the Southern Judiciary," *Saint Louis University Law Journal* 48 (Spring 2004): 1051–57.

132. "Klan-Indian Violence Is Feared in North Carolina Area," *New York Times,* January 17, 1958, 10.

133. "Raid by 500 Indians Balks North Carolina Klan Rally," *New York Times,* January 19, 1958, 1.

134. Luther Hodges, "Statement by Governor Luther H. Hodges," January 30, 1958, Box 312, Folder: "Segregation: Miscellaneous," Luther Hodges Papers, NCSA.

135. Ibid.

136. Ibid.

137. Ibid.

138. For the role of northern media in the civil rights struggle, see Gene Roberts and Hank Klibanoff, *The Race Beat: The Press, the Civil Rights Struggle, and the Awakening of a Nation* (New York: Alfred A. Knopf, 2006).

139. Agent L. E. Allen to Walter F. Anderson, "Ku Klux Klan Meeting, Klavern #8—Jamestown, N.C." July 20, 1958. Box 313, Folder: Segregation, KKK, Luther Hodges Papers, NCSA.

140. Agent L. E. Allen to The [S.B.I.] Director, "KKK Activities, Greensboro, North Carolina," January 27, 1958, Box 313, Folder: Segregation, KKK, Luther Hodges Papers, NCSA.

141. Ibid.

142. Luther Hodges, "Statement by Governor Luther H. Hodges," January 30, 1958, Box 312, Folder: Segregation, Miscellaneous, Luther Hodges Papers, NCSA.

143. Agent L. E. Allen to The [S.B.I.] Director, "KKK Activities, Greensboro, North Carolina," January 27, 1958, Box 313, Folder: Segregation, KKK, Luther Hodges Papers, NCSA.

144. Ibid.

145. Ibid.

146. Luther Hodges, "Statement by Governor Luther H. Hodges," January 30, 1958, Box 312, Folder: "Segregation: Miscellaneous," Luther Hodges Papers, NCSA. For example, on July 20, 1958, S.B.I. agent L. E. Allen sent a memo to the governor's office describing a recent meeting of a White Citizens Council in Greensboro, North Carolina. According to the memo, nineteen people were present, and the speaker, a Reverend George F. Dorsett, "made derogatory remarks toward Governor Luther Hodges

and Attorney General Malcolm B. Seawell." The informer at the meeting, according to the memo, was a local sheriff named O. T. Jones, who had been cooperating with the State Bureau of Investigation. Agent L. E. Allen to Walter F. Anderson, "White Citizens Council Meeting, June 17, 1958—Greensboro, North Carolina," July 20, 1958, Box 313, Folder: Segregation, Governor Luther Hodges Papers, NCSA.

147. Tyson, *Radio -Free Dixie*, 64.

148. Oscar L. Richardson to Luther Hodges, undated except for mention that original was sent to Mr. "T" Taylor, presumably of the Education Advisory Commission, on September 22, 1955. Box 39, Folder: Segregation, Advisory Commission on Education, Luther Hodges Papers, NCSA.

149. Tim Tyson recounts the "kissing case," as it came to be called, in considerable detail in *Radio-Free Dixie*, 90–136.

150. George L. Weissman, "The Kissing Case," *Nation*, Jan. 17, 1959, 46.

151. Luther Hodges to George V. Allen, February 12, 1959, Box 422, Folder: Segregation, Union County, General, Luther Hodges Papers, NCSA.

152. Mary L. Dudziak, "Desegregation as a Cold War Imperative," 41 *Stanford Law Review* (November 1988). For Cold War propaganda and race in North Carolina, Tyson, see *Radio-Free Dixie*, 68.

153. Luther Hodges to George V. Allen, February 12, 1959, Box 422, Folder: Segregation, Union County, General, Luther Hodges Papers, NCSA.

154. Ibid.

155. "Statement by Blaine M. Madison, Commissioner, Board of Correction and Training," January 2, 1959, Box 421, Folder: Monroe Kissing Case, Luther Hodges Papers, NCSA.

156. Ibid.

157. Luther Hodges to George V. Allen, February 12, 1959, Box 422, Folder: Segregation, Union County, General, Luther Hodges Papers, NCSA.

158. Luther Hodges to Canon L. John Collins, St. Paul's Cathedral, London, England, January 2, 1959, Box 421, Folder: Monroe Kissing Case, Luther Hodges Papers, NCSA.

159. Ibid.

160. Ibid.

161. Tyson, *Radio-Free Dixie*, 134–35.

162. Luther Hodges to Ellen Winston, Jan. 6, 1959, Box 358, Folder: Illeg. Children, Luther Hodges Papers, NCSA.

163. Ellen Winston to Luther Hodges, Feb. 3, 1959, Box 358, Folder: Illeg. Children, Luther Hodges Papers, NCSA.

164. Ibid.

165. Luther Hodges to Rachel Davis, 12 February 1959, Luther Hodges Papers, Box 358, Illegitimate Children Folder, NCSA.

166. Ibid.

167. The bill is described in a letter by Estelle Marie Deres to Luther Hodges, March 12, 1959, Box 358, Folder: Illeg. Children, Luther Hodges Papers, NCSA.

168. "Franklin's Jolly Headed Survival Unit," *Durham Morning Herald*, June 17, 1959, North Carolina Collection Clipping File through 1975, UNC–CH.

169. Ibid.

170. "Racial Flareup Winds Up Hearing on Sterilization," *News & Observer* (Raleigh), April 2, 1959.

171. "Lady Members Had Their Voice in 1959 Law-Making Session," *News & Observer* (Raleigh), June 16, 1959. Davis recommended that Alabama, Florida, Georgia, Louisiana, Mississippi, South Carolina, Tennessee, Virginia, Illinois, New York, and the District of Columbia also be joined in the study because they, like North Carolina, "have illegitimacy problems." See "Crime Study Group Proposed in Assembly," *News & Observer* (Raleigh), June 3, 1959, 3.

172. Guy B. Johnson was a social scientist at the University of North Carolina, Chapel Hill. He worked with sociologists like Howard Odum on the moderate, racially progressive Commission on Interracial Cooperation. See Kluger, *Simple Justice*, 312. He also participated in Gunnar Myrdal's writing of *An American Dilemma*; see Kluger, *Simple Justice*, 313, 343–44.

173. "The Problem of Births Out of Wedlock," report prepared by the Technical SubCommittee of the Committee on Children and Youths, North Carolina Conference for Social Service, Raleigh, April 1959. Rickie Solinger discusses the way in which formal adoption favored whites in *Wake Up Little Susie: Single Pregnancy and Race before* Roe v. Wade (New York: Routledge, 1992). According to her, "[a]doption, which was, of course, not an option for most blacks, was the most important factor in removing white children from would-be ADC families" (193).

174. "The Problem of Births Out of Wedlock," report prepared by the Technical Subcommittee of the Committee on Children and Youths, North Carolina Conference for Social Service, Raleigh, April 1959.

175. Ibid.

176. Davis summarized her personal views of culture before a group of sorority sisters at the University of North Carolina in Chapel Hill. "With the shifting ratios of humans to the earth's surface," Davis told a gathering of Chi Omegas, "rose our great social conscience, and our great sociological scientific concepts for a human culture composed of the providors [*sic*] and the dependants [*sic*]." Providers and dependents, Davis explained, referred to types of people. Providers were those who could "maintain and improve [their] genetic qualities [by] sublimat[ing] [their] breeding to the acquiring of the material, the intellectual, the cultural, the aesthetic and the non-genetic creative." Dependents, on the other hand, "know not and practice not genetic sublimation." The racial implications of Davis's speech were relatively clear. Blacks (and perhaps even some whites) constituted dependents. They did not create anything of value nor, implied Davis, would they. It was therefore imperative that white undergraduates perpetuate civilization through selective breeding. "Acquire learning," Davis told her young listeners, "develop perspectives with directions, find your opportunity—you

have one—and purposely with disciplined control live well, mate well and breed well, and breed with a genetic consciousness and with Eugenic responsibility." Rachel Davis, "The Need for Genetic Responsibility," address before Epsilon Beta of Chi Omega, University of North Carolina, Chapel Hill, upon being presented the North Carolina Distinguished Service Award. North Carolina Collection, University of North Carolina, Chapel Hill.

177. Lala Williams and Nannie Lyons to Luther Hodges, April 13, 1959, Box 358, Illegitimate Children Folder, Governor Luther Hodges Papers, North Carolina State Archives, Raleigh.

178. Ibid.

179. "Racial Flareup Winds Up Hearing on Sterilization," *News & Observer* (Raleigh), April 2, 1959.

180. Ibid.

181. Rickie Solinger discusses how services available to unwed mothers differed according to race, both in the South and nationally, in *Wake Up Little Susie*, 69–70.

182. Ibid.

183. Ellen Winston, "Unmarried Parents and Their Children: Services in the Decades Ahead," speech delivered by Ellen Winston to the Florence Crittenton Association, National Conference for Social Welfare, Grand Ballroom, Sheraton-Cleveland, Cleveland, Ohio, May 23, 1963 (p. 24). Ellen Winston Papers, UNC–G.

184. "Davis-Jolly Morals Bill Is Discarded," *News & Observer* (Raleigh), April 22, 1959, 1.

185. Ibid.

186. "Sterilized Illegitimacy Bill Okayed," *News & Observer* (Raleigh), May 30, 1959, 3.

187. "Davis-Jolly Morals Bill Is Discarded," *News & Observer* (Raleigh), April 22, 1959, 1.

188. "Mrs. Boyce Hunter of Charlotte, national president of the Florence Crittenden Home Assn., said a requirement for keeping records on illegitimate births with district solicitors could have harmful effects. The threat of disclosure, she explained, could drive unmarried pregnant women to move out of the state, go to abortionists, or have their babies at home rather than permit their names to go on records of welfare departments and district solicitors." "Other objections came from Blair Daily, Greensboro lawyer, speaking for the North Carolina Children's Home Society. . . . 'It would deny the families involved the opportunity to make a healthy adjustment,' he said. 'In 90 percent of the cases (of illegitimacy), the family makes its own adjustment and receives no welfare aid.'" "Davis-Jolly Substitute Is Opposed," *News & Observer* (Raleigh), May 7, 1959, 10.

189. H. Galt Braxton to Carl Venters, 12 May 1959. Box 358, Illegitimate Children Folder, Governor Luther Hodges's Papers, North Carolina State Archives, Raleigh.

190. H. Galt Braxton, "Such Legislation Would Be a Black Mark," *Kinston Daily Free Press*, May 11, 1959.

191. Ibid.

192. Ibid.

193. "Sterilized Illegitimacy Bill Okayed," *News & Observer* (Raleigh), May 30, 1959, 3.

194. Ibid.

195. "Davis-Jolly Morals Bill Is Discarded," *News & Observer* (Raleigh), April 22, 1959, 1.

196. "Crew Bill Debate Delayed," *News & Observer* (Raleigh), April 25, 1959, 3.

197. "Bill to Punish Unwed Mothers Passes Senate," *News & Observer* (Raleigh), May 1, 1959, 1.

198. Ibid.

199. "Senate Favors Crew Plan for Checking Illegitimacy," *News & Observer* (Raleigh), April 30, 1959, 1.

200. "Illegitimacy Bill Is Defeated," *News & Observer* (Raleigh), June 18, 1959, 8.

201. "Senate Enacts Davis-Jolly Sub," *News & Observer* (Raleigh), June 19, 1959, 6.

202. Luther H. Hodges, "Address by Governor Luther H. Hodges of North Carolina on State-wide Radio-Television Network," August 8, 1955, Box 39, Folder: Segregation Advisory Committee on Integration," Luther Hodges Papers, NCSA.

203. "Coleman Sees Lessening of Desegregation Pressure," *Jackson Daily News*, February 17, 1956.

Chapter Three

1. For more on the Tallahassee boycott, see Glenda Alice Rabby, *The Pain and the Promise: The Struggle for Civil Rights in Tallahassee, Florida* (Athens: University of Georgia Press, 1999); Aldon Morris, *The Origins of the Civil Rights Movement: Black Communities Organizing for Change* (New York: Free Press, 1984), 63–68.

2. For accounts of the attacks, see Rabby, *Pain*; and Wagy, *Governor LeRoy Collins*. For the leadership of C. K. Steele and Daniel Speed, see Morris, *Origins*, 42.

3. LeRoy Collins, Proclamation Regarding Suspension of Bus Service in Tallahassee, January 1, 1957, LeRoy Collins Papers, Box 116, Folder 12, Florida State Archives (FSA), Tallahassee, Florida.

4. Luther Hodges to LeRoy Collins, January 3, 1957, Box 116, Folder 12, FSA.

5. This was a common view among journalists at the time, and it persists in academic treatments of Collins's career. See, for example, "Florida's Governor LeRoy Collins," *Time*, December 19, 1955; William C. Havard and Loren P. Beth, *The Politics of Mis-Representation: Rural-Urban Conflict in the Florida Legislature* (Baton Rouge: Louisiana State University Press, 1962); Reed Sarratt, *The Ordeal of Desegregation* (New York: Harper & Row,

1966); Helen L. Jacobstein, *The Segregation Factor in the Florida Democratic Gubernatorial Primary of 1956* (Gainesville: University of Florida Press, 1972); Black, *Southern Governors*, 93–96; David R. Colburn and Richard K. Scher, *Florida's Gubernatorial Politics in the Twentieth Century* (Tallahassee: University Presses of Florida, 1980); Wagy, *Governor LeRoy Collins*; Numan V. Bartley, *The New South, 1945–1980* (Baton Rouge: Louisiana State University Press, 1985); David R. Colburn, "Florida's Governors Confront the Brown Decision: A Case Study of the Constitutional Politics of School Desegregation, 1954–1970" in *An Uncertain Tradition: Constitutionalism and the History of the South*, Kermit L. Hall and James W. Ely Jr., eds. (Athens: University of Georgia Press, 1989); Chappell, *Inside Agitators*.

6. Steven F. Lawson, David R. Colburn, and Darryl Paulson, "Groveland: Florida's Little Scottsboro" in *The African American Heritage of Florida*, David R. Colburn and Jane L. Landers, eds. (Gainesville: University Press of Florida, 1995), 318.

7. "Governor LeRoy Collins: Inaugural Address," January 8, 1957, LeRoy Collins Papers, FSA.

8. Frances Fox Piven and Richard A. Cloward, *Regulating the Poor: The Functions of Public Welfare*, 2nd ed. (New York: Vintage, 1993), 139–40.

9. LeRoy Collins, "Statement by Governor LeRoy Collins," February 2, 1956, LeRoy Collins Papers, Box 140, Folder: Unmarked, University of South Florida, Tampa, Florida.

10. Ibid.

11. LeRoy Collins, Press Conference, Thursday, February 12, 1959. LeRoy Collins Papers, Claude Pepper Library, Florida State University, Tallahassee, Florida.

12. Chappell, *Inside Agitators*, xxv.

13. David L. Chappell is correct when he argues that Collins's moderation gave black activists some leverage in making demands. However, Chappell underestimates the extent to which this moderation prevented more substantive change at the constitutional level. See *Inside Agitators*, 212–27.

14. LeRoy Collins, "Statement by Governor LeRoy Collins to Conference on Segregation," March 21, 1956, Box 140, Folder F, LeRoy Collins Papers, University of South Florida, Tampa, Florida.

15. Assessments of Collins's gubernatorial career range from Reed Sarratt's laudatory praise in *The Ordeal of Desegregation* to Tom R. Wagy's more substantial but not particularly critical *Governor LeRoy Collins*. See also Colburn, "Florida's Governors Confront the *Brown* Decision"; Colburn and Scher, *Florida's Gubernatorial Politics*; Black, *Southern Governors*, 93–96; and Chappell, *Inside Agitators*, 84–96. Not surprisingly, the most critical account of Collins comes from a civil rights movement perspective; see Rabby, *The Pain and the Promise*.

16. Eastman was founded by Poughkeepsie Mayor Harvey G. Eastman, a contemporary of Matthew Vassar, in 1859, during an era when business education was left to private interests. For more on Collins's background,

see LeRoy Collins and Robert H. Akerman, *The Man in the Middle: A Story of America's Race Crisis*, unpublished manuscript, LeRoy Collins Papers, Claude Pepper Library, Florida State University; and Wagy, *Governor LeRoy Collins*, 3–34.

17. Collins and Akerman, *The Man in the Middle*, 42.

18. Ibid.

19. Wagy, *Governor LeRoy Collins*, 18–33.

20. Collins ran successfully for the State House of Representatives in 1934, shortly after graduating from law school. At the time, he was only twenty-five. From 1935 until his election to governor in 1954, with a brief hiatus during World War II, Collins served in the state legislature, first as a representative and then as a senator. See Wagy, *Governor LeRoy Collins*, 3–17.

21. Collins and Akerman, *The Man in the Middle*, 44–45.

22. Ibid., 47.

23. Collins's willingness to reflect on his early views of segregation, something that he did in his unpublished memoirs, provides a rare window into the mind of a moderate southern governor in the 1950s. It is also worthy of some comment. Unlike Luther Hodges and J. P. Coleman, who never expressed any regret or remorse over the racial views they held in the 1950s, Collins underwent something of a public transformation in his racial views in the 1960s. This transformation, which helps to explain why he lost a race for the Senate in 1968, began gradually in the early 1960s and coincided roughly with the victories of the civil rights movement. As Collins later explained it, these victories educated him about the plight of blacks in the South. Prior to this education, he admitted willingly, he simply had not seen segregation in a discriminatory light, nor had he seen African Americans as an oppressed class. One of Collins's first public assertions that segregation was morally wrong occurred during a 1960 speech after the first round of sit-ins in Tallahassee. LeRoy Collins, Interview, Jack Bass and Walter De Vries, May 19, 1974, Tallahassee, Florida, Southern Oral History Program, #4007, Southern Historical Collection, University of North Carolina at Chapel Hill; Collins and Akerman, *The Man in the Middle*, 47.

24. LeRoy Collins, *Forerunners Courageous: Stories of Frontier Florida* (Tallahassee: Colcade, 1971).

25. This became obvious during a sociological study conducted by Lewis M. Killian over the summer of 1954. See Lewis M. Killian, *Black and White: Reflections of a White Southern Sociologist* (Dix Hills, N.Y.: General Hall, 1994), 80–81.

26. Gilmore, *Gender & Jim Crow*.

27. For a brief discussion of national attitudes toward Reconstruction during the first two decades of the twentieth century, see Woodward, *Strange Career*, 69–74. Claude Bowers, *The Tragic Era* (New York: Houghton Mifflin, 1929). For one of the first challenges to the argument that Reconstruction was corrupt, see W. E. B. DuBois, *Black Reconstruction* (New York: Harcourt Brace, 1935).

28. For more on Jim Crow's impact in Florida, see Paul Ortiz, *Emancipation Betrayed: The Hidden History of Black Organizing and White Violence in Florida from Reconstruction to the Bloody Election of 1920* (Berkeley: University of California Press, 2005). See also Nancy A. Hewitt, *Southern Discomfort: Women's Activism in Tampa, Florida, 1880s–1920s* (Urbana: University of Illinois Press, 2001).

29. Collins called integration ridiculous in an article written for *Look* magazine in 1958. See LeRoy Collins, "How It Looks from the South," *Look*, May 27, 1958.

30. Wagy, *Governor LeRoy Collins*, 32.

31. Collins and Akerman, *The Man in the Middle*, 40.

32. "Governor LeRoy Collins: Address to the Legislature," April 1955, reprinted in "Excerpts from Report of Saul A. Silverman, Staff Assistant to the Fowler Commission on Race Relations," LeRoy Collins Papers, Claude Pepper Library, Florida State University.

33. LeRoy Collins, Interview, Jack Bass and Walter De Vries, May 19, 1974, Tallahassee, Florida, Southern Oral History Program, #4007, Southern Historical Collection, University of North Carolina at Chapel Hill, 12.

34. For more on the study, see Killian, *Black and White*, 76. For a brief description of Florida's cabinet system, see Colburn and Scher, *Florida's Gubernatorial Politics*, 110. Members of the governor's cabinet, like the attorney general, were not appointed by the governor but independently elected. This meant that cabinet members could remain in office even as governors changed, resulting in a bizarre type of seniority over state governors.

35. Lewis M. Killian, "The Report and Conclusions," filed with "Amicus Curiae Brief of the Attorney General of Florida," *Brown et al. v. Board of Education of Topeka*, October 1, 1954.

36. Ibid.

37. Richard W. Ervin, "Amicus Curiae Brief of the Attorney General of Florida," *Brown et al. v. Board of Education of Topeka*, October 1, 1954.

38. Ibid.

39. Ibid.

40. Ibid. Quoting Hodding Carter, "The Court's Decision and the South," *Reader's Digest*, September 1954.

41. Ibid.

42. Ibid.

43. For more on *Brown II*, see Richard Kluger, *Simple Justice*, 714–44; Michael J. Klarman, *From Jim Crow to Civil Rights*, 312–20.

44. "Governor LeRoy Collins: Inaugural Address, January 4, 1955," LeRoy Collins Papers, FSA.

45. "Excerpts from Report of Saul A. Silverman, Staff Assistant to the Fowler Commission on Race Relations," LeRoy Collins Papers, Claude Pepper Library, Florida State University.

46. LeRoy Collins, "Race Relations 1954–1960: Excerpts from Report of Saul A. Silverman, Staff Assistant to the Fowler Commission on Race

Relations," Special Collections, Claude Pepper Library, Florida State University, Tallahassee, Florida.

47. Collins and Akerman, *Man in the Middle*, 48.

48. LeRoy Collins to Leo Mindlin, February 12, 1957, Series 776, Box 37, LeRoy Collins Papers, FSA.

49. LeRoy Collins to Reverend Richard I. Brown, 17 May 1955, LeRoy Collins Papers, Series 776, Box 37, Segregation Folder, FSA.

50. Ibid.

51. Ibid.

52. Ibid.

53. Ibid.

54. Ibid.

55. Ibid.

56. Ibid.

57. Both seemed to adopt, at least publicly, a vision of the law very similar to that endorsed by William Graham Sumner in his classic *Folkways: A Study of the Sociological Importance of Usages, Manners, Customs, Mores, and Morals* (Boston: Ginn, 1906).

58. *Brown v. Board of Education (II)* 349 U.S. 294 (1955).

59. LeRoy Collins to Lee Davis, July 15, 1955, Series 776, Box 37, Folder: Segregation, LeRoy Collins Papers, FSA.

60. Michael Klarman (*From Jim Crow to Civil Rights*, 314–16) reveals that the Supreme Court supported gradualism more than the NAACP realized.

61. Parker's opinion in *Briggs* was handed down on July 15, 1955. See *Briggs v. Elliott*, 132 F. Supp. 776 (1955).

62. Jack Bass describes the manner in which Parker's opinion in *Briggs* opened the door for a substantial revision of *Brown*. See Jack Bass, *Unlikely Heroes: The Dramatic Story of the Southern Judges Who Translated the Supreme Court's Brown Decision into a Revolution for Equality* (New York: Simon & Schuster, 1981), 123–24. The Fifth Circuit endorsed Parker's view on January 9, 1957, in *Avery v. Wichita Falls*, 241 F.2d 230 (1957).

63. Bass, *Unlikely Heroes*, 124.

64. LeRoy Collins to Lee Davis, July 15, 1955, Series 776, Box 37, Folder: Segregation, LeRoy Collins Papers, FSA.

65. Collins and Akerman, *The Man in the Middle*, 48.

66. Collins signed the bill into law on May 30, 1955. See Chap. 29746, *Laws of Florida 1955*. Daniel J. Meador missed Florida's first placement act, prompting him to assert that Florida did not endorse pupil placement until 1956. See Meador, "The Constitution and the Assignment of Pupils," 527. For evidence that Florida's law was inspired by North Carolina's statute, see the discussion of pupil placement in Florida in "Call Due by Tomorrow to Enact School Plan," *Tallahassee Democrat*, July 17, 1956, 1.

67. Some take Collins's initial threat to veto pupil placement as evidence that he did not support it. However, a close look at his correspondence suggests that he did support it but was afraid it might derail the success of

the Ervin Brief. Once the Court accepted the arguments set forth in that brief, Collins endorsed pupil placement. LeRoy Collins to Lee Davis, July 15, 1955, Series 776, Box 37, Folder: Segregation, LeRoy Collins Papers, FSA.

68. Though governors usually serve four years, Collins's first term only lasted two years because his predecessor, Dan McCarty, had died in office, suddenly, in 1953. This meant that Collins, who took McCarty's place in 1955, only served one year before facing the prospect of running again in 1956. See Wagy, *Governor LeRoy Collins*, 35, 62.

69. Jacobstein, *The Segregation Factor*, 27.

70. Ibid.

71. LeRoy Collins, "Statement by Governor LeRoy Collins," February 2, 1956, Box 140, Folder unmarked, LeRoy Collins Papers, University of South Florida.

72. Ibid.

73. *Florida Ex. Rel. Hawkins v. Board of Control*, 350 U.S. 413 (1956).

74. *Sweatt v. Painter*, 339 U.S. 629 (1950). For a discussion of both *Sweatt* and its relations to Virgil Hawkins's case, see Klarman, *From Jim Crow to Civil Rights*, 253–58.

75. *Florida Ex. Rel. Hawkins v. Board of Control*, 350 U.S. 413 (1956).

76. LeRoy Collins, "Statement by Governor LeRoy Collins to Conference on Segregation," March 21, 1956, Box 140, Folder unmarked, LeRoy Collins Papers, University of South Florida, Tampa, Florida.

77. Ibid.

78. Further evidence of what transpired during the March 21, 1956, conference can be found in an untitled memo, dated April 12, 1956, in LeRoy Collins Papers, Series 776, Box 32, Folder, "Segregation Resolution," FSA. See also LeRoy Collins to Millard B. Smith, April 17, 1956, Series 776, Box 32, Folder, "Segregation Commission," FSA.

79. Ibid.

80. "Collins Plans Legislature Call if Needed: Pledges Step at Race-Mix Session Here," *Tallahassee Democrat*, May 1, 1956, 1.

81. Ibid.

82. "Florida Policy Switches to Resistance after Court's Ruling," *Southern School News*, April 1956, 9.

83. *Sweatt v. Painter*, 339 U.S. 629 (1950).

84. *Florida Ex. Rel. Hawkins v. Board of Control*, 350 U.S. 413 (1956).

85. Michael J. Klarman summarizes the Autherine Lucy case in *From Jim Crow to Civil Rights*, 258–59; see also Bartley, *Rise of Massive Resistance*, 146.

86. Morris, *Origins of the Civil Rights Movement*, 63–68; Wagy, *Governor LeRoy Collins*, 75–76.

87. "4-Point Legislative Plan Recommended; Supreme Court Hit," *Tallahassee Democrat*, July 16, 1954, 1.

88. "Special Session Called Monday: Governor Lists 5 Matters," *Tallahassee Democrat*, July 18, 1956, 2.

89. Ibid.

90. Malcolm Johnson, "Under the Dome," *Tallahassee Democrat*, July 26, 1956, 1.

91. "School Assignment Bill Passes House by 93–1, Senate Approves Four Race Bills," *Tallahassee Democrat*, July 24, 1956, 1.

92. Ibid.

93. "House Passes Resolution on State's Rights," *Tallahassee Democrat*, July 26, 1956, 1.

94. "NAACP Blasts School Plan," *Tallahassee Democrat*, July 24, 1956, 1.

95. "John Orr Says Segregation Is Morally Wrong," *Tallahassee Democrat*, July 26, 1956, 1.

96. "School Assignment Bill Passes House by 93–1, Senate Approves Four Race Bills," *Tallahassee Democrat*, July 24, 1956, 1.

97. "$7.5 Million Is Voted in Emergency Funds," *Tallahassee Democrat*, July 24, 1956, 2.

98. Ibid.

99. Lawson, Colburn, and Paulson, "Groveland: Florida's Little Scottsboro," 318.

100. *Shepherd v. Florida*, 341 U.S. 50 (1951).

101. Lawson, Colburn, and Paulson, "Groveland: Florida's Little Scottsboro," 315.

102. Klarman, *From Jim Crow to Civil Rights*, 275–77; Lawson, Colburn, and Paulson, "Groveland: Florida's Little Scottsboro."

103. Lawson, Colburn, and Paulson, "Groveland: Florida's Little Scottsboro," 318.

104. Collins and Akerman, *Man in the Middle*, 54–60.

105. "Call Due By Tomorrow to Enact School Plan: Session May Halt Mixing," *Tallahassee Democrat*, July 17, 1956, 1; "Segregation Group to Report Monday: Legislature's Call Depends on Findings," *Tallahassee Democrat*, July 12, 1956, 1.

106. "Experts Ask Program to Slow Racial Mixing," *Tallahassee Democrat*, July 16, 1956, 1.

107. Ibid.

108. Ibid.

109. "Call Due by Tomorrow to Enact School Plan: Session May Halt Mixing," *Tallahassee Democrat*, July 17, 1956, 1.

110. "Collins Urges Approval of Segregation Action: Governor Sees Best Plan of Any State; Warns of New Bills," *Tallahassee Democrat*, July 23, 1956, 1.

111. "School Assignment Bill Passes House by 93–1: Senate Approves Four Race Bills," *Tallahassee Democrat*, July 24, 1956, 1; "Collins Finds a Strange Session," *Tallahassee Democrat*, July 29, 1956, 2. That Collins enjoyed such success in the legislature is remarkable. Generally, deep divisions between representatives from the Panhandle and representatives from more urban, South Florida districts resulted in legislative clashes. See Havard and Beth, *The Politics of Mis-Representation*.

112. "Collins Finds a Strange Session," *Tallahassee Democrat*, July 29, 1956, 2.

113. "Call Due by Tomorrow to Enact School Plan: Session May Halt Mixing," *Tallahassee Democrat*, July 17, 1956, 1. David R. Colburn, "Florida's Governors Confront the Brown Decision," 333.

114. "Lowry Tells Collins to Use Interposition," *Tallahassee Democrat*, July 23, 1956, 1.

115. "Segregation Suggestions," *Tallahassee Democrat*, July 15, 1956, 6.

116. Announcement issued by Governor Collins, August 29, 1956, LeRoy Collins Papers, Series 776, Box 32, Segregation Commission Folder, FSA.

117. Ibid.

118. For an account of the ICC in Tallahassee, see Rabby, *The Pain and the Promise*; Morris, *The Origins of the Civil Rights Movement*.

119. Gaither, an employee of a state-funded university, and therefore at the mercy of state government for his salary, also stood to lose his football team if integration occurred. He feared that larger white schools would recruit his players, at that time some of the best in the country. Interview, James Eaton, Curator, Black Archives, Florida A&M University, September 2001. Notes in the author's possession.

120. Ibid.

121. Turning to a mildly coercive tone, Pompey implied that if the state did not help them gain their own beach, good relations between the races would break down, resulting in more agitation. "[T]he men, judging from the response to your message of yesterday and the good which is sure to eventuate from your expected report to Mr. Collins when he returns to the state, are perfectly content and willing to wait even longer, give the city all the time practible [*sic*] to negotiate the deal," they wrote. The concession hid within its language a mildly coercive threat. If the city did not negotiate a deal, then the Civic League would have no choice but to reactivate legal agitation, threatening Collins's interest in maintaining peace. "Moreover," the letter continued, "we strongly feel that with some urging from the state level there will be no need for further legal action and that the fine relations between the races which is the desire of us all will be reestablished and maintained." C. Spencer Pompey to A. S. Gaither, 29 May 1956, LeRoy Collins Papers, Series 776, Box 32, Segregation Folder, FSA.

122. Bob Saunders to Roy Wilkins, June 16, 1956, Part 20, Reel 6, NAACP Papers.

123. "Governor Raps NAACP Stand," *Tallahassee Democrat*, July 3, 1956, 1.

124. Ibid.

125. Ibid.

126. Morris, *Origins of the Civil Rights Movement*, 65.

127. R. J. Strickland, "Memorandum Report," Box 140, Folder: Tallahassee Bus Boycott, LeRoy Collins Papers, University of South Florida. For evidence that Strickland worked for the Legislative Investigation

Committee, see *Gibson v. Florida Legislative Comm.*, 372 U.S. 539 (1963). Rabby (*The Pain and the Promise*, 35) notes that Strickland also worked for the Tallahassee Police Department.

128. Strickland, "Memorandum Report."

129. Ibid.

130. Collins's role in founding the committee should not be overstated. It was really the brainchild of Charley Johns, Collins's opponent in the 1954 gubernatorial campaign. For a description of its work, see Steven F. Lawson, "The Florida Legislative Investigation Committee and the Constitutional Readjustment of Race Relations, 1956–1963," in *An Uncertain Tradition: Constitutionalism and the History of the South*, Kermit L. Hall and James W. Ely Jr., eds. (Athens: University of Georgia Press, 1989). See also Musselman to Collins, June 14, 1956, LeRoy Collins Papers, Series 776, Box 32, Segregation Folder, FSA.

131. Notes on Meeting of Bi-Racial Commission, November 20, 1956, LeRoy Collins Papers, Series 776, Box 32, Segregation Folder, FSA, 9.

132. John T. Wigginton to Joe Grotegut, 3 October 1956, LeRoy Collins Papers, Series 776, Box 32, Segregation Folder, FSA.

133. Ibid.

134. Ibid.

135. LeRoy Collins, "Law-Enforcement Agencies Should Be Proud of Teamwork," *St. Petersburg Times*, September 5, 1988, copy in Collins Papers, Box 466, Folder: "St. Pete Times Articles by Collins, 1988," University of South Florida, Tampa.

136. Ibid. On October 6, 1956, Collins's assistant, Joe Grotegut, asked John Wigginton to contact the Sheriff's Bureau and go ahead with the plan of notifying police about potential protests—but not to advertise it. "[T]he Sheriffs contacted," Grotegut ordered, "should understand, of course, the necessity for treating the matter on a confidential basis." Joe Grotegut to John Wigginton, October 6, 1956, LeRoy Collins Papers, Series 776, Box 32, Segregation Bi-Racial Commission Folder.

137. Kasper ignited what historian Michael Belknap would later call the worst outbreak of anti-integration violence that fall. See Michal R. Belknap, *Federal Law and the Southern Order: Racial Violence and Constitutional Conflict in the Post-;Brown South* (Athens: University of Georgia Press, 1987), 29.

138. Memo from Joe Grotegut to LeRoy Collins, 11 September 1956, LeRoy Collins Papers, Series 776, Box 32, Segregation Bi-Racial Commission Folder, FSA.

139. Ibid.

140. Ibid. Written in longhand by governor on memo.

141. "Notes on Meeting of Bi-Racial Commission, November 20, 1956, LeRoy Collins Papers, Series 776, Box 32, Segregation Folder, FSA, 4.

142. Minutes from Meeting of Governor's Advisory Commission on Bi-Racial Problems, March 5, 1957, LeRoy Collins Papers, Series 776, Box 117, Segregation Race Relations Folder, FSA, 7.

143. Ibid.

144. Ibid.

145. Ibid.

146. Ibid.

147. "Governor's Committee on Race Relations Operating Procedure," attached to letter from John Wigginton to Joe Grotegut, March 11, 1957, LeRoy Collins Papers, Series 776, Box 117, Segregation/Race Relations Folder, FSA.

148. Ibid.

149. Ibid.

150. "Statement by Governor Collins," November 19, 1956, LeRoy Collins Papers, Series 776, Box 32, Segregation Folder, FSA.

151. Ibid.

152. Ibid.

153. Lewis M. Killian, "Hypocrisy of 'Delay.'" *New South* 11 (June 1956): 3.

154. Ibid., 1.

155. "Suggested Studies Related to Negro Citizens," memorandum to Governor LeRoy Collins from Advisory Committee on Race Relations, January 4, 1957, LeRoy Collins Papers, Series 776B, Box 117, FSA.

156. Ibid.

157. Joe Grotegut, administrative assistant for LeRoy Collins, to Doak Campbell, L. L. Fabisinski, J. R. E. Lee, John T. Wigginton, J. Lewis Hall, John Blair, Thomas N. Morgan. No specified date, LeRoy Collins Papers, FSA.

158. Minutes from meeting of Governor's Advisory Commission on Bi-Racial Problems, March 26, 1957, LeRoy Collins Papers, Series 776B, Box 117, Segregation Race Relations Folder, FSA.

159. Ibid.

160. "The Governor's Message to the Legislature," April 2, 1957, Collins Papers, Box 2, Folder 1: Governor's Speeches, Claude Pepper Library, FSU. It is also possible that his views changed between January and March. On January 9, for example, five days after the Fabisinski Commission received its research assignment, the Fifth Circuit handed down an opinion endorsing Fourth Circuit Judge John Parker's reasoning in *Briggs v. Elliott, Avery v. Wichita Falls*, 241 F.2d 230 (5th Cir. 1957). In the ruling, the court all held that *Brown* did not require schools to integrate, only that students be allowed to choose the schools they wanted to attend. Dual schools, in other words, were legal not only in the relatively intransigent Fourth Circuit but also in the more forward-looking Fifth Circuit. Jack Bass (*Unlikely Heroes*, 123) mentions the manner in which the Fifth Circuit adopted the "Briggs dictum" in *Avery*.

161. Ibid.

162. LeRoy Collins, "How It Looks from the South," *Look*, May 27, 1958, 90.

163. Ibid.

164. Ibid.

165. *Carson v. Warlick*, 238 F.2d 724 (4th Cir. 1956) cert. denied, 353 U.S. 910 (1957).

166. This letter is mentioned in the Tallahassee City Commission Minutes, March 13, 1958.

167. Smoky Hollow was home to Wallace Amos, creator of Famous Amos cookies, as well as jazz musicians Nat and Cannonball Adderly. See "Past Is Preserved in Smoky Hollow," *Tallahassee Democrat*, Dec. 16, 2000, 2A. In 1958, for example, two Tallahassee state legislators proposed that the entire neighborhood be cleared. While interests across the state protested the plan, claiming that it would encourage the condemnation and sale of private property to private developers throughout Florida, Collins helped the legislators get an exception for Tallahassee. Tallahassee City Commission Minutes, March 13, 1958; "Slum Clearance Bill Is Dead," *Tallahassee Democrat*, June 2, 1959; "City Looks Ahead as Urban Renewal Proposal Passes," *Tallahassee Democrat*, June 5, 1959; "Urban Renewal Fight Is Seen," *Tallahassee Democrat*, April 17, 1961; Tallahassee City Commission Minutes, February 2, 1961.

168. African Americans like Sandra Palmer Williams, a former resident of Smoky Hollow, asserted that LeRoy Collins's brother, Marvin Collins Jr., owned the house she rented in the Hollow. Sandra P. Williams to Bob Jones, December 21, 1999; included in "Application to Place Smoky Hollow on the National Register of Historic Places," filed with the National Park Service, U.S. Department of the Interior, 2000. Elrea Dean Wilson, another former resident of Smoky Hollow, claimed that LeRoy Collins and his father owned approximately twenty-five houses in the district; see Elrea Dean Wilson to Bob Jones, January 21, 2000, included in "Application to Place Smoky Hollow on the National Register of Historic Places," filed with the National Park Service, U.S. Department of the Interior, 2000.

169. Minutes, Meeting of Governor's Advisory Commission on Bi-Racial Problems, March 5, 1957, LeRoy Collins Papers, Series 776B, Box 117, FSA.

170. *Meet the Press*, May 25, 1958, NBC Television, Lawrence Spivak, moderator. For other examples of this type of language, see LeRoy Collins to Reverend Richard I. Brown, May 17, 1955, LeRoy Collins Papers, Series 776, Box 37, Segregation Folder, FSA; "Race Relations 1954–1960, Quoted Excerpts from Governor's Speeches," LeRoy Collins Papers, Claude Pepper Library Special Collections, Florida State University, Tallahassee.

171. "Study of Illegitimacy," *Ocala Star Banner*, November 5, 1958, Florida Clipping Service, Tampa, in LeRoy Collins Papers, Series 776, Box 143, Welfare Illegitimacy Folder, FSA.

172. "Study of Illegitimacy Asked; Governor's Approval Accepted," *Palmetto News*, November 13, 1958, Florida Clipping Service, Tampa, in LeRoy Collins Papers, Series 776, Box 143, Welfare Illegitimacy Folder, FSA.

173. "Study of Illegitimacy," *Ocala Star Banner*, November 5, 1958, Florida Clipping Service, Tampa, in LeRoy Collins Papers, Series 776, Box 143, Welfare Illegitimacy Folder, FSA.

174. LeRoy Collins to Judge William M. Maness, January 16, 1959, LeRoy Collins Papers, Series 776, Box 143, Welfare Illegitimacy Folder,

FSA. Identical letters were sent out to eleven private citizens, all nominated to join the committee.

175. "The State Department of Public Welfare," wrote Collins to potential committee members, "as one of the agencies vitally concerned with this problem, will provide whatever funds and facilities the work of the Committee may require." Ibid.

176. House Bill No. 437, Chap. 59–120, 1959 Laws of Florida, May 25, 1959.

177. House Bill No. 312, Chap. 59–202, 1959 Laws of Florida, May 29, 1959.

178. Ibid.

179. Ibid.

180. Piven and Cloward, *Regulating the Poor*, 2d ed., 139–40.

181. Ibid.

182. "Senators Get Ready for Fight," *Meet the Press*, May 23, 1957, 4.

183. "Morals Bill Action Taken," *Tallahassee Democrat*, May 29, 1957, 13.

184. These protections began to emerge quickly, not only in the form of limits on what children could read but also a general tightening of moral codes. During the same 1957 legislative session, for example, the Florida House of Representatives voted in favor of banning common law marriage in the state. The proposed ban echoed Mississippi's invalidation of common law marriage, one year earlier, yet garnered some resistance. See "House Votes Common Law Marriage Ban," *Tallahassee Democrat*, April 10, 1957, 9. Although it passed the House, the ban on common law marriages would actually not come until 1964 in Florida. However, the institution was more strictly regulated, in particular in regard to individuals attempting to claim welfare benefits. A 1959 law was passed, for example, stating that "when the existence of a common-law marriage is called into question in any matter pertaining to payment to Aid to Dependent Children, it shall not be subject to proof except by prior registration of the marriage in a 'Register of Common-Law Marriage,' to be maintained by the office of the county judge." From "New Legislation and a Summary of Its Effect" *Florida Public Welfare News*, July 1959, Florida State Library, F361.6s P9, p. 11. Representative Crews of Baker County opposed the bill, for example, arguing that it would disproportionately affect African Americans "who legally marry under the common law or 'turpentine law,' as it is called in North Florida." See "House Votes Common Law Marriage Ban," *Tallahassee Democrat*, April 10, 1957, 9.

185. "Interposition 'Lie' Says Gov. Collins," *Tallahassee Democrat*, April 21, 1957, 1.

186. Ibid.

187. Minutes from meeting of Governor's Advisory Commission on Bi-Racial Problems, March 26, 1957, LeRoy Collins Papers, Series 776B, Box 117, Segregation Race Relations Folder, FSA, 13.

188. "Interposition's Foes Delay Vote in Senate by Parliamentary Step," *Tallahassee Democrat*, April 17, 1957, 1.

189. "Collins Asserts State Is Made to Look Foolish," *Tallahassee Democrat*, April 19, 1957, 2.

190. Ibid.

191. Ibid.

192. Rabby, *The Pain and the Promise*, 51.

193. Danielle L. McGuire, "'It Was Like All of Us Had Been Raped': Sexual Violence, Community Mobilization, and the African American Freedom Struggle," *Journal of American History* 91 (December 2004); Rabby, *The Pain and the Promise*, 77–79.

194. McGuire, "It Was Like All of Us Had Been Raped.'"

195. Rabby, *The Pain and the Promise*, 81–108, 97.

196. Ibid., 101–2.

197. Ibid.

198. "Remarks by Governor LeRoy Collins," March 20, 1960, LeRoy Collins Papers, Box 96, Folder: Race Relations, Part 2," University of South Florida, Tampa, Florida.

199. Ibid.

200. "Text of Collins' Address," *Miami Daily News*, March 21, 1960.

201. Ibid.

202. "Statistical Developments from 1954," *Statistical Summary of School Segregation-Desegregation in the Southern and Border States, 1966–1967* (Nashville: Southern Education Reporting Service, 1967).

203. Application for Pupil Placement for Mary Call Collins for 1958–59 School Year, LeRoy Collins Papers, Box 458, Folder: "Collins Family 1958," University of South Florida, Tampa.

Chapter Four

1. Transcript, *Open End with David Susskind*, Channel 13, WNTA Television, New York City, April 3, 1960. James Jackson Kilpatrick Papers, Series 6626-b, Box 62, Folder: "1959," Special Collections, University of Virginia, Charlottesville, Virginia. The panel also included James McBride Dabbs, president of the Southern Regional Conference and author of a forward-looking book endorsing the end of segregation, *The Southern Heritage* (New York: Alfred A. Knopf, 1958).

2. Ibid.

3. Joseph J. Thorndike, "'The Sometimes Sordid Level of Race and Segregation': James J. Kilpatrick and the Virginia Campaign against *Brown*" in *The Moderates' Dilemma: Massive Resistance to School Desegregation in Virginia*, Matthew J. Lassiter and Andrew B. Lewis, eds. (Charlottesville: University of Virginia Press, 1998), 51–71; Robert Gaines Corley, *James Jackson Kilpatrick: The Evolution of a Southern Conservative, 1955–1965*, M.A. thesis , University of Virginia, 1971. See also James Jackson Kilpatrick, *The Sovereign States: Notes of a Citizen of Virginia* (Chicago: Henry Regnery, 1957). Six states actually passed interposition resolutions: Florida, Virginia, Mississippi, Georgia, Alabama, and Arkansas. North Carolina, Texas, and Tennessee

enacted similarly worded statements of protest. See Bartley, *The Rise of Massive Resistance*, 131. For Bartley, interposition was the "battle cry" of massive resistance (126, 2nd ed.).

4. Transcript, *Open End*.

5. Ibid.

6. "Collins Decries Curbs by Stores: Florida Governor Declares It 'Unfair' Not to Treat All Customers Alike," *New York Times*, March 21, 1960, 37; "South's Mood: Florida's Governor Sounds New Integration Note," *New York Times*, March 27, 1960, E8.

7. Transcript, *Open End*.

8. James Jackson Kilpatrick to Edward E. Lane, January 7, 1960, James Jackson Kilpatrick Papers, Series # 6626b, Box 31, Folder: "Correspondence," Special Collections, University of Virginia, Charlottesville.

9. For the collapse of massive resistance, see Bartley, *Rise*, 320–39. For the political constraints Kennedy faced, see Carl M. Brauer, *John F. Kennedy and the Second Reconstruction* (New York: Columbia University Press, 1997), 30–60; Hugh Davis Graham, *The Civil Rights Era: Origins and Development of National Policy* (New York: Oxford University Press, 1990), 63–67; Nick Kotz, *The Bystander: John F. Kennedy and the Struggle for Black Equality* (New York: Basic Books, 2006), 225–42.

10. For a concise explanation of how electoral politics affect the Court, see Robert Post and Reva Siegel, "Popular Constitutionalism, Departmentalism & Judicial Supremacy," 92 *California Law Review* (2004): 1027. Alexander Bickel discusses political constraints placed on the Supreme Court in *The Least Dangerous Branch: The Supreme Court at the Bar of Politics* (Indianapolis: Bobbs-Merrill, 1962), 247–54. For a more recent discussion, see Klarman, *From Jim Crow to Civil Rights*, 463.

11. This is true even though the Fifth Circuit was showing resistance to placement plans. Not only would the Fifth Circuit's membership change over the course of the 1960s but also the South proved able to devise a variety of other methods, most notably the freedom of choice plan, that was not attacked by the Supreme Court until well after the direct-action strategies of the civil rights movement shifted national support in favor of more aggressive enforcement of civil rights. Peter Irons, *Jim Crow's Children: The Broken Promise of the Brown Decision* (New York: Viking, 2002), 199–200.

12. For more on the direct-action phase of the movement, see Morris, *The Origins of the Civil Rights Movement*, 188–94; Garrow, *Protest at Selma*; David J. Garrow, *Bearing the Cross: Martin Luther King, Jr. and the Southern Christian Leadership Conference* (New York: Random House, 1986); Raymond Arsenault, *Freedom Riders: 1961 and the Struggle for Racial Justice* (New York: Oxford University Press, 2006).

13. Owen M. Fiss, "Groups and the Equal Protection Clause," *Philosophy and Public Affairs* 5 (1976): 107–8.

14. As Clayborne Carson writes, "Many black activists of the 1960s saw themselves as a part of a liberation struggle for collective advancement rather than simply a movement for individual rights and opportunities."

Clayborne Carson, "Review of Steven F. Lawson, *In Pursuit of Power: South-ern Blacks and Electoral Politics, 1965–1982*," in *Journal of American History* 72 (December 1985): 736–37. Coleman's jurisprudence bolsters the findings of constitutional scholars like Reva Siegel, who note the manner in which segregationists abandoned "group-categorical distinctions" to reinforce ra-cial stratification in the post-*Brown* era. See Siegel, "Discrimination in the Eyes of the Law," 109–11.

15. Michael Klarman shows how Hollings began to retreat from defiance in 1962. See Klarman, *Jim Crow to Civil Rights*, 400–405. Klarman shows, for example, that Virginia, Arkansas, Florida, Texas, and Tennessee dis-tanced themselves from massive resistance in 1959 (400); Georgia aban-doned massive resistance in 1961–62 (404–5); North Carolina continued its moderate path with the election of Terry Sanford in 1961; and South Carolina moved away from massive resistance under Hollings in 1962 (406). See also Bartley, *Rise*, 320–39.

16. Black, *Southern Governors*, 128–29. Black (130) calls Connally's ap-proach a "new" one. While this might be true for Texas, Connally's approach was not much different from the stances that Collins, Coleman, and Hodges took in their states, five years earlier.

17. Ibid., 119–22.

18. "Kennedy Moves to Ease the Transition," *New York Times*, November 20, 1960, E5. "Excerpts from Kennedy-Hodges Parley," *New York Times*, December 4, 1960, 58.

19. For more on Kennedy's need for southern support, see Brauer, *Kennedy*, 30–60; Nick Bryant, *The Bystander: John F. Kennedy and the Struggle for Black Equality*(New York: Basic Books, 2006), 218–19.

20. "Kennedy Planning to Give Bowles Foreign Policy Job," *New York Times*, November 30, 1960, 30. It was no secret that Luther Hodges en-dorsed segregation. See, for example, "Hodges, the Amateur in Politics, Won 2 Reputations as Governor," *New York Times*, December 4, 1960, 59.

21. For desegregation data, see "Statistical Developments from 1954," *Statistical Summary of School Segregation-Desegregation in the Southern and Border States, 1966–1967* (Nashville: Southern Education Reporting Service, 1967).

22. Though Collins was not in the race, Bryant attacked him neverthe-less, in part for finding moral value in the student sit-ins. Colburn and Scher, *Florida's Gubernatorial Politics*, 80–81.Folsom and Long are some-times considered liberals for their interest in increasing social services to blacks and whites, not to mention their reliance on class-based biracial coalitions of voters and emphasis in New Deal–style, redistributive politics. In calling them moderates, I borrow from Numan V. Bartley, who notes that "their class-based assumptions dictated racial moderation." Bartley, *New South*, 206. For a summary of gubernatorial elections, see Black, *Southern Governors*, 212, 216; For Ross Barnett, see Crespino, *Another Country*, 35.

23. For Folsom, see Carl E. Grafton, *Big Mules and Branchheads: James E. Folsom and Political Power in Alabama* (Athens: University of Georgia Press,

1985); see also Bartley and Graham, *Southern Politics*, 67; and Bartley, *Rise*, 281–86. For Long's struggle to keep blacks on the rolls, see Bartley and Graham, *Southern Politics*, 58–59.

24. Transcript, "Session on History of the Integration Situation in North Carolina," Saturday, Sept. 3, 1960, Southern Oral History Program, #4007, Wilson Library, University of North Carolina, Chapel Hill. This might explain why Numan V. Bartley noted that of LeRoy Collins, Orval Faubus, and Luther Hodges, only Hodges "appeared to hold a serious personal commitment to Jim Crow." Bartley, *New South*, 217.

25. For Coleman's defeat, see Black, *Southern Governors*, 170. One explanation for why voters turned on Collins and Coleman may have been a relatively dramatic rise in voter turnout among less affluent, less educated voters across the South, beginning in 1956. See Bartley and Graham, *Southern Politics*, 112.

26. This can be seen in the decline of support that Carlton received not just in conservative North Florida but also in South Florida in 1960. See Bartley and Graham, *Southern Politics*, 64.

27. Colburn and Scher, *Florida's Gubernatorial Politics*, 78; Bartley, *Rise*, 342.

28. Though this number may seem high, it was still only 2.67 percent of all eligible school-age black children. "Statistical Developments from 1954," *Statistical Summary of School Segregation-Desegregation in the Southern and Border States, 1966–1967* (Nashville: Southern Education Reporting Service, 1967).

29. For Patterson, see "Montgomery under Martial Law; Troops Called after New Riot; Marshals and Police Fight Mob," *New York Times*, May 22, 1961, 1. See also Arsenault, *Freedom Riders*, 228. For Jimmie Davis, see Liva Baker, *The Second Battle of New Orleans: The Hundred-Year Struggle to Integrate the Schools*(New York: HarperCollins, 1996); see also Bass, *Unlikely Heroes*, 128. For Barnett's theatrics, see Crespino, *Another Country*, 42.

30. The stated goal of the freedom rides was to push for enforcement of the 1960 Supreme Court ruling ordering the desegregation of interstate bus terminals. *Boynton v. Commonwealth of Virginia*, 364 U.S. 454 (1960); "Bi-Racial Buses Attacked, Riders Beaten in Alabama," *New York Times*, May 15, 1961, 1; J. Mills Thornton, *Dividing Lines: Municipal Politics and the Struggle for Civil Rights in Montgomery, Birmingham, and Selma* (Tuscaloosa: University of Alabama Press, 2002), 240–50; Bass, *Unlikely Heroes*, 139; Arsenault, *Freedom Riders*, 205.

31. "Freedom Riders Attacked by Whites in Montgomery," *New York Times*, May 21, 1961, 1; "Montgomery under Martial Law; Troops Called after New Riot; Marshals and Police Fight Mob," *New York Times*, May 22, 1961, 1; Arsenault, *Freedom Riders*, 226–27; Bass, *Unlikely Heroes*, 143.

32. Quoted in Garrow, *Bearing the Cross*, 156.

33. Arsenault, *Freedom Riders*, 166.

34. "Freedom Riders Reach Carolina: Raleigh Calm as Two Groups Arrive on Way to Florida," *New York Times*, June 14, 1961, 19. See also Covington and Ellis, *Terry Sanford*, 283.

35. Thomas J. Pearsall to Terry Sanford, May 29, 1961, Terry Sanford Papers, North Carolina State Archives, Raleigh, North Carolina.

36. "Police Guard 32 on Freedom Ride: 3 Groups Are Unmolested on Trip in Carolinas," *New York Times*, June 15, 1961, 38. Ernest F. Hollings, the increasingly moderate governor of South Carolina, took similar measures. After a gang of whites attacked a bus in one of the first freedom rides, he ordered state police to escort future buses. In June, riders were followed by unmarked South Carolina Law Enforcement Division cars as they traveled through the state. Even in Mississippi, things remained quiet, due in part to the intervention of J. P. Coleman. Following the violence in Birmingham and Montgomery, Coleman personally called Robert Kennedy, warning him that Ross Barnett might try something similar in Jackson. Kennedy, no doubt suspecting Coleman to be right, contacted Mississippi Senator James O. Eastland and asked him to guarantee the freedom riders' safety. Eastland, who held considerable sway over Barnett in Mississippi, promised Kennedy that the riders would not be harmed but also warned that they would be arrested. True to his word, police met the riders at the bus station in Jackson and promptly took them into custody. There was no extremism, no violence, and no federal intervention. Bass, *Unlikely Heroes*, 143; "27 Bi-Racial Bus Riders Jailed in Jackson, Miss., as They Widen Campaign," *New York Times*, May 25, 1961, 1. According to historian Adam Fairclough, "The [federal] government's conduct during the Freedom Rides—intervening in Alabama, where Klan mobs had been permitted to run amok, but adopting a 'hands-off' policy towards Mississippi, where police had kept order and carried out 'peaceful' arrests—sent a coded but clear message to Southern segregationists: federal intervention could be avoided if the authorities kept violence in check." See Adam Fairclough, "Martin Luther King, Jr. and the Quest for Nonviolent Social Change," 47:1 *Phylon* (Winter 1986): 6.

37. On May 9, 1962, a relatively modest civil rights bill seeking to remove literacy requirements from southern polls failed to muster the two-thirds vote needed in the Senate to stop a southern filibuster. See "Senate Rejects Bid for Closure; Rights Bill Dead," *New York Times*, May 10, 1962, 1.

38. These were among the complaints enumerated by W. G. Anderson in *Anderson v. City of Albany*, 321 F.2d 649 (5CA 1963).

39. When Dr. William G. Anderson, president of the Albany Movement, invited Martin Luther King Jr. to join the protests in an attempt to draw media attention to the town, Albany Police Chief Laurie Pritchett was waiting. "We had a bodyguard with [King] all the time," Pritchett later explained, "When he would enter the city limits, we'd escort him, take him out of his car, and he would volunteer to leave his car and come into our car. We'd take him everywhere he wanted to go. Where he spent the night, we had people there all the time. We afforded him protection. This caused some criticism that we were payin' taxpayers money to protect this man, and I felt it was proper. As I told them, if this man was killed in Albany, Georgia, the fires would never cease." Laurie Pritchett interview with

Howell Raines, reprinted in *My Soul Is Rested: Movement Days in the Deep South Remembered*(New York: Putnam, 1977), 365.

40. *Anderson v. City of Albany*, 321 F.2d 649 (5CA 1963). The executive branch of the federal government also did not intervene substantially in Albany. The Department of Justice filed a "friend-of-the-court" brief opposing the city's request for an injunction prohibiting further protests, but otherwise the executive branch did not intervene physically, as it had in Montgomery. See "U.S. Intervenes on Negroes' Side in Georgia Cases: Justice Department Opposes Albany's Plea for Ban on Segregation Protests," *New York Times*, August 9, 1962, 1.

41. "Georgia Defeat Angers Negroes," *New York Times*, July 5, 1963, 33.

42. Historian David L. Chappell calls Albany a failure and an exception to the rule that moderates actually created possibilities for change. Yet, Chappell fails to note the success that the movement had locally in Albany, particularly the removal of segregation ordinances. He also fails to draw links between Albany and Tallahassee, where the movement also won local concessions but failed to initiate the kind of national change that occurred following both the Montgomery bus boycott and the Freedom Rides. See Chappell, *Inside Agitators*, 84–96, 122–143.

43. See Robert D. Loevy, *To End All Segregation: The Politics and Passage of the Civil Rights Act of 1964* (Lanham, Md.: University Press of America, 1990). For the decreasing solidarity of southern Democrats, see Kari Fredrickson, *The Dixiecrat Revolt and the End of the Solid South, 1932–1968* (Chapel Hill: University of North Carolina Press, 2001).

44. For a discussion of these measures, see Bass, *Unlikely Heroes*, 218–20. For federal district judges, see J. W. Peltason, *Fifty Eight Lonely Men: Southern Federal Judges and School Desegregation*(New York: Harcourt Brace, 1961).

45. Garrow, *Cross*, 228; See also Adam Fairclough, "Martin Luther King, Jr.," 3.

46. Garrow, *Cross*, 248–50.

47. "Dogs and Hoses Repulse Negroes in Birmingham," *New York Times*, May 4, 1963, 1.

48. "Celler and Javits Demand U.S. Intervene in Alabama Violence," *New York Times*, May 10, 1963, 14.

49. For Kennedy's initial approach to Birmingham, see "JFK's Moderate Strategy in Birmingham," *New York Times*, May 10, 1963, 32; "Federal Role: Government's Power Is Limited but It Plays an Active Role behind the Scenes," *New York Times*, May 12, 1963, E3. See also Thornton, *Dividing Lines*.

50. For Wallace's "stand in the school house door," see Dan T. Carter, *Politics of Rage: George Wallace, the Origins of the New Conservatism, and the Transformation of American Politics* (Baton Rouge: Louisiana State University Press, 1995), 142–51.

51. For Medgar Evers's murder, see Adam Nossiter, *Of Long Memory: Mississippi and the Murder of Medgar Evers* (Reading, Mass.: Addison-Wesley, 1994), 128–29.

52. For examples of national outrage, see "Rallies Support Negroes' Effort: 500 Pickets in Philadelphia Protest over Birmingham, 300 March in Los Angeles," *New York Times*, May 12, 1963, 52. For international outrage, see "Africa Aides Demand a Unity Charter: Racial Bias Fought," *New York Times*, May 22, 1963, 10; "Uganda Denounces U.S. on Racial Bias," *New York Times*, May 24, 1963, 1.

53. Garrow, *Cross*, 272.

54. "Address," President John F. Kennedy, H. Doc. 124, 88th Cong. 1st Sess. June 20, 1963.

55. Ibid.

56. "Kennedy Speeds Civil Rights Bill; Plans a Message," *New York Times*, June 3, 1963, 1; "Kennedy Asks Broad Rights Bill as 'Reasonable' Course in Crisis; Calls for Restraint by Negroes," *New York Times*, June 20, 1963, 1. Glenn Eskew stresses the centrality of Birmingham to the 1964 Civil Rights Act in his study *But for Birmingham*, 299–331, as does Thornton, in *Dividing Lines*,378. But see Garrow, *Protest at Selma*, 135–49.

57. Loevy, *To End All Segregation*.

58. Ibid., 313.

59. Civil Rights Act of 1964, Title X. Sec. 1002.

60. "Civil Rights Bill Provides a $20,000 'Peacemaker,'" *Chicago Tribune*, February 28, 1964, 1.

61. Laurence Tribe, *American Constitutional Law*, 3rd ed. (New York: Foundation, 2000), 807–25.

62. Ibid.

63. Brauer, *John F. Kennedy*, 278.

64. Loevy, *End All Segregation*, 122–23.

65. According to certain students of the bill, the inclusion of the CRS was a clear concession to conservatives who wanted to limit the potential impact of the CRA. See Charles Whalen and Barbara Whalen, *The Longest Debate: A Legislative History of the 1964 Civil Rights Act*(Cabin John, Md.: Seven Locks Press, 1985), 120. See also Bertram Levine, *Resolving Racial Conflict: The Community Relations Service and Civil Rights, 1964–1989* (Columbia: University of Missouri Press, 2005), 13.

66. Finally, Johnson, a former senator from Texas, was himself a southern moderate who had long advocated the need for a federal agency capable of intervening in local matters and reconciling civil rights disputes. In fact, he first expressed interest in such an agency following the Montgomery bus boycott, in 1957.

67. Julia Sullivan Chapman discusses Hodges's recommendation of Collins in her thesis, "A Southern Moderate Advocates Compliance: A Study of LeRoy Collins as the Director of the Community Relations Service," M.A. thesis, University of South Florida, 1974, 21, 26. "Collins Is Offered Major Rights Post," *New York Times*, June 26, 1964, 1.

68. Collins recounted some of the details of his meeting with then Senator Lyndon Johnson during a press conference February 12, 1959. "Of course we talked at great length about his overall interest in civil rights

and his program in that area," Collins told reporters. "He was very anxious to get the ideas that I had in respect to that, and I shared my feelings with him very freely." LeRoy Collins, Press Conference, February 12, 1959, LeRoy Collins Papers, Speeches, Claude Pepper Library, Florida State University, Tallahassee, Florida.

69. Loevy, *To End All Segregation*, 214, 221. It also did not hurt that Luther Hodges, now secretary of Commerce, endorsed Collins as director of the CRS. Julia Sullivan Chapman, "A Southern Moderate Advocates Compliance." See also "An Informal Legislative History of the Community Relations Service," Box 314, Folder: "CRS Legislation," LeRoy Collins Papers, Special Collections, University of South Florida.

70. For a discussion of response to the stall-in at the World's Fair, see Alexander M. Bickel, *Politics and the Warren Court* (New York: Harper & Row, 1965), 86.

71. "Nomination of LeRoy Collins to be Director, Community Relations Service, Department of Commerce," U.S. Senate Commerce Committee, July 7, 1964.

72. Whalen and Whalen, *The Longest Debate*, 215.

73. Transcript, "Nomination of LeRoy Collins to be Director, Community Relations Service, Department of Commerce," U.S. Senate Commerce Committee, July 7, 1964.

74. As if this were not bad enough, many suspected that local sheriff, L. O. Davis, was deputizing members of the Ku Klux Klan to deal with the protestors. See "Police-Klan Ties Hinted at in Florida," *New York Times*, June 3, 1964; "2 Hurt in Clash in St. Augustine," *New York Times*, May 29, 1964, 10. While local police claimed to be protecting the demonstrators, evidence suggests that some participated in, or at the very least allowed, attacks against them. See "Nightriders Fire on Dr. King's Aide," *New York Times*, May 30, 1964, 14. Partly in response to this, Governor Farris Bryant sent state troopers into the city to reinforce local police. See "Florida Sheriff Called Klan Ally," *New York Times*, June 4, 1964; "Marchers Beaten in St. Augustine," *New York Times*, June 10, 1964, 1; "Race Groups Attacked in 2 Cities," *Chicago Tribune*, June 10, 1964, 1.

75. "Nomination of LeRoy Collins to Be Director, Community Relations Service, Department of Commerce," U.S. Senate Commerce Committee, July 7, 1964.

76. "Police Rout Mob at St. Augustine: Tear Gas and Dogs Disperse Whites Attacking Negroes," *New York Times*, June 11, 1964, 23; Garrow, *Cross*, 330.

77. "3 States Reject Plea by Collins," *New York Times*, July 24, 1964, 10.

78. "Police Rout Mob at St. Augustine: Tear Gas and Dogs Disperse Whites Attacking Negroes," *New York Times*, June 11, 1964, 23; "50 More Demonstrators Jailed in St. Augustine," *New York Times*, June 17, 1964, 50; "Whites Repulsed in St. Augustine," *New York Times*, June 20, 1964, 12; "New Racial Clash Halted in Florida: Police Guard Integrationists at Beach and on March," *New York Times*, June 24, 1964, 19; "Florida Battles for

Protest Ban: Sees Action by U.S. Court as Leading to Tragedy," *New York Times*, June 28, 1964, 48.

79. Memorandum, "Report of Nine-State Trip of Secretary Hodges and Governor Collins and Governor Ellington" (July 7, 8, 9, 10, 1964), Box 336, Folder: WHCF Name File, Lyndon Johnson Library, Austin, Texas.

80. "3 States Reject Plea by Collins," *New York Times*, July 24, 1964, 10.

81. "President's Rights Team Tours States," *Chicago Tribune*, July 9, 1964, W4. Hodges would resign as secretary of Commerce in January 1965. "Hodges Will Direct Research Institution in North Carolina," *New York Times*, January 22, 1965, 13.

82. "Hodges Hopeful Protests Can End: Says Negroes Can Turn to New Rights End," *New York Times*, July 9, 1964.

83. Nick Kotz, *Judgment Days: Lyndon Baines Johnson, Martin Luther King, Jr., and the Laws That Changed America* (New York: Mariner, 2005), 244.

84. Garrow, *Protest*, 34–35.

85. "Voting Is Crux of Civil Rights Hopes, *New York Times*, February 14, 1965, E5.

86. Abernathy, *The Walls Came Tumbling Down*,308.

87. "Southerners and Other in U.S. Protest Selma Police Methods," *New York Times*, March 9, 1965, 23; "Alabama Police Use Gas and Clubs to Rout Negroes," *New York Times*, March 8, 1965, 1.

88. "Outrage at Selma," *Washington Post*, March 9, 1965.

89. Walter Mondale, "Shocking Brutality in Selma, Ala." *Congressional Record*, March 8, 1965, 4350.

90. Lyndon Johnson to Buford Ellington, phone conversation, March 8, 1965, 8:29 A.M., reprinted in Michael Beschloss, ed., *Reaching for Glory: Lyndon Johnson's Secret White House Tapes, 1964–1965*(New York: Simon & Schuster, 2001), 218. On Ellington's work with Collins and Hodges for Johnson, see Levine, *Resolving Racial Conflict*, 17.

91. Garrow, *Protest*, 85–86; for more on Johnson and civil rights, see Kotz, *Judgment Days;* Robert Dallek, *Flawed Giant: Lyndon Johnson and His Times, 1961–1973*(New York: Oxford University Press, 1998); Doris Kearn Goodwin, *Lyndon Johnson and the American Dream*(New York: Harper & Row, 1976); and Robert A. Caro, *The Path to Power*(New York: Knopf, 1982); *Means of Ascent*(New York: Knopf, 1990); and *The Years of Lyndon Johnson* (New York: Knopf, 1982).

92. Garrow, *Protest*, 36–38.

93. For Johnson's encouragement of King, see Kotz, *Judgment Days*, 252–53.

94. For Collins's side of the story, see his *Man in the Middle*, 145–50. For Collins's suggestion that King hold a symbolic demonstration, see LeRoy Collins's interview with Jack Bass and Walther Devries, May 19, 1974, Southern Oral History Program, Southern Historical Collection, University of North Carolina, Chapel Hill. For King's comments that Collins discipline police and also that he would not order marchers through a police line, see Testimony of Martin Luther King Jr., trial transcript, *Hosea Williams, et al. v.*

The Honorable George Wallace, Civ. Action No. 2181-N, U.S. Dist. Ct. of Alabama, Northern Division, March 11, 1965, p. 63. Papers of Martin Luther King Jr., Ser. III Speeches, Sermons, etc. March 1, 1965–July 3, 1965. Bertram Levine presents a slightly different account of events than that found in Collins's memoirs, one that places more emphasis on Andrew Young and Andrew Secrest. See Levine, *Resolving Racial Conflict*, 64–67.

95. Though Bruce Ackerman does not focus on Selma, his distinction between normal lawmaking and higher lawmaking provides a useful mode of analyzing what the movement was trying to accomplish in Alabama, namely, a push to draw public attention to black voting rights claims. See Bruce Ackerman, *We the People 2: Transformations*(Cambridge: Harvard University Press, 1998), 5.

96. Jack Bass, *Taming the Storm: The Life and Times of Judge Frank M. Johnson, Jr. and the South's Fight for Civil Rights* (New York: Doubleday, 1993), 238.

97. Martin Luther King Jr., *Williams v. Wallace*, trial transcript, 68. According to Collins, he met with Al Lingo and Jim Clark, told them about the turnaround idea, and asked them to refrain from violence. Both men, upon conferring, then called an unknown party, who Collins thought might be George Wallace, before they agreed to the plan. Upon agreeing, they drove Collins back to the front of the march in a patrol car. LeRoy Collins, *Man in the Middle*, 147. Collins later wrote that Clark and Lingo had agreed with the turnaround on the condition that the marchers (1) follow a map drawn by them and (2) stop on the bridge no longer than twenty minutes. LeRoy Collins, *Man in the Middle*, 147.

98. Ibid. See also Garrow, *Cross*, 403.

99. King's realization that the protest was doomed held true, even though the Alabama authorities moved to clear the way to Montgomery once they saw the demonstrators stop and begin to turn around. Marching to Montgomery had never been the primary goal of the demonstration. See Garrow, *Cross*, 404.

100. Martin Luther King Jr., *Williams v. Wallace*, trial transcript, 65.

101. Lyndon B. Johnson, "Special Message to Congress: The American Promise," March 15, 1965, *Public Papers of the Presidents: Lyndon Johnson, 1965*, 281–87. Six months later, the Voting Rights Act was passed, effectively dismantling the last overt vestige of Jim Crow and effectively granting African Americans their civil rights. Most scholars also support a link between Birmingham and the Civil Rights Act of 1964: Eskew, *But For Birmingham*, 310–312, Thornton, *Dividing Lines*, 378; Fairclough, "Martin Luther King, Jr.," 7–9. But see David J. Garrow, *Protest*, 135–49, who challenges the notion that Birmingham led to federal legislation.

102. "Nomination of James P. Coleman," Hearings before a Special Subcommittee of the Committee on the Judiciary, United States Senate, Eighty-Ninth Congress, First Session, July 12 and 13, 1965 (Washington, D.C.: U.S. Government Printing Office, 1965), 19.

103. Ibid., 39–40.

104. This statement appears to have been prepared as part of a press release. It can be found on an undated document in a file designated "Speeches, Sermons, Etc ... 11/1/1964–2/28/1965," Box 7, King Papers, Atlanta, Georgia.

105. Coleman's tendency to uphold certain civil rights claims has led scholars like James T. Read and Lucy McGough to take a relatively uncritical view of Coleman's jurisprudence. See James T. Read and Lucy McGough, *Let Them Be Judged: The Judicial Integration of the Deep South* (Metuchen, N.J.: Scarecrow, 1978), 443.

106. *Hartfield v. Mississippi*, 367 F.2d 362 (CA5 1966), citing *Georgia v. Rachel*, 384 U.S. 780 (1966). Jack Bass notes how *Rachel* was itself a limitation on the removal power forged by Tuttle. See Bass, *Unlikely Heroes*, 291.

107. *Guyot v. Pierce*, 372 F.2d 658 (CA5 1967); *Strother v. Thompson*, 372 F.2d 654 (CA5 1967).

108. *Wilkins v. United States*, 376 F.2d 552 (CA5 1967).

109. Ibid.

110. Coleman did not sit on the initial panel of three that heard Jefferson County: *United States v. Jefferson County Board of Education*, 372 F.2d 836 (1966). He did, however, write a cautionary concurring opinion when the case was reheard before the entire court (*United States v. Jefferson County*, 380 F.2d 385 (CA5 1967).

111. J. Harvie Wilkinson, *From Brown to Bakke: The Supreme Court and School Integration, 1954–1978* (New York: Oxford University Press, 1979), 113.

112. For example, Wisdom invoked guidelines devised by the Department of Health, Education and Welfare, in his opinion, guidelines generated as part of the implementation of the 1964 Civil Rights Act. Wilkinson, *Brown to Bakke*, 104–7, 112. See also James T. Patterson, *Brown v. Board of Education: A Civil Rights Milestone and Its Troubled Legacy* (New York: Oxford University Press, 2001), 145.

113. Coleman, concurring opinion, *United States v. Jefferson County*, (II) 380 F.2d 385 (CA5 1967).

114. J. P. Coleman, concurring opinion, *United States v. Jefferson County*, (II) 380 F.2d 385 (CA5 1967).

115. *Singleton v. Jackson Municipal Separate School District*, 425 F.2d 1211 (CA5 1970). This was a later *Singleton* case, different from *Singleton* I and II, in which Wisdom began to lay the foundations for *Jefferson County*. See Bass, *Unlikely Heroes*, 301.

116. The case Coleman lamented was *Carter v. West Feliciana Parish*, 396 U.S. 290 (1970), a decision that enforced *Alexander v. Holmes County*, 396 U.S. 19 (1969) demanding immediate integration.

117. *Singleton*, 425 F.2d 1211, 1215.

118. *Green v. County School Board of New Kent County, Va.*, 391 U.S. 430 (1968).

119. Coleman used *Green v. New Kent County* as ammunition against civil rights plaintiffs in *Singleton v. Jackson Municipal Separate School District*, 425 F.2d 1211 (CA5 1970), and also in *Gordon v. Jefferson Davis Parish School Board*, 446 F.2d 266 (CA5 1971).

120. *Singleton*, 425 F.2d 1211 (1970).

121. Ibid., 1216.

122. Ibid.

123. Ibid. For the next four years, as Judges Wisdom and Tuttle would intervene more and more boldly in local school matters, Coleman would file Cassandra-like dissents. On February 5, 1970, he filed a dissenting opinion against Wisdom lamenting his invalidation of a freedom of choice plan that drew white students to predominantly black schools on a part-time basis so that they could pursue specially designed courses like remedial reading, homemaking, and driver education.See *Bivins v. Bibb County Board of Education*, 424 F.2d 97 (1970). On March 6, 1970, Coleman wrote the first of a string of dissents that objected to the Supreme Court's sudden demand, pursuant to *Carter v. West Feliciana Parish*, that integration happen during the middle of the school year. According to Coleman, this was a "wholly unreasonable requirement" that would only result in "these schools [being] torn up in the middle of the semester." See *Hall v. St. Helena Parish School Board*, 424 F.2d 320 (CA5 1970). See also Coleman's dissenting opinions in *United States v. Board of Education of Baldwin County*, 423 F.2d 1013 (CA5 1970); *Youngblood v. Board of Public Instruction of Bay County*, 430 F.2d 625 (CA5 1970).

124. Coleman, dissent, *Henry v. Clarksdale Municipal Separate School District*, 433 F.2d 387 (CA5 1970).

125. Coleman, dissent, *Cisneros v. Corpus Christi Independent School District*, 467 F.2d 142 (CA5 1972).

126. *Swann v. Mecklenburg County*, 402 U.S. 1 (1971).

127. *Milliken v. Bradley*, 418 U.S. 717, 742 (1974). For a discussion of the pre-*Milliken* antibusing protests, see Peter Irons, *Jim Crow's Children*, 223–33.

128. *Milliken v. Bradley*, 418 U.S. 717, 727.

129. Ibid. at 742. For Thurgood Marshall, who dissented, the majority's opinion was "a giant step backwards," for *Brown*. Marshall, dissent, *Milliken v. Bradley*, 418 U.S. 717, 742 (1974).

130. Milliken, 418 U.S. at 742, citing *San Antonio School District* v. *Rodriguez*,411 U.S. 1, 50 (1973).

131. *Oklahoma City v. Dowell*, 498 U.S. 237 (1991).

132. *Freeman v. Pitts*, 503 U.S. 467 (1992).

133. Ibid.

134. Coleman protested integrating schools mid-year. *Hall v. St. Helena Parish School Board*, 424 F.2d 320 (CA5 1970); *United States v. Board of Education of Baldwin County, Georgia*, 423 F.2d 1013 (CA5 1970). Coleman also protested forced integration in situations involving "unreasonable methods." *United States v. Hale County Board of Education*, 445 F.2d 1330 (CA5 1971).

135. J. Harvie Wilkinson notes the legalist turn in *Milliken*, away from equitable concern for "compensatory justice" and toward "legalism." See Wilkinson III, *From Brown to Bakke*, 222–23.

136. *Palmer v. Thompson*, 391 F.2d 324 (1967).

137. Ibid.

138. *Palmer v. Thompson*, 403 U.S. 217 (1971).

139. The story of this move is complex. The MFDP first brought a lawsuit in 1965, challenging Mississippi's congressional districts on the grounds that they were malapportioned. (The largest district, with a population of 608,441 possessed the same congressional representation as the smallest district, with a population of 296,072.) The district court upheld this challenge and ordered the state legislature to redistrict. In response to this order, and to the rising number of registered black voters in the state, the legislature then cut the Delta, the largest black district, into three parts, attaching each part to larger white districts. See Frank R. Parker, *Black Votes Count: Political Empowerment in Mississippi after 1965*(Chapel Hill: University of North Carolina Press, 1990), 78–101.

140. *Connor v. Johnson*, 279 F.Supp. 619 (S.D. Miss. 1966).

141. Ibid.

142. *Reynolds v. Sims*, 377 U.S. 533 (1964).

143. *Connor v. Johnson*, 279 F.Supp. 619 (S.D. Miss. 1966).

144. *Connor v. Johnson*, 386 U.S. 483 (1967). According to Frank R. Parker, "The Supreme Court's refusal to address the racial gerrymandering issue in *Connor v. Johnson* had an enduring political impact for black voters in Mississippi" (*Black Votes Count*, 88–90).

145. Coleman, dissenting opinion, *Morrow v. Crisler*, 491 F.2d 1053 (CA5 1974).

146. Ibid.

147. Ibid.

148. Ibid.

149. *Washington v. Davis*, 426 U.S. 229 (1976).

150. Jack Bass describes *Washington v. Davis* as a significant setback to civil rights in *Unlikely Heroes*, 325. On February 19, 1977, Coleman relied on *Washington v. Davis* to argue against a black school principal in Clarksdale, Mississippi, who had resigned from his position to achieve an advanced degree but was then passed over by whites who were arguably less qualified. Citing *Davis*, Coleman argued that "statistics alone could not carry the day" and that the black appellant needed to prove discriminatory intent. See Coleman, dissent, *Hardy v. Porter*, 546 F.2d 1165 (CA5 1977).

151. J. P. Coleman, dissenting opinion, *Golden v. Biscayne Bay Yacht Club*, 521 F.2d 344 (CA5 1975), 353.

152. Ibid.

153. The case was *Perkins v. Mississippi*, 455 F.2d 7 (CA5 1972). The Supreme Court had approved Tuttle's innovations, albeit in a somewhat restricted form, in *Greenwood v. Peacock*, 384 U.S. 808 (1966) and *Georgia v. Rachel*, 384 U.S. 780 (1966).

154. *Perkins v. Mississippi*, 455 F.2d 7 (CA5 1972).

155. Ibid.

156. Ibid., 26.

157. Ibid., 157. Brown rooted his dissent in two Supreme Court opinions: *Greenwood v. Peacock*, 384 U.S. 808s (CA5 1966) and *Georgia v. Rachel*, 384 U.S. 780 (CA5 1966).

158. *Perkins*, 455 F.2d 7, 11.

159. Critical to this was evidence that the demonstrators who did return from Mendenhall issued an "alarm" regarding the arrest of the appellants, leading the ministers to visit the jail. Such confrontation, Coleman suggested, should be discouraged, not constitutionally protected. *Perkins*, 455 F.2d 7, 8.

160. For more on Cox's segregationist views, see Neil R. McMillen, "Black Enfranchisement in Mississippi: Federal Enforcement and Black Protest in the 1960's," *Journal of Southern History* 43 (August 1977): 357–58.

161. *Smith v. Grady*, 411 F.2d 181 (CA5 1969).

162. Ibid.

163. In December 1969, Coleman issued a similar ruling, this time upholding the right of a university to suspend students for engaging in direct-action protest. In this case, brought by students suspended from Southwest Texas State University for mounting demonstrations, Coleman broke from the majority and held that colleges had the right to tell students when and where they could protest. See *Bayless v. Martine*, 430 F.2d 872 (CA5 1969).

164. Coleman, dissent, *Brown v. Thompson*, 430 F.2d 1214 (1970). For further mention of this case, see Clayborne Carson, *In Struggle: SNCC and the Black Awakening of the 1960s* (Cambridge, Mass.: Harvard University Press, 1981), 255; and Dittmer, *Local People*, 413–14.

165. Ibid.

166. *Wyche v. Hester*, 431 F.2d 791 (CA5 1970). Wyche was the president of the Madison Parish Voters League in Madison Parish, Louisiana. He would go on to become the first black sheriff of Tallulah County. See "Top Cop in Tallulah," *Nation*, March 2, 1970.

167. Ibid.

168. Ibid.

169. Ibid.

170. *Perkins v. Mississippi*(I), 455 F.2d 7 (CA5 1972) and *Perkins v. Mississippi*(II), 470 F.2d 1371 (CA5 1972).

171. *Perkins v. Mississippi*(II), 470 F.2d 1371 (CA5 1972).

172. *Greenwood v. Peacock*, 384 U.S. 808 (1966); *Georgia v. Rachel*, 384 U.S. 780 (1966).

173. Bass, *Unlikely Heroes*, 326.

174. Bureau of Justice Statistics, *Sourcebook of Criminal Justice Statistics–1994* (Washington, D.C.: Government Printing Office, 1995), 305.

175. For more on the tradition of black armed self-defense in the South, see Christopher B. Strain, *Pure Fire: Self-Defense as Activism in the Civil Rights Era* (Athens: University of Georgia Press, 2005); Lance E. Hill, *The Deacons for Defense: Armed Resistance and the Civil Rights Movement* (Chapel Hill: University of North Carolina Press, 2004); and Tyson, *Radio Free Dixie*.

176. Carson, *In Struggle*, 209–10.

177. See William L. Van Deburg, *New Day in Babylon: The Black Power Movement and American Culture, 1965–1975* (Chicago: Chicago University Press, 1992).

178. Nixon's Fifth Circuit appointees included George Harrold Carswell, Charles Clark, Thomas Gee Gibbs, Joe McDonald Ingraham, and Paul Hitch Raney.

179. "Nomination of George Harrold Carswell, of Florida, to Be Associate Justice of the Supreme Court of the United States," Hearings before the Committee on the Judiciary, United States Senate, 91st Congress, February 2, 1970.

180. The plan was so flagrantly evasive that even J. P. Coleman, together with John Minor Wisdom, declared it unconstitutional. See *Steele v. Board of Public Instruction of Leon County*, 421 F.2d 1382 (1969 CA5).

181. "Nomination of George Harrold Carswell," Senate Judiciary Committee, Tuesday, January 27, 1970.

182. St. John De Crevecoeur, *Letters from an American Farmer* (London: T. Davies, 1782).

183. Ibid.

184. Ibid.

Conclusion

1. LeRoy Collins, "LeRoy Collins and Selma '65: The Epic Fight for Civil Rights," *St. Petersburg Times*, December 10, 1978 (reviewing Garrow, *Protest at Selma*).

2. Ibid.

3. Ibid.

4. Lyndon B. Johnson, "Special Message to Congress: The American Promise," March 15, 1965, *Public Papers of the Presidents: Lyndon Johnson, 1965*, 281–87.

5. The Court declared that deliberate speed had come to an end in *Griffin v. County School Board of Prince Edward County*, 377 U.S. 430 (1964) (holding unconstitutional the closing of public schools to avoid desegregation).

6. The Court did not take a close look at pupil placement plans until 1968, in *Green v. County School Board of New Kent County*, 391 U.S. 430 (1968).

7. *Milliken v. Bradley*, 418 U.S. 717 (1974).

8. Ibid.

9. Ibid.

10. Paul A. Johnson, "Transcription [of] Session on History of the Integration Situation in North Carolina," September 3, 1960, Governor's Office, State Capitol, Raleigh. Southern Oral History Program, Southern Historical Collection, University of North Carolina, Chapel Hill.

11. Constitutional scholar Reva Siegel notes how efforts to reform status regimes lead defenders of those regimes to modify both their rhetoric and

their rule structure in the hopes of achieving a type of "preservation through transformation." See Reva Siegel, "Why Equal Protection No Longer Protects: The Evolving Forms of Status-Enforcing State Action," 49 *Stanford Law Review* (1997): 1113; and "The Rule of Love: Wife Beating as Prerogative and Privacy," 105 *Yale Law Journal* (1996): 2120.

12. For a discussion of the motivations of suburban southerners, see Lassiter, *The Silent Majority*, 28.

13. Thomas J. Pearsall, "Transcription [of] Session on History of the Integration Situation in North Carolina," September 3, 1960, Governor's Office, State Capitol, Raleigh. Southern Oral History Program, Southern Historical Collection, University of North Carolina, Chapel Hill. See also Paul and Coates, *The School Segregation Decision*, 118–19.

14. For more on the relationship between social movements and constitutionalism, see Balkin and Siegel, "Principles, Practices, and Social Movements," 927.

15. Daniel Patrick Moynihan, *The Negro Family: The Case for National Action* (Washington, D.C.: Office of Policy Planning and Research, 1965); see also Daryl Scott, *Contempt and Pity: Social Policy and the Image of the Damaged Black Psyche, 1880–1996* (Chapel Hill: University of North Carolina Press, 1997).

16. "'Welfare Queen' Becomes Issue in Reagan Campaign," *New York Times*, February 15, 1976, 51. For the manner in which black illegitimacy rates became politicized in the 1980s and 1990s, see Dorothy Roberts, *Killing the Black Body: Race, Reproduction, and the Meaning of Liberty* (New York: Vintage, 1999), 202–45; Kenneth Nuebeck and Noel A. Cazanave, *Welfare Racism: Playing the Race Card against America's Poor* (New York: Routledge, 2001), 70–76, 112–13, 138–39, 163–65.

17. "Senate Panel Approves Welfare Plan: Clinton, Who Pushed Bill, Lauds Action," *Arkansas Democrat-Gazette*, April 21, 1988.

18. "Right on for the New Right," *Time*, October 3, 1977.

19. The rise in moderation was not just the product of moderate leaders but of larger historical forces like corporate migration and suburbanization. See, for example Lassiter, *The Silent Majority*, 226. For books on the relationship between the South and the nation, see Earl Black and Merle Black, *The Rise of Southern Republicans* (Cambridge, Mass.: Belknap, 2002); John Egerton, *The Americanization of Dixie: The Southernization of America* (New York: Harper's Magazine Press, 1974); Peter Applebome, *Dixie Rising: How the South Is Shaping American Values, Politics, and Culture* (New York: Times Books, 1996).

20. Bartley, *Rise*, 142; Klarman, *From Jim Crow*, 396–97.

21. Early historians of southern state politics in the 1950s, Numan V. Bartley, Hugh D. Graham, Dewey Grantham, and Earl Black, for example, base their research almost entirely on newspaper accounts and electoral data, not archival evidence. See, for example, Bartley, *Rise*; Black, *Southern Governors*; Bartley and Graham, *Southern Politics;*Dewey W. Grantham, *The Life and Death of the Solid South: A Political History* (Lexington: University

Press of Kentucky, 1988). This is also true for Jack Bass and Walter DeVries, who augment their work with personal interviews. See Jack Bass and Walter DeVries, *The Transformation of Southern Politics: Social Change and Political Consequence Since 1945* (New York: Basic Books, 1976). Historians who have looked at primary sources, conversely, are critical of these leaders. See, for example, Timothy B. Tyson's discussion of Luther Hodges in *Radio Free Dixie*. See also David L. Chappell, *Inside Agitators*; Joseph Crespino, *In Search of Another Country*, 19–30.

22. "Most officials," notes Michael J. Klarman, "including those who were ordinarily inclined toward racial moderation, became more extremist to survive, and those few who resisted were generally destroyed." Michael J. Klarman, "Why Massive Resistance" in *Massive Resistance: Southern Opposition to the Second Reconstruction*, Clive Webb, ed. (New York: Oxford University Press, 2005), 23.

23. Martin L uther King, Jr., *"Letter from Birmingham Jail," Reprinted in Martin Luther King, Jr.*, Why We Can't Wait (New York: Signet, 2000), 73.

BIBLIOGRAPHY

Manuscript Sources

J. P. Coleman Papers. Mississippi Department of Archives and History (MDAH). Jackson, Mississippi.

LeRoy Collins Papers. Florida State Archives (FSA). Tallahassee, Florida.

LeRoy Collins Papers. Claude Pepper Library, Florida State University, Tallahassee, Florida.

LeRoy Collins Papers, University of South Florida, Tampa, Florida.

Luther H. Hodges Papers. North Carolina Division of Archives and History (NCDAH). Raleigh, North Carolina.

Guion Johnson Papers, Special Collections. Louis Round Wilson Library. University of North Carolina, Chapel Hill, North Carolina.

Albert Galloway Keller Papers. Documents, Manuscripts, and Archives. Sterling Memorial Library, Yale University, New Haven, Connecticut.

James Jackson Kilpatrick Papers. Special Collections. Alderman Library, University of Virginia, Charlottesville, Virginia.

Martin Luther King Jr. Papers. The King Center. Atlanta, Georgia.

Mississippi State Sovereignty Commission Files. Mississippi Department of Archives and History, Jackson, Mississippi.

NAACP Papers. Library of Congress. Washington, D.C.

David W. Robinson Papers. University of South Carolina School of Law, Columbia, South Carolina.

Walter Sillers Papers, Delta State University Archives, Cleveland, Mississippi.

Ellen Black Winston Papers. Special Collections. University of North Carolina-Greensboro, Greensboro, North Carolina.

Interview Sources

Brady, Thomas Pickens. Interview with Orley B. Caudill, March 4, 1972. Center for Oral History and Cultural Heritage. University of Southern Mississippi, Hattiesburg, Mississippi.

Brady, Thomas Pickens. Interview with Orley B. Caudill, May 17, 1972. Center for Oral History and Cultural Heritage. University of Southern Mississippi, Hattiesburg, Mississippi.

Coleman, J. P. Interview with Orley B. Caudill. November 12, 1981. Center for Oral History and Cultural Heritage. University of Southern Mississippi, Hattiesburg, Mississippi.

Coleman, J. P. Interview with John Egerton. September 5, 1990. Southern Oral History Program, Southern Historical Collection, University of North Carolina, Chapel Hill.

Collins, LeRoy. Interview with Jack Bass and Walter De Vries, May 19, 1974. Southern Oral History Program, Southern Historical Collection, University of North Carolina, Chapel Hill.

Government Documents and Court Cases

Alexander v. Holmes County, 396 U.S. 19 (1969).

Anderson v. City of Albany, 321 F.2d 649 (CA5 1963).

Brown v. Board of Education, 347 U.S. 483 (1954).

Brown v. Board of Education, 349 U.S. 294 (1955)—"*Brown II*"

Butler's Estate v. McQuarters, 48 So. 2d 617 (1950).

Bush v. Orleans Parish School Bd., 138 F. Supp. 337 (E.D. La. 1956).

Bush v. Orleans Parish School Bd., 242 F.2d 156 (CA5 1957).

Carson v. Warlick, 238 F.2d 724 (CA4 1956).

Carter v. West Feliciana Parish, 396 U.S. 290 (1970).

Cooper v. Aaron, 358 U.S. 1 (1958).

Florida Ex. Rel. Hawkins v. Board of Control, 350 U.S. 413 (1956).

General Laws of the State of Alabama, 1954–1960.

General Laws of the State of Arkansas, 1954–1960.

General Laws of the State of Florida, 1954–1960.

General Laws of the State of Louisiana (Louisiana Acts), 1954–1960.

General Laws of the State of Mississippi, 1954–1960.

General Laws of the State of Georgia, 1953–1960.

General Laws of the State of North Carolina (N.C. Session Laws), 1954–1960.

General Laws of the State of South Carolina (S.C. Session Laws), 1954–1960.

General Laws of the State of Virginia, 1954–1960.

Georgia v. Rachel, 384 U.S. 780 (1966).

Green v. County School Board of New Kent County, 391 U.S. 430 (1968).

Guyot v. Pierce, 372 F.2d 552 (CA5 1967).

Hartfield v. Mississippi, 367 F.2d 362 (CA5 1966).

"Investigation of Public School Conditions," Report of the Subcommittee to Investigate Public School Standards and Conditions and Juvenile Delinquency in the District of Columbia; Committee on the District of

Columbia. House of Representatives. Washington, D.C.: United States Government Printing Office, 1957.

Moynihan, Daniel Patrick. *The Negro Family: The Case for National Action.* Washington, D.C.: Office of Policy and Planning, United States Department of Labor, March 1965.

"Obscene and Pornographic Literature and Juvenile Delinquency," Interim Report, Subcommittee to Investigate Juvenile Delinquency. Senate Committee on the Judiciary. Washington, D.C.: United States Government Printing Office, 1956.

The Problem of Births Out of Wedlock. Raleigh: North Carolina Conference for Social Services, 1959.

School Board of Newport News v. Atkins, 246 F.2d 325 (CA4 1957).

Shepherd v. Florida, 341 U.S. 50 (1951).

Shuttlesworth v. Birmingham, 358 U.S. 101 (1958).

Shuttlesworth v. Birmingham, 162 F. Supp. 372 (N.D. AL. 1958).

Sims v. Sims, 85 So. 73 (1920).

Singleton v. Jackson Municipal Separate School District, 425 F.2d 1211 (CA5 1970).

Strother v. Thompson, 372 F.2d 654 (CA5 1967).

Sweatt v. Painter, 339 U.S. 629 (1950).

"Time to Tell Mississippi's Welfare Story," *Mississippi State Board of Public Welfare Annual Report.* July 1, 1955–June 30, 1956.

U.S. Department of Health Education and Welfare. *Vital Statistics of the United States.* 1954–1964.

United States v. Jefferson County Board of Education, 372 F.2d 552 (CA5 1967).

United States v. Jefferson County Board of Education, 380 F.2d 385 (CA5 1967) *(II, en banc).*

Wilkins v. United States, 376 F.2d 552 (CA5 1967).

Pamphlets

Brady, Tom P. *Black Monday.* Greenwood, Miss.: Citizens' Councils Press, 1955.

Joint Statement of United States Senator James O. Eastland, Judge Tom P. Brady, and Congressman John Bell Williams," Jackson, Mississippi, December 12, 1955.

M Is for Mississippi and Murder, NAACP. 1956.

Paul, James C. N., *The School Segregation Decision: A Report to the Governor of North Carolina on the Decision of the Supreme Court of the United States on the 17th of May 1954.* Chapel Hill, N.C.: Institute of Government, 1954.

Woodside, Moya. *Sterilization in North Carolina: A Sociological and Psychological Study.* Chapel Hill: University of North Carolina Press, 1950.

Periodicals

The Citizens' Council (Jackson, Mississippi)
Clarion-Ledger (Jackson, Mississippi)

Constitution (Atlanta, Georgia)
Daily Free Press (Kinston, North Carolina)
Daily News (Jackson, Mississippi)
Daily World (Atlanta, Georgia)
Defender (Chicago, Illinois)
Delta Democrat-Times (Greenville, Mississippi)
Democrat (Tallahassee, Florida)
Morning Advocate (Baton Rouge, Louisiana)
Morning Herald (Durham, North Carolina)
Nation
News & Courier (Charleston, South Carolina)
News & Observer (Raleigh, North Carolina)
News Leader (Richmond, Virginia)
New York Times
Race Relations Law Reporter
Shreveport Times
Southern School News
State Times (Jackson, Mississippi)
Time
Times Picayune (New Orleans, Louisiana)

Books

Abernathy, Ralph. *And the Walls Came Tumbling Down: An Autobiography.* New York: Harper & Row, 1989.

Arsenault, Raymond, *Freedom Riders: 1961 and the Struggle for Racial Justice.* New York: Oxford University Press, 2006.

Baker, Liva. *The Second Battle of New Orleans: The Hundred Year Struggle to Integrate the Schools.* New York: Harper Collins, 1996.

Bartley, Numen V. *The New South: The Story of the South's Modernization, 1945–1980.* Baton Rouge: Louisiana State University Press, 1995.

———. *The Rise of Massive Resistance*, 2nd ed. Baton Rouge: Louisiana State University Press, 1969.

———, and Hugh D. Graham. *Southern Politics and the Second Reconstruction.* Baltimore: Johns Hopkins University Press, 1975.

Bass, Jack. *Taming the Storm: The Life and Times of Judge Frank M. Johnson, Jr., and the South's Fight over Civil Rights.* New York: Doubleday, 1993.

———. *Unlikely Heroes: The Dramatic Story of the Southern Judges Who Translated the Supreme Court's Brown Decision into a Revolution for Equality.* New York: Simon & Schuster, 1981.

———, and Walter DeVries. *The Transformation of Southern Politics: Social Change and Political Consequences since 1945.* New York: Basic Books, 1976.

Belknap, Michal R. *Federal Law and the Southern Order: Racial Violence and Constitutional Conflict in the Post-Brown South.* Athens: University of Georgia Press, 1987.

Bell, Derrick. *Silent Covenants:* Brown v. Board of Education *and the Unful-filled Hopes for Racial Reform.* New York: Oxford University Press, 2004.

Bell, Winifred. *Aid to Dependent Children.* New York: Columbia University Press, 1965.

Beschloss, Michael, ed. *Reaching for Glory: Lyndon Johnson's Secret White House Tapes, 1964–1965.* New York: Simon & Schuster, 2001.

Bickel, Alexander. *The Least Dangerous Branch: The Supreme Court at the Bar of Politics.* Indianapolis, Ind.: Bobbs-Merrill, 1962.

———. *Politics and the Warren Court.* New York: Harper & Row, 1965.

Black, Earl. *Southern Governors and Civil Rights: Racial Segregation as a Campaign Issue in the Second Reconstruction.* Cambridge, Mass.: Harvard University Press, 1976.

Bowers, Claude. *The Tragic Era.* New York: Houghton Mifflin, 1929.

Brauer, Carl M. *John F. Kennedy and the Second Reconstruction.* New York Columbia University Press, 1977.

Brown, Sarah Hart. *Standing against Dragons: Three Southern Lawyers in an Era of Fear.* Baton Rouge: Louisiana State University Press, 1998.

Bryant, Nick. *The Bystander: John F. Kennedy and the Struggle for Black Equality.* New York: Basic Books, 2006.

Burt, Al. *The Tropic of Cracker.* Gainesville: University Press of Florida, 1999.

Carson, Clayborne. *In Struggle: SNCC and the Black Awakening of the 1960's.* Cambridge, Mass.: Harvard University Press, 1981.

Carter, Dan. *The Politics of Rage: George Wallace, the Origins of the New Conservatism and the Transformation of American Politics.* Baton Rouge: Louisiana State University Press, 1995.

———. *Scottsboro: A Tragedy of the American South.* Baton Rouge: Louisiana State University Press, 1979.

Carter, Hodding III. *The South Strikes Back.* Garden City, N.Y.: Doubleday, 1959.

Cecelski, David. *Along Freedom Road: Hyde County, North Carolina, and the Fate of Black Schools in the South.* Chapel Hill: University of North Carolina Press, 1994.

Cell, John W. *The Highest Stage of White Supremacy: The Origins of Segregation in South Africa and the American South.* Cambridge, U.K.: Cambridge University Press, 1982.

Chafe, William Henry. *Civilities and Civil Rights: Greensboro, North Carolina, and the Black Struggle for Freedom.* New York: Oxford University Press, 1980.

Chalmers, David M. *Hooded Americanism: The History of the Ku Klux Klan,* 3rd ed. Durham, N.C.: Duke University Press, 1981.

Chappell, David L. *Inside Agitators: White Southerners in the Civil Rights Movement.* Baltimore: Johns Hopkins University Press, 1994.

———. *A Stone of Hope: Prophetic Religion and the Death of Jim Crow.* Chapel Hill: University of North Carolina Press, 2004.

Cobb, James. *Industrialization and Southern Society, 1877–1984.* Lexington: University Press of Kentucky, 1984.

Cobb, James. *The Most Southern Place on Earth: The Mississippi Delta and the Roots of Regional Identity.* New York: Oxford University Press, 1992.

———. *The Selling of the South: The Southern Crusade for Industrial Development. 1936–1980,* 2nd ed. Baton Rouge: Louisiana State University Press, 1982.

Colburn, David R., and Jane L. Landers. *The African American Heritage of Florida.* Gainesville: University Press of Florida, 1995.

Colburn, David R. and Richard K. Scher, *Florida's Gubernatorial Politics in the Twentieth Century.* Tallahassee: University Presses of Florida, 1980.

Collins, LeRoy. *Forerunners Courageous: Stories of Frontier Florida.* Tallahassee: Colcade, 1971.

Cook, James Graham. *The Segregationists.* New York: Appleton, 1962.

Covington, Howard E., Jr., and Marion A. Ellis, *Terry Sanford: Politics, Progress, and Outrageous Ambitions.* Durham, N.C.: Duke University Press, 1999.

Crespino, Joseph. *In Search of Another Country: Mississippi and the Conservative Counterrevolution* (Princeton, N.J.: Princeton University Press, 2007).

Cushman, Barry. *Rethinking the New Deal Court: The Structure of a Constitutional Revolution.* New York: Oxford University Press, 1998.

Dailey, Jane, Glenda Elizabeth Gilmore, and Bryant Simon, eds. *Jumpin' Jim Crow: Southern Politics from Civil War to Civil Rights.* Princeton, N.J.: Princeton University Press, 2000.

Daniel, Pete. *Lost Revolutions: The South in the 1950's.* Chapel Hill: University of North Carolina Press, 2000.

Davis, Townsend. *Weary Feet, Rested Souls: A Guided History of the Civil Rights Movement.* New York: Norton, 1998.

Dittmer, John. *Local People: The Struggle for Civil Rights in Mississippi.* Urbana: University of Illinois Press, 1995.

Douglas, Davison M. *Reading, Writing, and Race: The Desegregation of Charlotte Schools.* Chapel Hill: University of North Carolina Press, 1995.

DuBois, William E. Burghardt. *Black Reconstruction.* New York: Harcourt Brace, 1935.

Dudziak, Mary L. *Cold War Civil Rights: Race and the Image of American Democracy.* Princeton, N.J.: Princeton University Press, 2000.

Dunbar, Anthony. *Against the Grain: Southern Radicals and Prophets, 1929–1959.* Charlottesville: University of Virginia Press, 1981.

Eagles, Charles W., *Jonathan Daniels and Race Relations: The Evolution of a Southern Liberal.* Knoxville: University of Tennessee Press, 1982.

———. ed. *The Civil Rights Movement in America.* Jackson: University Press of Mississippi, 1986.

Egerton, John. *Speak Now against the Day: The Generation before the Civil Rights Movement in the South.* New York: Knopf, 1994.

Ely, James W., Jr. *The Crisis of Conservative Virginia: The Byrd Organization and the Politics of Massive Resistance.* Knoxville: University of Tennessee Press, 1978.

Eskew, Glenn T. *But for Birmingham: The Local and National Movements in the Civil Rights Struggle.* Chapel Hill: University of North Carolina Press, 1997.

Fairclough, Adam. *To Redeem the Soul of America: The Southern Christian Leadership Conference and Martin Luther King, Jr.* Athens: University of Georgia Press, 1987.

Frederickson, George. *The Black Image in the White Mind: The Debate on Afro-American Character and Destiny, 1817–1914.* Middletown, Conn.: Wesleyan University Press, 1971.

———. *White Supremacy: A Comparative Study in American and South African History.* Oxford: Oxford University Press, 1981.

Fredrickson, Kari, *The Dixiecrat Revolt and the End of the Solid South, 1932–1968.* Chapel Hill: University of North Carolina Press, 2001.

Garrow, David. *Bearing the Cross: Martin Luther King, Jr., and the Southern Christian Leadership Conference.* New York: Morrow, 1986.

———. *Protest at Selma: Martin Luther King, Jr., and the Voting Rights Act of 1965.* New Haven: Yale University Press, 1978.

Gates, Robbins. *The Making of Massive Resistance: Virginia's Politics of School Desegregation, 1954–1956.* Chapel Hill: University of North Carolina Press, 1962.

Gilmore, Glenda Elizabeth. *Gender and Jim Crow: Women and the Politics of White Supremacy in North Carolina, 1896–1920.* Chapel Hill: University of North Carolina Press, 1996.

Gordon, Linda. *Pitied but Not Entitled: Single Mothers and the History of Welfare, 1890–1935.* Cambridge, Mass.: Harvard University Press, 1995.

Grafton, Carl E. *Big Mules and Branchheads: James E. Folsom and Political Power in Alabama.* Athens: University of Georgia Press, 1985.

Graham, Hugh Davis. *The Civil Rights Era: Origins and Development of National Policy.* New York: Oxford University Press, 1990.

Gray, Osha Davidson. *The Best of Enemies: Race and Redemption in the New South.* New York: Scribner's, 1996.

Green, Adwin. *The Man Bilbo.* Westport, Conn.: Greenwood, 1976.

Greenberg, Jack. *Crusaders in the Courts: How a Dedicated Band of Lawyers Fought for the Civil Rights Revolution.* New York: Basic Books, 1994.

Greene, Christina. *Our Separate Ways: Women and the Black Freedom Movement in Durham, North Carolina.* Chapel Hill: University of North Carolina Press, 2005.

Hall, Jacquelyn Dowd, James Leloudis, Robert Korstad, Mary Murphy, Lu Ann Jones, and Christopher B. Daly. *Like a Family: The Making of a Southern Cotton Mill World.* Chapel Hill: University of North Carolina Press, 1987.

Hall, Kermit L., and James W. Ely Jr. *An Uncertain Tradition: Constitutionalism and the History of the South.* Athens: University of Georgia Press, 1989.

Hampton, Henry, Steve Fayer, and Sarah Flynn, eds. *Voices of Freedom: An Oral History of the Civil Rights Movement from the 1950s to the 1980s.* New York: Bantam, 1990.

Havard, William C. *Changing Politics of the South.* Baton Rouge: Louisiana State University Press, 1985.

———, and Beth, Loren P. *The Politics of Mis-Representation: Rural-Urban Conflict in the Florida Legislature.* Baton Rouge: Louisiana State University Press, 1962.

Henry, Aaron. *The Fire Ever Burning.* Jackson: University Press of Mississippi, 2000.

Hewitt, Nancy. *Southern Discomfort: Women's Activism in Tampa, Florida, 1880s–1920s.* Urbana: University of Illinois Press, 2001.

Highsaw, Robert B., and Charles N. Fortenberry. *The Government and Administration of Mississippi.* New York: Thomas Y. Crowell, 1954.

Hodges, Luther H. *Businessman in the Statehouse: Six Years as Governor of North Carolina.* Chapel Hill: University of North Carolina Press, 1962.

Irons, Peter. *Jim Crow's Children: The Broken Promise of the Brown Decision.* New York: Viking, 2002.

Jacobstein, Helen L. *The Segregation Factor in the Florida Democratic Gubernatorial Primary of 1956.* Gainesville: University of Florida Press, 1972.

Jacoway, Elizabeth, and David R. Colburn, eds. *Southern Businessmen and Desegregation.* Baton Rouge: Louisiana State University Press, 1982.

Katagiri, Yasuhiro. *The Mississippi State Sovereignty Commission: Civil Rights and States' Rights.* Jackson: University Press of Mississippi, 2001.

Katz, Michael. *The Undeserving Poor: From the War on Poverty to the War on Welfare.* New York: Pantheon, 1989.

Kevles, Daniel J. *In the Name of Eugenics: Eugenics and the Uses of Human Heredity.* New York: Alfred A. Knopf, 1985.

Key, V.O., Jr. *Southern Politics in State and Nation.* New York: Vintage, 1949.

Killian, Lewis M. *Black and White: Reflections of a White Southern Sociologist.* Dix Hills, N.Y.: General Hall, 1994.

Kilpatrick, James Jackson. *The Southern Case for School Segregation.* New York: Crowell-Collier, 1962.

———. *Sovereign States: Notes of a Citizen of Virginia.* Chicago: Regnery, 1957.

King, Martin Luther, Jr. *Stride toward Freedom: The Montgomery Story.* New York: Harper, 1958.

Klarman, Michael, *From Jim Crow to Civil Rights: The Supreme Court and the Struggle for Racial Equality.* New York: Oxford, 2004.

Kluger, Richard. *Simple Justice: The History of* Brown v. Board of Education *and Black America's Struggle for Equality.* New York: Alfred A. Knopf, 1977.

Korstad, Robert Rodgers. *Civil Rights Unionism: Tobacco Workers and the Struggle for Democracy in the Mid-Twentieth Century South.* Chapel Hill: University of North Carolina Press, 2003.

Kotz, Nick. *Judgment Days: Lyndon Baines Johnson, Martin Luther King, Jr. and the Laws That Changed America.* New York: Mariner, 2005.

Kousser, Morgan. *Colorblind Injustice: Minority Voting Rights and the Undoing of the Second Reconstruction.* Chapel Hill: University of North Carolina Press, 1999.

———. *The Shaping of Southern Politics: Suffrage Restriction and the Establishment of the One-Party South, 1880–1910.* New Haven, Conn.: Yale University Press, 1974.

Kruse, Kevin M. *White Flight: Atlanta and the Making of Modern Conservatism.* Princeton, N.J.: Princeton University Press, 2005.

Larson, Edward J. *Sex, Race, and Science: Eugenics in the Deep South.* Baltimore: Johns Hopkins University Press, 1995.

Lassiter, Matthew D. *The Silent Majority: Suburban Politics in the Sunbelt South.* Princeton, N.J.: Princeton University Press, 2006.

———, and Andrew B. Lewis, eds., *The Moderates' Dilemma: Massive Resistance to School Desegregation in Virginia.* Charlottesville: University Press of Virginia, 1998.

Lawson, Steven F. *Black Ballots: Voting Rights in the American South, 1944–1969.* New York: Columbia University Press, 1976.

Leloudis, James L. *Schooling the New South: Pedagogy, Self, and Society in North Carolina, 1880–1920.* Chapel Hill: University of North Carolina Press, 1996.

Levine, Bertram. *Resolving Racial Conflict: The Community Relations Service and Civil Rights, 1964–1989.* Columbia: University of Missouri Press, 2005.

Loevy, Robert D. *To End All Segregation: The Politics and Passage of the Civil Rights Act of 1964.* Lanham, Md.: University Press of America, 1990.

Martin, John Bartlow. *The Deep South Says "Never."* New York: Ballantine, 1957.

McMillen, Neil R. *The Citizens' Council: Organized Resistance to the Second Reconstruction, 1954–1964.* Urbana: University of Illinois Press, 1971.

Meier, August, and Elliot Rudwick. *CORE: A Study in the Civil Rights Movement, 1942–1968.* Urbana: University of Illinois Press, 1973.

Metress, Christopher, ed. *The Lynching of Emmett Till: A Documentary Narrative.* Charlottesville: University of Virginia Press, 2002.

Moon, Henry Lee. *Balance of Power: The Negro Vote.* Garden City, N.Y.: Doubleday, 1948.

Morgan, Chester M. *Redneck Liberal: Theodore G. Bilbo and the New Deal.* Baton Rouge: Louisiana State University Press, 1985.

Morris, Aldon. *Origins of the Civil Rights Movement: Black Communities Organizing for Change.* New York: Free Press, 1984.

Muse, Benjamin. *Ten Years of Prelude: The Story of Integration since the Supreme Court's 1954 Decision.* New York: Viking, 1964.

———. *Virginia's Massive Resistance.* Bloomington: Indiana University Press, 1961.

Neubeck, Kenneth J., and Noel A. Cazenave. *Welfare Racism: Playing the Race Card against America's Poor.* New York: Routledge, 2001.

Newby, I. A., ed. *The Development of Segregationist Thought.* Homewood, Ill.: Dorsey, 1968.

———. *Challenge to the Court: Social Scientists and the Defense of Segregation, 1954–1966.* Baton Rouge: Louisiana State University Press, 1967.

———. *Jim Crow's Defense: Anti-Negro Thought in America, 1900–1930.* Westport, Conn.: Greenwood, 1965.

Nossiter, Adam. *Of Long Memory: Mississippi and the Murder of Medgar Evers.* Reading, Mass.: Addison-Wesley, 1994.

O'Brien, Gail Williams. *The Color of the Law: Race, Violence, and Justice in the Post–World War II South.* Chapel Hill: University of North Carolina Press, 1999.

Omi, Michael, and Howard Winant. *Racial Formation in the United States from the 1960s to the 1990s,* 2nd ed. New York: Routledge, 1994.

Ortiz, Paul. *Emancipation Betrayed: The Hidden History of Black Organizing and White Violence in Florida from Reconstruction to the Bloody Election of 1920.* Berkeley: University of California Press, 2005.

Patterson, James T. *Brown v. Board of Education: A Civil Rights Milestone and Its Troubled Legacy.* Oxford: Oxford University Press, 2001.

Paul, James C. N., and Albert Coates. *The School Segregation Decision.* Chapel Hill: University of North Carolina Press, 1954.

Payne, Charles M. *I've Got the Light of Freedom: The Organizing Tradition and the Mississippi Freedom Struggle.* Berkeley: University of California Press, 1995.

Peltason, J. W. *Fifty Eight Lonely Men: Southern Federal Judges and School Desegregation.* New York: Harcourt Brace, 1961.

Perman, Michael. *The Road to Redemption: Southern Politics, 1869–1879.* Chapel Hill: University of North Carolina Press, 1984.

Piven, Frances Fox, and Richard Cloward. *Regulating the Poor: The Functions of Public Welfare,* 2nd ed. New York: Random House, 1971.

Powe, Lucas A., Jr., *The Warren Court and American Politics.* Cambridge, Mass,: Belknap, 2000.

Powledge, Fred. *Free At Last? The Civil Rights Movement and the People Who Made It.* New York: HarperCollins, 1991.

Rabby, Glenda Alice. *The Pain and the Promise: The Struggle for Civil Rights in Tallahassee, Florida.* Athens: University of Georgia Press, 1999.

Raines, Howell. *My Soul Is Rested: Movement Days in the Deep South Remembered.* New York: Putnam, 1977.

Rainwater, Lee, and William L. Yancey. *The Moynihan Report and the Politics of Controversy.* Cambridge, Mass.: Massachusetts Institute of Technology Press, 1967.

Read, James T., and Lucy McGough, *Let Them Be Judged: The Judicial Integration of the Deep South.* Metuchen, N.J.: Scarecrow, 1978.

Roberts, Dorothy. *Killing the Black Body: Race, Reproduction and the Meaning of Liberty.* New York: Vintage, 1997.

Roberts, Gene, and Hank Klibanoff. *The Race Beat: The Press, the Civil Rights Struggle, and the Awakening of a Nation.* New York: Alfred A. Knopf, 2006.

Romano, Renee C., and Leigh Raiford, eds. *The Civil Rights Movement in American Memory.* Athens: University of Georgia Press, 2006.

Rosenburg, Gerald N. *The Hollow Hope: Can Courts Bring about Social Change?* Chicago: University of Chicago Press, 1991.

Sarratt, Reed. *The Ordeal of Desegregation.* New York: Harper & Row, 1966.

Schattsneider, E. E. *The Semisovereign People.* New York: Holt, Rinehart & Winston, 1960.

Schoen, Joanna. *Choice and Coercion: Birth Control, Sterilization, and Abortion in Public Health and Welfare.* Chapel Hill: University of North Carolina Press, 2005.

Scott, Daryl. *Contempt and Pity: Social Policy and the Image of the Damaged Black Psyche, 1880–1996.* Chapel Hill: University of North Carolina Press, 1997.

Shoemaker, Don, ed. *With All Deliberate Speed: Segregation-Desegregation in Southern Schools.* New York: Harper & Brothers, 1957.

Siefert, Harvey. *Conquest through Suffering.* Philadelphia: Westminster, 1965.

Solinger, Rickie. *Wake Up Little Susie: Single Pregnancy and Race before* Roe v. Wade. New York: Routledge, 1992.

Sosna, Morton. *In Search of the Silent South: Southern Liberals and the Race Issue.* New York: Columbia University Press, 1977.

Summers, Cecil L. *The Governors of Mississippi.* Gretna, LA: Pelican, 1980.

Sumner, William Graham. *Folkways: A Study of the Sociological Importance of Usages, Manners, Customs, Mores, and Morals.* Boston: Ginn, 1906.

Taylor, Stephen Wallace. *The New South's New Frontier: A Social History of Economic Development in Southwestern North Carolina.* Gainesville: University Press of Florida, 2001.

Thornton, J. Mills. *Dividing Lines: Municipal Politics and the Struggle for Civil Rights in Montgomery, Birmingham, and Selma.* Tuscaloosa: University of Alabama Press, 2002.

Tumin, Melvin. *Desegregation: Resistance and Readiness.* Princeton, N.J.: Princeton University Press, 1958.

Tushnet, Mark. *Making Civil Rights Law: Thurgood Marshall and the Supreme Courts, 1936–1961.* New York: Oxford University Press, 1994.

———. *The NAACP's Legal Strategy against Segregated Education, 1925–1950.* Chapel Hill: University of North Carolina Press, 1987.

Tyson, Timothy B. *Radio Free Dixie: Robert F. Williams and the Roots of Black Power.* Chapel Hill: University of North Carolina Press, 1999.

Wagy, Tom R. *Governor Leroy Collins of Florida: Spokesman of the New South.* Tuscaloosa: University of Alabama Press, 1985.

Ward, Brian and Tony Badger, eds. *The Making of Martin Luther King, Jr. and the Civil Rights Movement.* New York: New York University Press, 1996.

Webb, Clive, ed. *Massive Resistance: Southern Opposition to the Second Reconstruction.* New York: Oxford University Press, 2005.

Whalen, Charles, and Barbara Whalen, *The Longest Debate: A Legislative History of the 1964 Civil Rights Act.* Cabin John, Md.: Seven Locks Press, 1985.

Whitfield, Stephen J. *A Death in the Delta: The Story of Emmett Till.* Baltimore: Johns Hopkins University Press, 1988.

Wilhoit, Francis M. *The Politics of Massive Resistance.* New York: George Braziller, 1973.

Wilkinson, J. Harvie, III. *From Brown to Bakke: The Supreme Court and School Integration, 1954–1978.* New York: Oxford University Press, 1979.

Woodward, C. Vann. *The Strange Career of Jim Crow,* 3rd rev. ed. New York: Oxford University Press, 1974.

Workman, William D. *The Case for the South.* New York: Devin-Adair, 1960.

Young, Andrew. *An Easy Burden: The Civil Rights Movement and the Transformation of America.* New York: HarperCollins, 1996.

Zinn, Howard. *Albany: A Study in National Responsibility.* Atlanta: Southern Regional Council, 1962.

Articles

Badger, Anthony J., "Southerners Who Refused to Sign the Southern Manifesto," *Historical Journal* 42 (June 1999): 517–34.

Balkin, Jack, M., and Reva Siegel, "Principals, Practices, and Social Movements," *University of Pennsylvania Law Review* 54 (April 2006).

Carson, Clayborne, "Review of Steven F. Lawson, *In Pursuit of Power: Southern Blacks and Electoral Politics, 1965–1982,*" *Journal of American History* 72 (December 1985).

Colburn, David R. "Florida's Governors Confront the Brown Decision: A Case Study of the Constitutional Politics of School Desegregation, 1954–1970," in *An Uncertain Tradition: Constitutionalism and the History of the South,* edited by Kermit L. Hall and James W. Ely Jr. Athens: University of Georgia Press, 1989.

Coleman, James P. "The Origin of the Constitution of 1890," *Journal of Mississippi History* 19 (April, 1957).

Collins, LeRoy, "How It Looks from the South," *Look,* May 27, 1958.

Cooper, Weldon. "The State Police Movement in the South," *Journal of Politics* 1 (November 1939): 414–33.

Dailey, Jane, "The Theology of Massive Resistance: Sex, Segregation, and the Sacred after Brown," in *Massive Resistance: Southern Opposition to the Second Reconstruction,* edited by Clive Webb. New York: Oxford University Press, 2005.

Dudziak, Mary L. "Desegregation as a Cold War Imperative," *Stanford Law Review* 41 (November 1988).

Ehrmann, Winston. "Illegitimacy in Florida II: Social and Psychological Aspects of Illegitimacy." *Eugenics Quarterly* 3 (December 1956): 223–27.

Eskridge, William N., Jr. "Channeling: Identity-Based Social Movements and Public Law," *University of Pennsylvania Law Review* 150 (2001).

————. "Some Effects of Identity-Based Social Movements on Constitutional Law in the Twentieth Century," *Michigan Law Review* 100 (August 2002).

Fairclough, Adam. "Martin Luther King, Jr. and the Quest for Nonviolent Social Change," *Phylon* 47 (Winter 1986).

Fiss, Owen M. "Groups and the Equal Protection Clause," *Philosophy and Public Affairs* 5 (1976): 107.

Friedman, Barry. "Mediated Popular Constitutionalism," *Michigan Law Review* 101 (August 2003).

Killian, Lewis M. "Hypocrisy of Delay," *New South* 11 (June 1956).

Klarman, Michael, "*Brown*, Racial Change, and the Civil Rights Movement," *Virginia Law Review* 80 (February 1994).

————. "How *Brown* Changed Race Relations: The Backlash Thesis," *Journal of American History* 81 (June 1994).

Lawson, Steven F. "The Florida Legislative Investigation Committee and the Constitutional Readjustment of Race Relations, 1956–1963," in *An Uncertain Tradition: Constitutionalism and the History of the South*, edited by Kermit L. Hall and James W. Ely Jr. Athens: University of Georgia Press, 1989.

Lawson, Steven F., David R. Colburn, and Darryl Paulson. "Groveland: Florida's Little Scottsboro," in *The African American Heritage of Florida*, edited by David R. Colburn and Steven F. Lawson. Gainesville: University Press of Florida, 1995.

McCauley, Patrick M. "Be It Enacted," in *With All Deliberate Speed: Segregation-Desegregation in Southern Schools*, edited by Don Shoemaker. New York: Harper & Brothers, 1957.

McGuire, Danielle L. "'It Was Like All of Us Had Been Raped': Sexual Violence, Community Mobilization, and the African American Freedom Struggle," *Journal of American History* 91 (December 2004).

McKay, "'With All Deliberate Speed': Legislative Reaction and Judicial Development, 1956–1957," *Virginia Law Review* 43 (1957).

Meador, Daniel. "The Constitution and the Assignment of Pupils to the Public Schools," *Virginia Law Review* 45 (May 1959), 517–71.

Morrison, Joseph L. "Illegitimacy, Sterilization, and Racism: A North Carolina Case History," *Social Service Review*, March 1965.

Paul, Julius, "The Return of Punitive Sterilization Proposals: Current Attacks on Illegitimacy and the AFDC Program," *Law and Society Review* 3 (1968): 77–92.

Ransone, Coleman B., Jr., "Political Leadership in the Governor's Office," *Journal of Politics* 26 (February 1964): 197–220.

Schattsneider, E. E. "Intensity, Visibility, Direction and Scope," *American Political Science Review* 51 (December 1957).

Services to and Characteristics of Unwed Mothers, Based on Florence Crittenton Association of America Two-Year Reporting Project, 1961–1962. Chicago: Florence Crittenton Association of America, 1963.

Siegel, Reva, "Why Equal Protection No Longer Protects: The Evolving Forms of Status-Enforcing State Action," *Stanford Law Review* 49 (May 1997).

———. "Discrimination in the Eyes of the Law: How 'Color Blindness' Discourse Disrupts and Rationalizes Social Stratification," *California Law Review* 88 (January 2000): 109–111.

"Suffer Little Children," *Nation,* September 24, 1960.

Tushnet, Mark, "The Significance of *Brown v. Board of Education,*" *Virginia Law Review* 80 (February 1994).

Walker, Anders. "Raising the Bar: *Brown* and the Transformation of the Southern Judiciary," *Saint Louis University Law Journal* 48 (Spring 2004).

Wilkinson, J. Harvie, III, "The Supreme Court and Southern School Desegregation, 1955–1970," *Virginia Law Review* 64 (1978): 485.

Unpublished Sources

Corley, Robert Gaines. "James Jackson Kilpatrick: The Evolution of a Southern Conservative, 1955–1965," M.A. Thesis, University of Virginia, 1971.

Schoen, Johanna. "A Great Thing for Poor Folks: Birth Control, Sterilization, and Abortion in Public Health and Welfare in the Twentieth Century." Dissertation, Department of History, University of North Carolina, Chapel Hill, North Carolina, 1995.

INDEX

Killian, Lewis M., 93, 108, 114
Kilpatrick, James Jackson, 21, 22, 23, 98, 117–119, 123
King, Clennon, 30, 31
King, Martin Luther, Jr., 26, 31, 117, 129, 135, 137, 156
  Black moral standards and, 43
  Coleman, J. P. and, 141
  Collins LeRoy and, 138
  Moderates and, 162
King, Slater, 129
Kissing case, 74–77
Klarman, Michael, 7, 39, 194*n*43, 195*n*60, 196*n*85, 197*n*102, 205*n*15, 160, 218*n*20, 219*n*22
Klibanoff, Hank, 187*n*138
Kluger, Richard, 188*n*172, 194*n*43
Korstad, Robert Rodgers, 178*n*6
Kotz, Nick, 204*n*9, 211*nn*83, 93
Kousser, Morgan, 167*n*25
Kruse, Kevin, 164*n*7
Ku Klux Klan, 51, 71–74, 92, 135
Kunstler, William, 136

Lake, Beverly, 61, 63
Larson, Edward, 186*n*120
Lassiter, Matthew, 163*n*5, 164*n*7, 165*n*16, 183*n*69, 218*nn*12, 19
Law Enforcement, 27, 28, 29, 30, 35, 36, 73, 101–102, 129, 136
Lawson, Steven, 192*n*6, 197*n*99, 199*n*130
Lee, George W., 24
Lee, J.R.E., 103
Legal Education Advisory Committee, 22, 39, 158
Leloudis, James, 182*n*46
Levine, Bertram, 209*n*65, 211*n*94
Lewis, Andrew B., 165*n*16
Lewis, John, 141
Lincoln, Abraham, 96
Lingo, Al, 137, 139
Liston, William, 32
Little Rock, 3
Little Three, 22, 23
Liuzzo, Viola, 143
Loevy, Robert, 208*n*43, 209*n*57, 210*n*69
Long, Earl K., 125, 126

Louisiana, 125, 128
Lowry, Sumter, 88, 98, 103
Lucy, Autherine, 100
Lumbee Indians, 71

M Is for Mississippi and Murder, 24, 37
Mackel, A.M. 33
Maggs, Douglas, 63
Mansfield, Texas, 64
Marriage, 41–42,
Marshall, Thurgood, 5, 12, 25, 33, 156
Massive Resistance, 4, 6, 20, 118, 119, 161
McCall, Willis, 102
McGee, Willie 18, 25
McGuire, Danielle, 203*n*193
McMillen, Neil R., 168*n*39, 216*n*160
Meador, Daniel, 195*n*66
Meredith, James, 127
Milliken v. Bradley, 214*nn*127, 128, 215*n*129, 217*n*7
Minton, Sherman, 17
Mississippi, 11–47, 125, 126, 128
Mississippi Freedom Democratic Party, 142
Mondale, Walter, 137
Monroe, North Carolina, 74, 74–77
Montgomery Bus Boycott, 104–105
Moral Background, 41, 93
Morris, Aldon, 191*n*1, 198*nn*118, 126, 127, 204*n*12
Morrow v. Crisler, 215*n*145
Moynihan, Daniel Patrick, 161
Myrdal, Gunnar, 189*n*172

National Association for the Advancement of Colored People (NAACP), 13, 15, 24, 25, 26, 31, 33, 35, 45, 74–76, 101
Negro Civic League, 104
New Deal, 17, 90
Nixon, Richard, 4, 142, 152
North Carolina, 49–84, 55,123, 125, 129
North Carolina State Bureau of Investigation, 50, 73
Nossiter, Adam, 208*n*51
Nuebeck, Kevin, 218*n*16